PELICAN BOOKS

Pelican Library of Business and Management
Editor: T. Kempner

COMPUTERS, MANAGERS AND SOCIETY

Michael Rose was born in 1937 and educated at Sir William Borlase's School and Trinity College, Cambridge, where he read Economics and Social Anthropology, graduating in 1962. From 1962 to 1964 he worked as Research Assistant and Junior Research Officer at the University of Cambridge Department of Applied Economics on a study of the social status of manual workers led by Dr David Lockwood and J. H. Goldthorpe. In 1964 he was appointed Research Fellow, and subsequently Lecturer in Industrial Sociology, at the University of Salford, where he worked with Professor W. H. Scott and J. E. Hebden on a study of 'computerization' in industrial firms in the north-west of England. At present he is Lecturer in Industrial and Organizational Sociology at Bath University. He is an author, with W. H. Scott and J. E. Hebden, of papers on the process of 'computerization', and is currently engaged on further research in the sociology of work and occupations.

MICHAEL ROSE

COMPUTERS, MANAGERS
AND SOCIETY

PENGUIN BOOKS

Penguin Books Ltd, Harmondsworth, Middlesex, England
Penguin Books Inc., 7110 Ambassador Road, Baltimore, Maryland 21207, U.S.A.
Penguin Books Australia Ltd, Ringwood, Victoria, Australia

—

First published 1969

—

—

Made and printed in Great Britain by
Richard Clay (The Chaucer Press) Ltd,
Bungay, Suffolk
Set in Monotype Times

Contents

Foreword

THIS book grew out of my connexion, between 1964 and 1968, with an industrial research study of the introduction of computers in firms in the north-west of England under the leadership of Professor W. H. Scott at the Department of Sociology, Government and Administration, University of Salford. Though it has terms of reference which go beyond this specialized piece of research, certain sections of the book owe a great deal to the work I did with Professor Scott and another former Salford colleague, John Hebden. Many other sections of the book have benefited considerably from the numerous general discussions we enjoyed together.

I should also like to take this opportunity to express my appreciation to a number of other people and organizations who helped in one way or another with the preparation of the book. Firstly, my other former colleagues at Salford, Lorraine Baric, Douglas Webster, Anthony Jackson, and John Lee, for their interest and consideration, and in particular Louis Turner for his criticisms of the manuscript, and John Hall (now of the Department of Transportation and Environmental Planning, University of Birmingham) who advised me on the sections on programming and wrote the specimen program appearing on page 69. Secondly, the industrial companies, computer suppliers, trade unions, managers, and data-processing specialists who provided information and interviews; especially the Elliott-Automation, English Electric Computers, and International Computers and Tabulators companies (now merged in International Computers Ltd); International Business Machines (U K) Ltd; the National Cash Register Company Ltd; the National Union of Bank Employees; the National and Local Government Officers' Association; the Clerical and Administrative Workers' Union. I am particularly indebted to Mr Mark Johns, formerly of the Electronic Engineering Association, for his assistance in making contact with the computer-manufacturing companies, and to

Mr P. Bowyer, of the National Cash Register Company, for his quite exceptional efforts on my behalf.

Thirdly, my editors at Penguin; in particular, Jillian Norman, who originally suggested the book; Andrew Pennycook; and the advisory editor of the series, Professor T. Kempner of the Management Centre, University of Bradford. Fourthly, Miss Anne Wilson and Mrs Maureen Knapkin, who typed the revised manuscript. Finally, my wife, who typed the whole first draft – a horrid job.

CHAPTER 1

Computers, Optimists and Pessimists

INTRODUCTION

To judge from the tone of most that is written about them it seems that it is hard to tackle the subject of computers without sounding either like a prophet of doom or like someone with something to sell. The machine has come of age as a standard industrial, commercial and scientific tool, and whether we like it or not it is here to stay. Because of its potentially extensive influence on the quantity and quality of our lives it is only right, indeed it is perhaps necessary, that we should all have an opinion about it. Most of the analysts and forecasters who would like to help us to make up our minds, however, adopt an extreme position : blithe enthusiasm on the one hand, uncritical pessimism on the other. The majority of us waver unhappily between the two, unable to come down firmly on one side or the other, or to arrive at a precise new position of our own, perhaps because we feel we are not fully capable of understanding the issues involved.

But there are many who feel no such handicap, and this being above all a subject that lends itself equally to emotionalism and oversimplification, the prophets, popularizers and PR men of both camps have subjected us to a growing cross-fire of tabloid thinking. In the 1950s, in the early days of the machine, the Jeremiahs had most of it their own way. With heart-rending verbal violin-music wailing in the background, science-fiction futures of massive unemployment in which human terminal values were totally eclipsed by technologically instrumental ones were conjured up. Mankind was to be relegated to an (admittedly well-heeled) helotry under the 'mighty electronic brain'. Such speculations continue, but meanwhile an important change in fashions of worrying has been occurring. It is far less popular nowadays to fret publicly about the dangers of exploiting the machine than about those of failing to exploit it, or failing to exploit it cleverly enough. The voice of the alarmed humanist romantic is being drowned by the stern admonitions of the technological utopian, who reminds us that what we seem to want above all is unlimited material abundance and insists that this is exactly what the machine will give us within a couple of generations if we throw away all our silly doubts and fears.[1]

Who should we listen to? One difficulty is that, stripped of its waffle and propaganda, each message is just about half-true. Computing technology, like any technology, nuclear included, is itself neutral, capable of both legitimate and improper methods of exploitation. The computer is not an electronic brain: but it can certainly be used by the unscrupulous to spy, control and manipulate. Nor is it a cornucopia: but boldly exploited it could probably put one or two percentage points on the UK economic growth-rate. Over twenty years that would add up to quite a bit. But neither outcome is an inevitable consequence of merely installing the machine. Ordinary individuals are quite capable of blocking the improper uses of the computer. On the other hand, we shall not reap the full economic benefit from the machine's valid uses without a good deal of ingenuity and hard work. And the first bit of hard work for most of us is to arrive at a broad appreciation of what the machine can and cannot do, has and has not done.

It is often suggested that because the computer will attain universal applicability, in industry and commerce, science, government, education, even in leisure life, familiarity with computing concepts and techniques will become as important as the traditional three Rs. We shall, as it were, need to be 'cybernate' as well as literate and numerate. This may be putting it a little strongly. But to get what we want from the computer while

1. The best known exponents of the pessimistic viewpoint are the late Norbert Wiener, and Donald Michael. See Wiener, N., *The Human Use of Human Beings*, Houghton Mifflin, New York, 1950 (also in paperback, Anchor Books, New York, 1954: in this edition Professor Wiener modified some of his earlier pessimism); Michael, D. N., *Cybernation: The Silent Conquest*, Center for the Study of Democratic Institutions, Santa Barbara, 1962.

The most enjoyable slice of technological utopianism known to the present writer is Terborgh, G., *The Automation Hysteria*, W. W. Norton & Co., New York, 1965.

keeping a weather eye open for abuses of its capabilities we all need to know a good deal more about it – not necessarily, it must quickly be added, about the complexities of its electronic innards : but about the key characteristics of the technology, what jobs the machine can do profitably, and how it affects the people involved.

This book is intended as a contribution towards this effort. Necessarily, however, in a subject of such considerable complexity, and one which is to some extent controversial and emotionally charged, it is impossible to cover everything properly and please everyone entirely, including perhaps oneself. Some selection is necessary, and inevitably the choice is partially a product of one's own interests and values. The present writer's occupational interests and competence are in the social sciences, which probably creates a predisposition to emphasize human and social as opposed to technological and economic problems. But such an emphasis, it should be pointed out here and now for those whose interests are otherwise, does not spring from any belief on the writer's part in the *necessary* contradiction between human values and the rationale of computing (or information) technology.

On the other hand it may be that for some people the approach adopted here will not be 'people-oriented' enough. For example, more might be welcome on the employment effects of computerization. It would be nice to be able to provide it. But even someone who is not a qualified labour economist can see that the present information we have on this critical issue is incomplete and supports conflicting interpretations.[2]

Again, there is a certain amount of commentary, some of it critical, on the rate and effectiveness of computerization in the United Kingdom. It will have to be taken on trust that this commentary is a sign much less of fellow-travelling with the technological utopians than of the impatience of a prospective beneficiary, as we all are, of the greater material prosperity which should follow more effective, but legitimate, exploitation of the machine.

2. See Stieber, J. (ed.), *Employment Problems of Automation and Advanced Technology: An International Perspective*, International Institute for Labour Studies, Geneva, and Macmillan, London, 1966; Ministry of Labour, *Computers in Offices* (Manpower Studies No. 4), HMSO, 1965.

THE COMPUTER REVOLUTION

Whether they are technological utopians or romantic humanists; the Duke of Edinburgh or the Premier; the Minister of Technology, Mr Edward Heath, or just plain Lord Snow, all who are given to occasional pronouncement on technological progress, and they are many, seem to agree on one point: that there is something called the Computer (Technological/Cybernetic/Second Industrial) Revolution. Central to this variously pictured momentous, menacing, or costive process is the *general-purpose electronic digital computer*.

The Computer

'Computer' is actually a generic term. Not all computers are electronic. A very important sub-class, *analog* computers, do not compute at all. If 'computer' has come to denote the electronic digital machine – and this in many ways unsatisfactory convention will be followed here – we should notice that it can embrace these other, rather different devices. But it is above all the digital computer and its ancillary equipment (which will be described more fully in the next chapter) which is being referred to when the Computer Revolution is invoked.

AUTOMATION, COMPUTERIZATION AND CYBERNATION

Another distinction needs mention at this point, that between automation and computerization. The word *automation* has been overworked almost to meaninglessness. The introduction of one-man buses has been called automation. So has the installation of tea-vending machines. In the factory it is applied indiscriminately to complex materials-handling equipment, sophisticated machine-tools, or simply larger-scale operations: a chemical works or oil refinery are pointed out as examples of 'automation'. But if the word is to mean anything more than 'advanced mechanization' it should refer to mechanisms or production-processes which are to some significant extent *self-regulating*, that is, able to function in a wide range of conditions without the constant attention of a human minder.

To achieve such servo-mechanical autonomy in complex equipment usually demands the coupling to the mechanism of some form of computer. Generally this will be an analog machine. Automation in this more rigorous sense, contrary to popular belief, is still very restricted. This holds even for the United States, where the high manual wage rates which make it an economic proposition are much more common. The sales value of analog equipment in the UK is a small fraction of that of digital machines, and there presumably it will stay until economic policies take on a more expansionist character.

If 'automation' can be reserved to denote the automatic handling of information and issue of control messages in self-regulating physical production processes, *computerization* can be used to embrace comparable procedures in the processes of administrative and professional work. The raw materials of such work are data and its chief product information, no less than the raw materials of a factory may be steel, rubber, glass and paint and its product a car. In the conventional office raw data such as the sales figures for a range of products are gradually processed by a team of clerks into information in the form of a sales report. Their job is the shaping and assembly of gross and undifferentiated matter into a meaningful configuration. This shaping and assembly process demands a multitude of particular operations as data are merged, condensed and redistributed. These operations can be performed automatically by the (digital) computer.

What goes for such simple clerical tasks holds for the more complex information handling work of the manager, engineer, scientist or civil servant. Computerization, then, basically implies *automatic data-processing* – though as we shall see (in Chapter 4) computers handle far more sophisticated work than is usually understood by the expression automatic data-processing (ADP).

Computerization is really just another aspect of automation, but since there has been such a striking difference in the rates at which manufacturing and administrative automation have occurred the special term 'computerization' enables us to make at least one important distinction. Finally it is worth noting that there is quite an influential lobby for the term *cybernation* as a blanket expression for all types of automation and computerization, and in particular for applications where the two are integrated in single overall control systems spanning factory and office.

COMPUTERIZATION IN THE UK

Three main things can be meant by an expression like 'Computer Revolution': spectacular advances in the technological apparatus; bold and ingenious applications of it; and its absorption of a major part of the work for which it is well adapted. In practice all three connotations get somewhat mixed up: hence much of the confusion over whether a Computer Revolution has in fact occurred. For while few would deny that computers have undergone revolutionary developments in their technology (see Chapter 2) and applications (see Chapter 4), it is stretching a point to assert that in terms of their economic contribution they have as yet had anything resembling a revolutionary impact, certainly as far as the United Kingdom goes.

In relative terms, of course, the machine's penetration is impressive. Less than twenty years ago the computer was still a rarity, by today's standards painfully slow in operation, technically unreliable for sustained running, and costly to use in terms of a given unit of capacity. It was to be found in a hallowed region of the mathematical or scientific laboratory, and there, shrouded in mystery (and often in dustsheets, thanks to its unreliable components) it seemed likely to remain.

A certain amount of bulk computation for the non-scientific user might be performed (for example, government or military statistical work) and a host of other applications could be conceived theoretically. But the worthwhile application of the machine to the everyday problems of administration and business decision-taking was generally believed to lie well in the future, dependent on elusive technical refinements, lower running costs, and – a serious difficulty, and one which has still to be decisively overcome – the simplification of *programming* (see Chapter 3).

But if the computing experts were cautious to predict an early graduation of the machine to direct economic usefulness, its potential users in business and industry were even more guarded. The same seems to have gone for the electrical equipment and office machinery manufacturers who were later to grow big on the crest of the business computer boom: in the late 1940s, International Business Machines (IBM), who currently supply more than seventy per cent of the world's computers, persistently forecast a dim immediate future for non-scientific computers. This, too, despite the fact that they had sponsored the development of the first (non-electronic) digital computer (the Advanced Sequence Controlled Calculator) some years before, and had a ready-made market for commercial calculating machines.

A celebrated illustration of the general scepticism about the feasibility of commercial computing is the case of *J. Lyons & Co*. In 1947 Lyons decided to investigate the possibility of computerizing such standard office jobs as payroll calculation and stock-control. They discovered that no suitable machine was envisaged in the United States – where they had assumed it would be found if at all – but that the EDSAC (Electronic Delay Storage Automatic Calculator) then being developed at the University of Cambridge Mathematical Laboratory would incorporate features which might enable its modification for the tasks they envisaged. LEO (Lyons Electronic Office), the first business computer, was developed in collaboration with the University and began work in late 1951. Encouraged by their progress and the hesitation of other possible manufacturers to exploit this new market Lyons diversified from tea shops to computers. Before these interests were disposed of in the early 1960s the LEO *marque* had established itself as something of a Bentley among British computers.

LEO I marks the take-off point for commercial computing, or *data-processing* (DP). But until the mid 1950s few firms on either side of the Atlantic made much effort to exploit the new technology. Yet the existence of even a modest demand and a growing awareness of the rich pickings to be had if it could be stimulated encouraged substantial new research and development efforts. Special attention was devoted to expanding and improving the operation of the computer's *store*, or *memory*, since rapid working and high-capacity storage is more important in business than in scientific computing. The adaptation of *magnetic tape* for bulk storage and the invention of high-speed *magnetic-core storage* (see Chapter 2) both attracted waves of new users.

American manufacturers were especially fortunate at this period in the support they received from the federal government, whose procurements of equipment for both general administration and military purposes financed development on a heroic scale. No less significant than the technical breakthroughs stimulated by this support were those in programming and systems design (see Chapter 3): military applications of the computer lie behind such advances as computerized *operations research* and the *integrated system* (see Chapter 4) in business. Perhaps the most productive single source of these applications breakthroughs was the SAGE computerized air-defence system initiated in the early 1950s.

In the last ten years the pace of technological advance has been even more rapid and each step has become so bewilderingly impressive that there is surprise when the next comes that there was any new frontier to cross. The same goes for applications. New ones are reported in the Press almost daily – 'Computer books airline seat/runs factory/selects wives' – and even allowing for journalistic licence they strengthen the impression of the machine's universal penetration. We have long since become accustomed to the computerized telephone account, gas bill, salary slip or bank statement. So much so that complaining letters to *The Times* on the machine's occasional idiocies in performing these chores have become as much an institution as broadsides against inflation or reports of the first cuckoo.

Official eyes have been turned to the manpower and employment effects of computerization to date and in the future. In 1965 the Ministry of Labour estimated that something like 50,000 clerical posts had been absorbed by the machine and that the total was likely to rise to several hundred thousand within ten years (see Chapter 6) as the machine absorbed more of the office work of banks, insurance companies, government and manufacturing. Another important report two years later charted the likely demand for computer staff by 1970 and concluded that a minimum of about 50,000 more of these various grades of specialists would be needed by then, and that, such is the present pace of computerization, staff shortages might occur and slow it artificially.

It is easy enough to read all these signs together as evidence of a revolution. But the United Kingdom is a long way from a computerized economy. This would be less of a cause for concern if our computer population were comparable to those of our industrial competitors, or if, given a relatively lower population, the majority of British computer users exploited the machine as effectively as, for example, such firms as British Petroleum or Rolls Royce. In fact, however, in both respects the UK shows up badly.

THE COMPUTER POPULATION

Statistics of computer populations are notoriously difficult to compile and different methods of calculation can make international comparisons very misleading. However, there were probably something like 3,000 installed digital computers in the UK by January 1968. When it is remembered that some of these installations represent computer systems with a capital cost running into several million pounds and that the average installation costs well over £100,000, this total is impressive in absolute terms. Again, ten years previously the British computer population had barely passed the hundred mark. But at the same date (January 1968) the United States had something like 50,000 installed machines. Even allowing for differences in population, geography, and industrial structure it is an invidious comparison. Worse still, West Germany, comparable to the UK on these scores, probably has something like 2,000 more machines in operation, and a faster underlying rate of installation. France, too, has marginally more machines, and in terms of machines per head of the employed population Sweden, Switzerland and Holland are well above Britain in the table.

It must be stressed once again that the statistical evidence for these unflattering comparisons is far from perfect. Definitions of a computer are typically elastic. Sometimes analog machines are included in a count without mention of the fact, though since so few computers of this type have been installed anywhere their inclusion does not seriously distort the total. A much more serious problem is the inclusion of simple calculating machines which although certainly electronic, digital, and designed for computation are not what is generally understood by an electronic digital computer (mainly because they do not follow a stored *program* of instructions). Similar confusion derives from failure to deduct scrapped machines from the total when adding their replacements, or to distinguish between machines actually installed and performing useful work, machines in the process of installation and trial (a period which can cover a number of months), machines sold but yet to be installed, and even machines which have not quite been sold but are confidently expected to be by manufacturers eager not to understate their share of the market. Given, too, the present continuous rapid growth in new installations, an estimate of a computer population for any year depends closely on which month it is made in.

A further complication is the enormous variation in size and capacity between computers. Some 'computers' are in fact gigantic hierarchical complexes of machines and 'peripheral' (see Chapter 2) information-translating and -storing equipment; others only just escape definition as the electronic calculators already referred to, and stand almost as inconspicuously on the top of a desk. For a strict comparison one would need to know the division of populations into broad categories such as 'large', 'medium' and 'small' machines. But published figures are not always very helpful in this respect.

COMPUTER USAGE

If one wished to defend the British record in computerization, stress on these confusions might take one a certain way, though it might equally well lead to further embarrassment. The same must be said for an alternative line of defence, namely that what counts in terms of economic advantage is not the sheer size of a national computer stock but its operational effectiveness: not the number of installations but the number of *successful* installations.

In the opinion of such well-placed observers as Mr John Diebold and Mr Dick Brandon, and it is supported by a number of independent surveys as well as their own experience as prominent international computer consultants, up to fifty per cent even of American installations fail to cut the operating costs of the organizations which possess them. A sizeable minority are significantly more expensive, sometimes ruinously so, than the 'manual' working systems they have superseded.

It takes a great deal of ingenuity and good planning to make any computer system pay. Until recently most commercial installations were restricted to a very narrow spectrum of applications, that is to say those which characterize the *office automation* approach (see Chapter 4) – accounting, invoicing and payroll work. The main economic advantage pursued at this level of utilization is the saving of salary costs through the elimination of a large body of office staff. But savings of this kind are far less spectacular than is usually imagined. In fact, for most organizations, the computer becomes a benefit only when it is worked around the clock on a large number of tasks. In considering the economic contribution of a computer population, then, one needs to consider how intensively the average machine is worked and how wide a range of applications are attempted on it.

The evidence here becomes even more sketchy, but it hardly suggests that the failure-rate of British schemes is any lower than in other countries or that our exploitation of the machine is more imaginative. Worldwide the computer has been misused and under-used. British failure in this respect cannot be written off as part of the general failure. In fact it is less understandable since we have begun using computers on a wide scale later than our industrial competitors and ought to have profited from their experience.

THE FUTURE

There has been nothing resembling a revolution in the economic exploitation of the computer in Britain. An important aspect of present official policy is indeed designed to procure it. One of the most severe obstacles to wider use of the machine is the difficulty and cost of programming it, with which is associated a shortage of the programming and systems design personnel who re-organize a business's information network to accommodate the computer in the most advantageous fashion. One of the main functions of the National Computing Centre at Manchester is to attack these problems, and since its establishment in 1965 it has made an increasingly influential contribution to alleviating them (see Chapter 9). Whether more direct official assistance should be given to prospective users is a tricky question. So far the most notable openings of the public purse-strings have been made to secure the British-owned computer-manufacturing industry. But in the long term its viability inevitably depends on how extensively the machine is used in the domestic market.

Nonetheless, at the time of writing there are a number of signs which seem to indicate that the pace of computerization in Britain, if not yet exactly revolutionary, has at least hotted up a good deal. During 1967 the computer population expanded by something like thirty per cent according to some reckonings and the growth had every appearance of being sustained. Important rationalizations were achieved in the British-owned sector of the computer-making industry, with more under discussion. One manufacturer, International Computers and Tabulators, which had been headed for bankruptcy four years before, announced the thousandth order for its present series of machines. Previous official estimates of growth-rates and the final size of the data-processing industry were being revised. In early 1968 the Ministry of Technology forecast that it would eventually account for something like five per cent of the gross national product, worth £1,600 million at 1967 prices. Even the more cautious projections of the computer manufacturers' own market researchers were predicting an annual growth of thirty-five per cent in orders up to 1972, with over 3,000 machines being delivered in that year alone.

MANAGEMENT AND THE COMPUTER

With the experience of the National Plan of 1965 behind us we are entitled to treat such optimistic forecasts with a good deal of reserve. Computerization at this rate will depend very much on the buoyancy of the economy as a whole. And while an expansionary atmosphere is a necessary precondition of rapid computerization it is by no means a sufficient one. The choice whether and when to computerize lies primarily with management. So also does responsibility for successful exploitation of the machine once the decision to use it has been made.

It has often been pointed out when the disappointing growth performance of the British economy since the war is under discussion that not only have we persistently invested a smaller percentage of our gross national product than most industrial competitors but, far more worrying, the return we gain from a given level of investment is relatively lower. This above all is a reflection on the quality of our management: foreign firms operating in Britain generally secure a level of return on investment which stands up to international comparison. Computerization is capital investment *par excellence*, and in connexion with the preceding remarks it is worth recording that foreign-owned firms in Britain have been much more willing to introduce the machine up to the present. It is noteworthy, too, that firms in the science-based growth industries, whatever their ownership, have been less hesitant than those in more traditional branches of manufacture. Their higher propensity to computerize and greater ability to do so successfully are closely related to their more highly qualified and versatile management teams.

The Computer Revolution is in fact very closely related to that other revolution – the Management Revolution – about which we have heard so much. It is no less true for being a cliché that the efficient operation of an advanced industrial economy can no longer depend on the gentleman part-timer, the gifted amateur, or the loyal, but ungifted, retainer. As well as competence in a specialism and experience of day-to-day practicalities the manager needs to acquire wider general planning, negotiating, financial and personnel skills. In other words he needs more in the way of a specifically managerial training. The provision of this kind of training depends largely on the spread of formal management education. Considerable effort is currently being put into its improvement and development. If these efforts succeed one would expect to see an increase in managerial professionalism.

The more professional manager tends to regard the computer as an essential management tool, to have greater familiarity with its worthwhile applications and some appreciation of the practical problems involved in putting it to work. As professionalism spreads, one would expect to see a wider and more skilful use of the machine. (However, we should recognize that tensions between the professional and managers with a more traditional background and outlook are largely inevitable. Conflicts between the new and the old guard can crystallize round the computer itself, to the detriment of a computerization scheme as a whole. See Chapter 8.)

RISKS OF COMPUTERIZATION

The title of this book endorses the view that successful exploitation of the computer is first and foremost a managerial responsibility, and, moreover, as will be argued later, that the machine's economic value derives primarily from its use as a tool which enhances the manager's own performance. The suggestion is also intended that this responsibility goes beyond securing purely economic benefits for society; for whoever exploits a new technology must shoulder some responsibility for ensuring that its potentialities are not misused.

Actual and possible misuses of the computer have sometimes, in the present writer's opinion, been somewhat overstated. But vigilance certainly needs to be exercised to prevent any relaxation of the at present generally ethical and humane exploitation of the machine. The policing of these standards of managerial conduct – and 'managers' is here used in its broadest sense to include administrators within government and its associated bureaucracies – rests largely with ordinary employees and members of the public. If managers, administrators and planners misuse the machine they will be to blame, but it will be partly our fault too.

The human and social risks of administrative automation can be classified in a number of ways but for the present purposes they may be conveniently grouped in four main categories.

Oversystematization

Computers operate most effectively in a world where communication is in a language of logically hermetic definitions and precise quantities. To exploit their quantifying and rationalizing potentialities it is always necessary to modify the content of some jobs, to redirect flows of work, and revise methods of doing it. This discipline can extend beyond the internal working arrangements of the individual concern to its dealings with customers and suppliers. Employees and clients have to fill in the authorized forms in the proper way at the correct time, both literally and metaphorically. In this respect computerization tends to reproduce the consequences – more repetitive, 'routinized' and 'machine-paced' work duties for employees and more standardized service to customers – of mass-production factory mechanization. As some observers have noted, at a time when factory automation brings the promise of reducing the prevalence of monotonous and 'estranging' work on the shop floor computerization could increase it in the office.[3]

Impersonality

Where the work system is designed with exclusive attention to the technical needs of its mechanical apparatus the relationships of workers to their work tasks, with each other, and with 'outsiders' such as customers become increasingly depersonalized. Computerization could finally eradicate the humanly satisfying 'personal touch' which has already been impressively eroded by the growth of large-scale organization.

An amusing but illuminating illustration of the reinforcement of this aspect of bureaucratization in industrial society is the handling of personal letters by the Billy Graham organization. On arrival each is scanned by a semi-skilled assistant, who underlines key passages in a marking ink which enables an

3. The most explicit attack on oversystematization can be found in Boguslaw, R., *The New Utopians: A Study of Systems Design and Social Change*, Prentice-Hall, New York, 1965. As the title suggests, it is also an indictment of technological utopianism as a whole, and traces some of the historical roots of the assumptions that many present-day systems designers bring to their work.

appropriate punched card to be coded. Fed into the computer each generates a letter by assembling a selection of the evangelist's own sentences recorded in the machine's files. A suitably uplifting biblical quotation is automatically inserted to complete the 'personalized' reply. Nowadays the saviour too is alienated from the means of salvation.[4]

Impersonality of this kind is irritating but relatively innocuous. More worrying is that which attaches to the computer's ability to make the analogue of a human decision. As we shall see later, such 'decisions' are of two main types. In the first the decision could be taken just as well by human decision-makers: building them into the computerized system merely saves the time of clerks or managers.

In the second, the computer produces answers to problems which, involving as they do the manipulation of a large number of factors and complex information, in practice a human being would be incapable of solving with comparable speed and precision – if in fact he could solve them at all. In both cases it follows a programmer's instructions, and the quality of its choice or solution depends directly on the quality of the program and the available information. (In the second case it also depends on the validity of the 'model' of the interdependent factors drawn up by operations researchers.) All too obviously on occasions it may mis-decide, either because it is fed with faulty information or because the 'best' choice or solution is excluded by the structure of the program.

In such cases who bears responsibility for the decision? The temptation is to place it on the machine. But this is patently ridiculous – and dangerous. A measure of automatic decision-taking is built into many modern weapons systems. As one alarmist saw it, 'Machine's Mistake May Doom World'.[5] In fact it would be the people who programmed and operated the machine who would be answerable.

This is obviously an extreme example. But similar lapses could

4. Quoted in Buckingham, W., *Automation: Its Impact on Business and People*, Mentor Books, New York, 1964, p. 33.
5. Headline of an article in the *New York Herald-Tribune*, 22 January 1958.

occur on a more mundane level. It is hard enough already to pin-point responsibility for a vast range of decisions in business and government which closely affect our lives. Increased use of the computer could widen the mask of impersonality and hence add to the risk of the irresponsible exercise of power by the faceless men who control the machine. Again, we are sometimes a little too willing to be impressed by the computer's achievements and power. We can even be dazzled into something approaching a belief in its infallibility. The unscrupulous could capitalize on this naïve mystique, representing as the 'objectively best' or 'impartial' ruling of the 'electronic brain' a decision which was entirely their own and designed to further their private aims or bolster their personal power. Such misuse could be extra-ordinarily difficult to detect. And because the machine is most certainly not infallible the culprits would have a strong line of defence if brought to book, being able to maintain that they merely acted in accordance with the machine's 'faulty' conclusions, in perfect good faith.

Centralized Control

The computer and its associated apparatus is an information-marshalling and -storing tool. The whole rationale of its use is to enhance control by exploiting these information-handling characteristics. Information and the use of information become more highly centralized. With regard to the purely technical functions of business or government administration this is for the most part beneficial and desirable. Top management armed with daily summaries of sales in all a firm's outlets is in a strong position to take corrective action as soon as deviations from forecasts occur. Direct transmission to a central computer of data on the movement of merchandise through the ports would bring comparable benefits to general economic management.

Reliable, comprehensive, up-to-the-minute information about events gives added power to control them. By the same token better information about persons makes it much easier to control them too. One of the most disturbing technical developments in computer technology from the point of view of civil liberties is the evolution of *mass random-access storage* (see Chapter 2).

'Information banks' can be built up for instant interrogation by the user. Those presently existing are used mainly to file such neutral information as an airline's seat bookings, or an engineering firm's technical design data. One hardly needs to be a Himmler or Beria, however, to visualize more imaginative applications: the compilation of a national security register, for example. A first step in this direction could be the perhaps politically acceptable consolidation of the numerous, but at present scattered, records which official bodies already keep on us.

Comparable, if more modest, aids to efficiency are equally available to any large organization. Some types of approach to administration already encourage the filing of information on the family and social life and personal opinions of an organization's managers. The computer makes possible the handling of the far greater volume of information which would be required for coding up every employee for such personal details.

Elitism

It has often been suggested that as computing grows in importance in the economy and society so will the prestige and power of the people – the systems designers and programmers – who understand and operate the machine or know how to exploit its potentialities. The money rewards of these personnel have already been climbing much faster than those of most industrial specialists, and will probably continue to do so. But so far they have been kept in an advisory staff role in most organizations. Indeed, one of their most common complaints, and it is largely valid, is that they usually have insufficient authority to push through many of their objectively necessary recommendations. They are a long way from becoming an elite in any but a narrowly economic sense.

Rather than becoming an elite themselves, however, they could help to foster elitism amongst management as a whole. An elite is not a group which simply has more money or power than others, but one whose prominence and authority are acknowledged by the majority as legitimately held. The elite needs to explain and justify its special position. It needs an ideology. Management can no longer justify its power by claiming it is a compensation for the risk it takes in investing personal capital in the enterprise. Such arguments are nowadays patently contradicted by the facts. Increasingly it has stressed its technical expertise in fostering wealth-creating efficiency. Computers can unquestionably enhance managerial effectiveness. If they are used successfully management takes the credit.

The growing realization by an elite of its rising prestige and influence is frequently soon followed by an increasing sensitivity to criticism and an increasing arrogance. Its high status, economic privileges and delegated prerogatives can soon be perceived more as a natural right than as society's rewards for outstanding services rendered. Its members may be tempted to extend their authority beyond their specialist fields and to intensify it within them. Such power-seeking is less easy to resist when the elite can point to an unquestioned competence within its own specialism. While management may not form a true or very prestigious elite at present, and specifically oligarchical objectives seem to be restricted to its otherwise more deviant luminaries only, there are many signs which point to the need for vigilance on the part of the rest of us in the coming years. At the very least, computerization, by improving managerial effectiveness, could stimulate managerial elitism sufficiently to reverse recent tentative movements towards the democratization of industrial and administrative control and the growth of 'consumer power'.

'*Drift*'

These are real, but mostly not immediate, dangers. How far computerization has resulted in oversystematized working conditions in the office will be discussed more fully in Chapter 6, but it is worth noting here that the machine can be exploited in such a way as to *reduce* the impingement of standardized work and the discipline of time on workers. Similarly, computerization can reduce the worrying impersonality of some decision-making because it enables the recording of data in such a way as to trace and pin-point responsibility. (But only if computer systems are *designed* to permit such identification.) It certainly encourages the centralization of control in organizations, but here it is necessary to distinguish between centralized control of operations and centralized control of persons. For the moment the technical difficulties of achieving the first are perhaps a cushion against the much more complicated second. And the computer has given scant support so far to greater managerial elitism: by and large it is clumsily used, bringing on its users much more ridicule than reverence.

True enough there are individual cases of misuse of the machine. One large American company was found to be operating a system which amounted to surveillance of individual workers. (It readily modified it, however, in the face of trade-union objection.) Professor Martin Greenburger of the Sloan School of Management, Massachusetts Institute of Technology, claims that computer technologists today find themselves in a position analogous to that of nuclear scientists after the discovery of atomic fission. There is also serious discussion in the United States of a code of computer usage, to be enforced by law.[6]

Perhaps such fears are extravagant. One reason for taking them seriously, however, is that widespread misuse of the machine could occur by default. As the French sociological philosopher Jacques Ellul has argued, the increasing acceptance of the primacy of technological convenience in general is not the product of some conspiracy on the part of a shadowy international fraternity of 'engineers', 'managers' or 'technocrats'. Mankind is *drifting* into subordination to technological and rational values. The erosion of human values is piecemeal, gradual and unconcerted. Along with the nuclear weapons systems, the synthetic food, our cities on wheels, supersonic civil aviation and mass-media entertainment go an increasingly detailed planning and organization of our lives, the pursuit of the 'one best method' in work and leisure alike.[7]

No individual or clique plots or masterminds the process. If they did, it would perhaps be easier to regulate. The drift continues with an apparently inexorable, almost Hegelian historical inevitability – a drift whose final political consequence is most probably dictatorship, albeit a materially benevolent one, since

6. See Professor Greenburger's article 'The Uses of Computers in Organizations', *Scientific American*, September 1966 ('Information' issue).
7. Ellul, J., *The Technological Society*, Cape, 1965.

political centrism can best marshal and deploy the fruits of technology and the means of production. Computerization can be viewed as an increasingly important ingredient in this prescription for the future.

But is the process really irreversible? Must the drive to exploit technology inevitably lead to the total primacy of technocratic values, producing types of person-to-person interaction, forms of social organization, and a distribution of power and prestige in society as a whole, which ride roughshod over fundamental human dignity? Dissenting from this kind of pessimism, the sociologist Alvin Gouldner has pointed out that we all too readily assume that a specific mode of organization and interaction is the inescapable product of technological advance. Too many social theorists, as he sees it, take one look at the historical trends, and, in a mesmerized state of 'metaphysical pathos', become 'morticians, eager to bury men's hopes'. Yet alternative structures, structures equally or almost as convenient for maximizing technological advantage and administrative efficiency but far more accommodating to human qualities, may be waiting to be discovered. Whether they finally prove to exist or not we should constantly search for them, instead of grumbling about the supposedly inescapable fate we so readily imagine we have let ourselves in for.[8]

Even more important, the imposition of any set of practices, procedures, or code of discipline depends ultimately on the consent of those who will be bound by them. Whether someone is attempting, in the name of 'progress', to impose on us a new supersonic airport, a dehydrated pudding mix, or a computerized national fingerprint index we can, as residents, consumers and citizens, say 'no'. The same goes for the organizational provisions and the petty but cumulatively substantial erosions of individual freedom that go along with, or in theory could go with, the more extensive use of computers.

The present economic difficulties of the United Kingdom have

8. Gouldner, A. W., 'Metaphysical Pathos and the Theory of Bureaucracy', *American Political Science Review*, 49, 1955, pp. 496–507; a shortened version is reprinted in Etzioni, A. (ed.), *Complex Organizations*, Holt, Rinehart & Winston, New York, 1964.

facilitated a measure of central control and direction unknown in peacetime. Recurrent crises have persuaded us to accept measures which would otherwise be firmly resisted. In such an atmosphere quite justifiable objections to some strategies for exploiting technology can be swept aside as minor economic treason or obscurantist chatter. The author would be the last to advocate universal resistance to computerization. But it would be catastrophic if such accusations of rocking the boat were to beat people into dumb acquiescence to the humanly improper.

Computerization – the type and range of applications attempted, and the working system which is erected around them – must be by actual or implicit consent: the consent of its employees and customers in the case of the enterprise, and of citizens in that of government departments. But consent can only be given or withheld realistically if the parties involved have some genuine appreciation of what the machine is, how it does its work, and how it will affect their own jobs and lives.

Further Reading

Boguslaw, R., *The New Utopians: A Study of Systems Design and Social Change*, Prentice-Hall, New York, 1965.

Burck, G., and the Editors of *Fortune*, *The Computer Age*, Harper & Row, New York, 1965.

Department of Scientific and Industrial Research, *Automation*, HMSO, 1956.

Diebold, J., *Automation: Its Impact on Business and Labor*, National Planning Association, Washington, 1959.

Ellul, J., *The Technological Society*, Cape, 1965.

Michael, D. N., *Cybernation: The Silent Conquest*, Center for the Study of Democratic Institutions, Santa Barbara, 1962.

Political and Economic Planning, *Attitudes in British Management*, Penguin, 1966.

Walker, C., 'Life in the Automatic Factory', *Harvard Business Review*, February 1958.

Wiener, N., *The Human Use of Human Beings*, Houghton Mifflin, New York, 1950 (Anchor Books, New York, 1954).

The most available regular guide to movements in the British computer population is *Computer Survey*, published by United Trade Press, London.

CHAPTER 2

Modern Computing Equipment

WHAT IS A COMPUTER?

BEFORE briefly reviewing the main items and characteristics of modern computing equipment (or *hardware*) it is necessary to say something further of the essential nature of the machine. One reason for this preliminary is the need to modify such coarse misconceptions of it as those conveyed by the expressions 'the glorified adding machine' or 'the electronic brain'.

A computer is an information engine, a mechanized *information*-converter, just as motive units such as a steam engine or electric motor are mechanized *energy*-converters. It operates completely mechanistically to convert a supply of information in a gross, unusable form to information in a refined and valuable form. Raw information, or *data*, is fed in one end; the engine interprets, classifies, counts, merges, sorts – i.e. *processes* – it; and processed information relevant to the needs of the user emerges at the other end. In essence this train of events is no more profound or mysterious than what happens when a supply of petrol is exploded in the engine of a car and we move forward: information is harnessed from data in one case, motion from fuel in the other.

Information conversion, or processing, includes but is not restricted to purely arithmetical calculation. As noted already, some computers do not compute at all, and the general-purpose digital computer can handle words or sentences (as in automatic language translation) or the lines of an engineer's or architect's design as readily as a set of numbers: in computing jargon it is *alpha-numeric*.

What distinguishes a computer from most other machines is this general-purpose nature and the fact that the information-converting process, once initiated by a human operator, is entirely self-supervised. This automaticity is achieved by including

31

in the information fed in a set of instructions, or program. Each instruction, read in turn, is designed to trigger a desired and known operation on the data to be handled – to add a number to another, or to move a word from one to another part of the machine, and so on. The program exploits the *basic operating software* of the machine, that is to say the logical repertoire built into it by its designer, which derives from the individual capacity and the planned interconnexions of its electronic components. This internal organization gives each machine specific and calculable functioning characteristics.

While the detailed structure of a particular machine determines what it can do best and how it does it, all digital computers have five basically distinct units or departments in common: *input*, *storage* (or memory), *control*, *arithmetic*, and *output* units.

Input

The computer handles information in a language of patterned electronic pulses. It cannot operate directly on the spoken or written symbols of human communication. To place information in the machine it is necessary to translate from human to machine language. This translation process consists of two phases. Computer language has two symbols only: 'pulse' and 'no-pulse' (of electricity), complex information being represented by combinations of the two. Each symbol can be represented in humanly intelligible form as '1' or '0', the two symbols of *binary* arithmetical notation or code. The first stage of translation is therefore to reduce data in other symbols to a binary form. For example, the numbers 3, 27 and 182 in decimal notation become 11, 11011, and 10110110 in binary. Letters of the alphabet can be coded by allocating each a decimal code number and then translating it to binary.

The second stage of translation involves the transformation of these coded data into electrical pulses. This is done by first punching specially designed paper tape or cards, a hole representing '1' and no-hole '0'. The data are now ready for presentation to the machine. As they are run through its input device the configurations of holes are sensed electronically and rendered into corresponding surges of patterned electronic pulses.

Storage

After entry through the input device, data, and equally important the program, are routed to the computer's store, or 'memory'. The store is analagous to a vast block of flats, each with an appropriate address number. Each item of data or program instruction is allocated its own set of addresses. On arrival at a storage address the electronic pulse is transformed into a magnetic charge in an appropriate material. It can be held in this form until required, when it is 'read', i.e. reconverted to a pulse or no-pulse as the case may be. The store of the machine is the key to its automatic nature. Each program instruction can be held ready for its turn to trigger an operation, and intermediate data generated during processing can be kept until they are required at a later stage. The intervention of a human operator is unnecessary.

Control

The control unit oversees the entry and exit of information from the machine and its transfer from one department to another. It does so in line with the instructions of the program, each of which is obeyed in turn. In effect it is a complex master-switch. Each program instruction is a code for setting the switch in a precise way: the control interprets the circuit-behaviour required and sets it in motion. After doing so it immediately calls for the next instruction.

Arithmetic

In purely mathematical work the arithmetic unit is that part of the machine where numbers withdrawn from the store are added, subtracted, multiplied and divided. But practically all that is required of the arithmetic unit is an ability to compare symbols for identity. It is around this simple operation that the complex logical operations of the machine in processing are erected. A major source of the machine's supposed intelligence is its ability to vary the sequence in which it executes the program instructions. Program instructions are punctuated with tests the outcome of which determines whether the next instruction will be followed in dealing with a particular case or whether a 'jump' or 'branch' will be made to an alternative, or later, set of instructions (see Chapter 3). These tests are for relations of equivalence. Two sets of symbols can be only identical or different. Hence the test is of a simple 'yes–no' kind. If A equals B then C will be done, if not D will be. By combining chains of such tests almost endless permutations of possible courses of action can be provided for.

Output

Once processing has finished the results or finished information must be communicated to the user. This involves a reverse process of translation from computer to human language. The output unit is a device responding to electronic stimuli to generate humanly intelligible symbols, most usually a printed document, though sometimes it punches paper tape which must then be passed through a reading device to make the output intelligible.

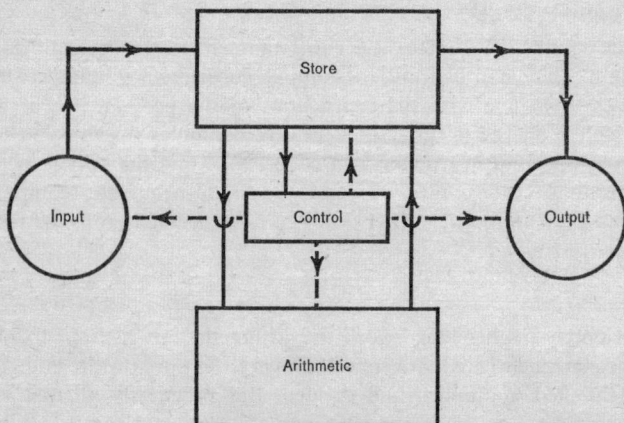

Figure 1. The functional relationships between the computer's five basic departments. Unbroken arrows indicate flows of data and information. Serrated arrows indicate control signals.

The functional relationships between the computer's five essential units are summarized in Figure 1, where bold arrows indicate flows of data and information and serrated arrows control signals. It should be emphasized that both the foregoing description and the diagram are highly schematic. In practice, the computer's main store, program control unit, and arithmetic unit are highly integrated physically. It is usual to refer to them jointly as the *central processing unit* (CPU). On the other hand input and output devices are physically detached from it (except for connecting cables) and for this reason, and others which will emerge subsequently, are termed *peripheral units*. Nonetheless in terms of physical bulk peripherals are far more space-taking and conspicuous than the CPU.

Besides their mechanistic nature, the outstanding general features of digital computers which can be summarized at this point are automaticity, accuracy, universality and speed.

Automaticity

In executing the program instructions the machine proceeds from one to another without any external cue. The instructions performed, and their sequence, can be varied to suit the particular circumstances of each one of a great many cases, because it can automatically consult and apply a set of rules for decision stored in its memory. In doing so it is subject to none of the delays or doubts which beset a human being performing a similar task. However, to perform so impressively it must be equipped with a program which has been carefully enough written to envisage and make allowance for every eventuality which may arise.

Accuracy

The computer is almost fiendishly accurate. Inaccuracy can stem only from faulty programming, faulty input data, or faulty components. The last possibility is nowadays almost small enough to ignore: most machines are designed to give warning of circuit faults, some diagnose where the fault is, and some even rectify it automatically. Errors from the first two sources can, and often do, seriously limit the practical value of the machine. Programs must be tested and retested ('debugged') to purge them of the programmer's fallible human illogicality. Source data must be collected, compiled and coded with scrupulous care: computing is subject to the so-called 'GIGO' ('garbage in–garbage out') principle, and without the most pernickety verification of input the machine generates nonsense. But both these sources of distortion originate not with the machine but with its users.

Universality

Provided a suitable program and reliable source data can be supplied the machine can perform an almost limitless series of heterogeneous tasks -- scientific, mathematical and technical computation (sometimes called 'number-crunching'), control of space vehicles, language translation, supervision of programmed learning, business problem-solving and so on. Wherever, in fact, the task can be reduced to a manageable number of interrelated steps leading inevitably to some final result or product, and source data can be presented in a codeable form, it will perform usefully. As experience in the analysis of problems and programming know-how accumulate, the range and number of applications must expand, especially in the administrative and decision-making areas of business and industry.

Speed

Fourth, and hardly in need of statement, the computer operates extremely rapidly, its speed deriving from its ability to handle information in the form of electronic pulses. However, as will be discussed later, the speed of the wholly electronic central processing unit is compromised by that of its relatively slower, partially mechanical – and therefore friction-prone – peripheral devices. Moreover, it is easily forgotten that not all computers are equally rapidly operating: the slowest are as slow beside the fastest as a human being is beside the slowest.

The 'Electronic Brain'

Because the computer is a universal information engine it is a narrow simplification to call it a 'glorified adding machine'. Such descriptions make little contribution to increasing its intelligibility or directing attention towards its most economically rewarding applications. The notion that it is an 'electronic brain' is even more obfuscating. This vulgar image relies on the fact that both brain and computer handle information and the computer can do work which we carelessly label 'mental' – e.g. arithmetic. There are of course parallels between the two entities, but because the computer can do some of the things a brain does it does not mean it does them in the same way or can do *everything* the brain does.

It has often been suggested that the comparison is anyway quite meaningless since present knowledge of the brain's structure and functioning is sketchy. Computer designers have perhaps imposed on the machine a method of functioning that we merely suppose the brain to follow when it is approaching specific problems. We know surprisingly little of how the brain tackles more complex problems. Hence we are not in a position to design a machine and write programs for these 'higher mental activities'. Contrary to popular belief the chess-playing computers are nowhere near the grand master class, and it is quite possible that no one will ever find out how to coach them to 'play' at this level. What little is known of the brain's own 'circuitry' indicates that it is several billion billion times more complex than that of the most advanced computer.

For these reasons there is very little possibility that it will ever surpass human beings in all-round information-handling. On specific tasks it is of course very much more rapid and accurate, and here – on tasks relatively trivial in terms of total human ability but demanding heavy slog – it serves a valuable complementary function. Finally, it is easily forgotten firstly that someone has to give a computer a program, feed it data, and switch it on; and secondly that the activity and comparative advantage of the brain are importantly, if obscurely, related to its containment in a total physical organism.

THE EVOLUTION OF COMPUTER HARDWARE

Generations

The speed of a computer's central processing unit inevitably depends on the speed of its individual components and on their size. Size is important because large components not only occupy a large volume of space but, becoming hotter in operation, demand additional ventilation space. Consequently the connexions between them must be longer, delaying the passage of electronic signals (which travel through a wire at approximately two thirds the speed of light). And the larger their size, the slower components function individually. Hence increases in central processor speeds have been largely dependent on the *miniaturization* of components. There have been three main phases of development, each associated with a characteristic component.

Computers of the first phase, or 'generation', were built around the *thermionic valve*. Although the first models of this generation were a thousand times faster than the first *non-electronic* computer (the Automatic Sequence Controlled Calculator), they were by present standards gigantic and ponderous. Their valves were slow in operation and liable to become very hot. Reliability was poor and maintenance expensive. Nowadays they tend to be written off as 'vacuum-tube monsters', though in fact improved valve technology enhanced their speed and reliability progressively until the mid 1950s and a few can still be found operating today.

The first major step towards miniaturization, ushering in the second generation of computers, was the adoption of *transistors*. Although the *point-contact transistor* had been invented as early as 1948 and the *junction transistor* in the early 1950s, the first proved too unreliable for the computer and the second too slow for its cost to offer successful competition to latter-day valves. Relative perfection, in the form of the *planar silicon transistor*, was not achieved until 1957, but within a couple of years a number of machines exploiting it were commercially available. The miniaturization permitted by these compact components helped to push speeds of second-generation computers to over a hundred thousand operations per second, and later refinements brought them not far short of the million mark.

It would probably be fair comment that many business computer users do not at present need speeds much in excess of this. However, the sheer momentum of development, one-up-manship amongst computer makers and designers, and, by no means least, military pressures continued to stimulate the quest for still smaller, faster components. By the early 1960s third-generation, *micro-miniaturized* computers performing millions of elementary operations per second were announced. The revolutionary component behind this new bout of contraction, the *micro-integrated-circuit*, is properly speaking the equivalent of a whole batch of components – transistors, resistors and capacitators – encrusted or engraved on a chip of material (e.g. silicon) sometimes not much larger than a full-stop on this page. Circuitry as powerful, but much faster, than that of a first-generation 'monster' can now be packed into the dimensions of the average suitcase.

Storage Technology

Advances in arithmetic speeds have tended to overshadow breakthroughs in computer storage, or memory, techniques. Yet a machine's capacity and range depend very closely on what storage facilities are available.

There are four main requirements of a computer memory. First, it should be as large as possible, and capable of further enlargement when a user's needs increase: the larger it is the more complex the programs and data which can be held internally, and the less troublesome programming becomes because the programmer does not have to worry so much about how to allocate a limited number of storage 'addresses'. Second, it should be *non-volatile*; that is, capable of retaining stored data without any risk of their fading away before they are required, or becoming lost when the current is switched off or interrupted accidentally. Third, it should offer *immediate access*, i.e. data or program instructions must be capable of being written into or read out of the store either by another part of the machine or by the user with almost zero delay.

The fourth requirement is that it should be cheap and easy to build. But unfortunately a store meeting even the first three requirements has proved elusive. ENIAC, the first electronic computer, could store a bare twenty 'words' of data. (A *word* of data consists of several *characters* each of several binary digits, or 'bits'.) Such capacity did not allow the storage of the program in the machine and it had to be represented by making numerous plug and socket connexions by hand. This time-consuming chore necessitated lengthy periods of computer inactivity in the turn-round from one job to another and limited severely the jobs which could be performed.

Suggestions for a computer with a memory of a thousand words, with the program being input from punched cards, were put forward by the designers of ENIAC at the University of Pennsylvania in 1946. The lavish funds needed to develop the idea were advanced promptly, mainly by the American Department of Defense. But teams working with more austere resources on this side of the Atlantic achieved the first successes.

In 1948 Professor F. C. Williams demonstrated his *cathode-ray-tube* store under laboratory conditions, and in the following year the Cambridge University Mathematical Laboratory incorporated the *mercury-delay-line* store in its EDSAC machine – the first computer to contain program and data in a single store. Both of these stores were, however, volatile and small. But a further storage technique, the *magnetic drum*, developed by A. D. Booth for the University of London's ARC machine at this time, although comparatively slower in operation, offered substantial capacity and has proved the most durable invention of the three.

The principle of operation of drum storage is to provide a rapidly rotating drum coated with a medium upon which electrical pulses can be induced from writing heads as magnetic dots. Once recorded the magnetized areas, or symbols, can only be removed by deliberately wiping them off or 'overwriting'. Reading is the reverse of writing, through a head which reconverts the magnetic charges to electrical pulses. A very large number of stored 'words' can be accommodated on the drum because the magnetized areas are microscopic. But access to a word is determined by its position relative to the reading head when it is required: on average it will take marginally more than half the time for a single revolution to read it. Speeding up average access time is a question of making the drum rotate faster – on which friction places practical limits.

On an electronic time-scale this irreducible delay is comparatively severe. In slow first-generation computers the penalty of delay was a fair exchange for the gain in storage space, but with faster components it became more urgent to develop an immediate-access store of reasonable capacity. The magnetic-drum store could always be used – and in fact, has been so used – as a rather slower, but more capacious, reserve memory backing the main immediate-access store.

The requisite breakthrough occurred in the mid 1950s, in the United States, in the form of the *magnetic-core* store which, first employed in latter-day valve computers, is still the orthodox main memory device in present machines.

Magnetic-core storage, or more usually *core* storage *tout court*, takes its name from its distinctive component, a minute, dough-nut-shaped ring of a magnetizable ceramic material (ferrite). A magnetic charge is 'written' into the core when electrical current is present in a wire passing through its central aperture. The direction of the magnetic charge, or polarity, can, depending on the nature of the current, run in either direction round the circumference of the core, and thus represent ideally the '0' or '1' of binary code. Reading is achieved by passing current through other wires threaded through the centre, leading to the firing, or the failure to fire, of a pulse along a 'sense' wire. (This does not remove the original magnetic charge from the core, which can only result from deliberate overwriting.) The access time for data is largely a function of the length of the wires connecting the cores with other parts of the machine. For practical purposes access is immediate.

Core stores are built up of arrays of individual 'doughnuts' meshed together by connecting wires in a single thin plane, several such 'matrix-planes' then being packed side by side to form a block through which each row of cores will store one word of data. This geometry of design has a number of advantages, the two most important being that it economizes on the number of connexions between the store and the rest of the machine, and allows an approach towards mass production in the manufacture of the store itself.

The invention of core storage soon made immediate-access stores of several thousand words a commercial proposition, and nowadays very much higher capacities are available. But a several-hundred-thousand-word immediate-access store is still very expensive. The ideal situation, where the commercial user can hold all the millions of items of data and information in his system in an immediately accessible form, is still a very long way off indeed.

Luckily, however, ways have been devised of getting by with a good deal less than perfection. Slower, but very much more capacious, and very much cheaper, 'backing' storage media can be articulated with the immediate-access store: information from these computer 'files' is then placed in it only when strictly needed there.

The two types of backing store or file exploited for this purpose are *magnetic discs* and *magnetic tapes*. (Magnetic drums may also be used.) Magnetic-disc stores, or files, consist of a pack of discs with a magnetizable coating, each one rather larger than a twelve-inch record, rotating at high speed on a common axle. Signals are written and read through traversing pick-up heads. Access time, usually at about twenty *milliseconds* (a millisecond is a thousandth of a second), is certainly not immediate since individual central processor operations are measured in *microseconds* (millionths of a second) or even *nanoseconds* (thousand-millionths). Discs are also much more expensive per million items of stored data than magnetic tapes. However, their great advantage for filing purposes is that items or blocks of data can be *randomly-accessed*, that is, retrieved quickly at will whenever they are required. They are analogous to a record-player, whose pick-up head can be moved directly to a chosen band: magnetic-tape files are similar to an ordinary tape-recorder, items being held along the length of the tape in sequence and requiring a delay for winding before access is achieved. Because of their random-access characteristics discs are most commonly used to hold records or programs which are continually required at short notice in the central processor (see, for example, *compilers*, page 62). It is, however, possible – though expensive and complicated to organize for such quantities – to employ them for bulk filing purposes.

More usually magnetic tapes – a cheap storage medium of almost infinite extensibility – come into their own when really vast quantities of data must be stored. As noted already these tapes are a rather broader version of those used in domestic tape-recorders and operate on exactly the same principle, the information being stored along their length and written and read by passing the tape through a head. During a processing run the tape has to be wound and rewound to gain access to data, and these delays can mean substantial under-utilization of central processing capacity. Consequently, much ingenuity must be applied to filing data on the tapes in sequences which reduce these hold-ups.

Efforts to develop new storage media and technologies are unremitting, and several more exotic types (such as *thin-film*, *cryogenic*, and *tunnel-diode* stores) are operational or undergoing refinement. This is not a book on computer technology nor the author a computer technologist, however, so they are not discussed here; and at present only one other storage medium, *magnetic-card* files, besides those described above is exploited on any scale in commercial computing systems.

Communication: Input, Output

A still more pressing problem than storage in exploiting the arithmetic speeds of third-generation central processors is that of getting information into and out of the system quickly. As noted, this information must be translated from human to machine language and back again. The crux of the problem is that most of the communication devices for these input and ouput formalities must be partially mechanical, and their possession of moving parts creates problems of friction and inertia which put an upper limit on their operating speeds low in relation to those of the central processor. The seriousness of the problem has been expressed as follows. If the speed of a modern central processor were slowed from around a million operations to a single operation a second, a communication device like an electrotypewriter which normally prints ten characters a second would print only one character a day. As one computer specialist put it, a computer accepting input from a gold-medal typist is in the same relative position as a man who receives one letter of an urgent telegram each morning for three weeks.

The classic communication media are *punch cards* and punched *paper tape*. Most punched cards are divided into eighty columns and twelve rows, making a total of almost a thousand possible punching spaces, holes being punched in line with a coding convention, and verified, by semi-skilled girl operatives. The verification stage is necessary to keep transcription errors to a manageable minimum. Stacks of prepared cards are fed into a card reader which senses the pattern of holes photoelectrically. A *card-punching* device, actuated by electronic signals, may be fitted to the output end. Paper-tape input is generated on a specialized typewriter (*flexo-writer*) and consists of a number of tracks (usually seven or eight) for holes distributed either side of a track of sprocket holes to help guide it through the input device (*paper-tape reader*), which winds in blocks of several hundred characters at a time rather like a bus conductor's ticket machine operating in reverse. Paper tape, too, may be punched automatically on the output end.

Both card and paper-tape reading and punching are necessarily slow, characters being transferred at one or two hundred per second at the most. There is the further inconvenience that before entry to and upon exit from the computer system they are not immediately intelligible to the human user. It is particularly irritating to have to wait while card or paper-tape output is fed through a further device to decode its holes into letters and numbers. A printing device is almost always linked directly to the central processor, generating print at a thousand lines or more per minute. For still higher-speed output a rather more costly device can produce whole pages at a time by transforming electronic signals to a xerographic (i.e. quasi-photographic) print image.

Progress in achieving the direct *input* of printed or written matter has been rather patchy. Two techniques, Optical Character Recognition (OCR) and Magnetic Ink Character Recognition (MICR), are, however, available. In MICR, documents must be prepared in an ink with a magnetic ingredient: a reading device can then convert the characters to electronic signals by sensing their outline. In OCR, written or printed documents are read photoelectrically by throwing a beam of light on to the page. Documents can be scanned at about fifteen hundred per minute. But so far the documents have had generally to be of a standardized size and layout and the amount of data on each one carefully rationed. They are easily scuffed or torn by the mechanism which presents them, and dust or smudges lead to errors. Both techniques have their specialized uses but the day is not here when the average computer will readily accept a wide range of typed or handwritten input. (Direct voice communication, another obvious goal, is even further off, despite impressive set-piece laboratory demonstrations.)

Direct electronic communication with the machine in a format intelligible to the user is of course the ideal both from the point of view of exploiting the computer's full capacity and from that of the user's convenience. So far the devices available for this are highly specialized and/or extremely expensive. The *graph-plotter*, for example, is a kind of electronic tracer which, when moved along the lines of a technical drawing, converts their co-ordinates to digital form and stores them in the computer's memory for later retrieval, when they are reproduced automatically. The *electronic stylus*, or 'light pen', goes one better. Passed over a cathode-ray screen by the draftsman it picks up the emissions and transmits them back to the computer. The machine interprets the shape of the figure being sketched and causes an immediate luminous outline of it to appear on the screen. The user can then send signals which delete, enlarge, contract, rotate, or even provide a three-dimensional image of the figure.

The most publicized, perhaps the most gimmicky, communication device so far available is the *cathode-ray display screen*. Similar to a small television screen it is wired into the main body of the computer. When the appropriate knobs and buttons are keyed in, tables, graphs, histograms and brief explanatory sentences can be captured directly from the machine's random-access files. It is likely that such equipment will become important in future high-level management planning. For the moment its utility is compromised by its limited range and the programming problems attaching to really productive man–machine 'dialogues'.

Peripheralization

Despite advances in communication methods, conventional (i.e. economically justifiable) input and output devices remain wasteful of the central processor's time and inconvenient to the user. A number of expedients have, however, helped to bridge the gap in operating speeds. The first stratagem to be applied was *peripheralization*.

The rationale of peripheralization is to remove the sluggish communication devices like paper-tape readers and card punches from immediate contact with the central processor, which no longer has to march at the pace of the slowest. An advantage of magnetic tape is that a given length of it can store a vastly greater amount of data than an equivalent length of paper tape. Thus although magnetic-tape reading devices do not operate much faster than paper-tape readers they transfer data into the machine, and accept output, at a much higher rate. Consequently slower devices can be operated *off-line*, i.e. segregated from the central processor, in conjunction with magnetic-tape units. Data can be placed on magnetic tape, or read from it, at convenient times, the magnetic tapes themselves being used as the main immediate communication medium with the processor. (At this point it is worth noting incidentally that it took some users a great deal of time to accept the fact that many output data could be held permanently on magnetic tape with no need to be reduced to a humanly intelligible form, since their relevance was to the internal requirements of certain processing runs only, and not the needs of the user.)

Radical peripheralization has, however, been overtaken by the techniques of *peripheral operating simultaneity*. All this mouthful means is getting a battery of peripherals linked to the central processor to function in parallel. Even with magnetic tape, input data enter the processor in blocks, between which on the processor's time-scale there are considerable pauses. The idea is to fill these interruptions by reverting to other work in the split second before a new block of data can be transferred in or out. This other work can be a transaction with another peripheral device. In this way a bevy of peripherals can be kept going simultaneously, feeding, and being fed by, a single processor. Further economies on the processor's time can be made by providing output devices with small 'buffer' memories which allow larger blocks of data to be output at each 'hesitation'.

Multiprogramming

The objective of *multiprogrammed* computing is to allow several programs as well as several peripherals to be handled simultaneously. The concept was first put forward in 1959 by Christopher Strachey of the University of Oxford Computing Laboratory, and first implemented a couple of years later on the ATLAS machine by the then International Computers and Tabulators Company.

A more publicity-conscious implementation, 'Project MAC', occurred subsequently at the Massachusetts Institute of Technology. (The 'MAC' acronym stands for 'multiple-access computer' – not to mention 'machine-aided cognition' and 'man and computer' – besides jokily punning on the American working-class term of address between familiar equals.) In the last five years multiprogramming has found commercial expression in the 'time-sharing' computer bureaux which provide access rights to a very powerful machine for numerous small or occasional users. And it is used increasingly to exploit the full capacity of large privately owned machines.

The precise technical details of achieving this multiple usage are not important here. There are two main strategies. In one, the processor executes a single instruction in turn of each of a number of programs. If a program is held up by a peripheral transfer it loses its turn and the machine skips to the next program. In the other, the processor continues executing the instructions of a single program until a delay for peripheral transfer occurs, when it turns its attention to the next program. In the latter system programs have to be given some kind of priority identification, and in both a very complex super-program (generally called an 'executive') has to be created to discipline the queue of programs and orchestrate peripherals.

On-line and Real-time Processing

Besides cutting the waste of central processing capacity, multiprogramming facilitates on-line and real-time processing. *On-line* computing is the transfer of information to and from the computer from 'remote' communication terminals over specially installed land-lines. (Limited volumes of data can even be transmitted over ordinary public telephone lines.) The user has a direct link with the distant central processor. Such links are extremely valuable in geographically dispersed organizations, since input does not have to be carried or posted to the computer centre with all the expense and – rather more important – the delay such journeys involve. (It has been jocularly suggested that the development of on-line computing will cut the accident-rate on the M1 and similar arteries by removing the dispatch-riders speeding from provincial offices to London headquarters *en masse* on Thursdays to 'get the payroll done'.)

Real-time computing implies the processing of data about on-going events sufficiently rapidly to obtain a reverse flow of feed-back information to influence the events while they are still occurring. Inevitably it is tied to on-line data transmission. Real time is of course a flexible and relative concept. The real-time control of a space vehicle must obviously involve two-way transmissions as near the instantaneous as possible. Real-time commercial computing does not and need not imply such breath-less and dramatic transactions. Yet in all cases the basic idea is to remove the delay in information-handling which can cause a wasteful or dangerous loss of control over events.

One of the best known commercial on-line, real-time applications is airline seat booking. The booking clerk, equipped with an interrogation console, transmits a request to a central computer file to check the availability of seats on the flight the customer requires. If a seat is available it is temporarily withdrawn from the pool while the customer confirms his order to prevent it being booked by another clerk meanwhile. Once the order is con-firmed a signal from the clerk removes it altogether. Details about the customer are then transmitted to the files to facilitate flight planning.

Similar, though more modest, kinds of system are operated by large insurance companies to advise customers on terms and premiums for (e.g. motor) policies while they wait. The London Stock Exchange is developing another to answer members' inquiries about the latest movements in security prices. The clearing banks are creating very elaborate systems to accelerate transfer of credits and balancing: it is bad news for many of us but the day is not far off when the clerk will be able to dial up an instant up-to-the-minute image of our account before he pays out.

Public information banks exploiting this aspect of the technology are an obvious future service industry of considerable scope and potential profitability. With the simplification of programming we may also find ourselves using such facilities to assist us with the increasingly complicated information-handling in our private decision-making – for instance, the calculations behind choosing a new car or house. Indeed, such *ad hoc* use of semi-public computers on-line and in real time is already taking root amongst commercial users. Computing bureaux providing access to large machines for small, occasional or specialist users for a standard fee per minute of machine-time have been a feature of the data-processing industry almost since its beginning.

But perhaps the most significant exploitation of on-line, real-time computing will be within individual large-scale industrial concerns. Successful managerial decision-making and control at all levels depends on the availability of relevant, up-to-date information. The growth in scale of modern industrial operations has rendered conventional methods for collecting this information inadequate. As the computing head of a large engineering concern has remarked: 'Perhaps the most difficult thing in a large modern engineering shop is to find out exactly what is going on.' The concern in question is attacking this problem by installing input terminals at key points on the factory floor to capture information on the movement of assemblies and parts at source, operatives dialling reports when items reach or leave their stations or certain operations are completed.

Two main impressions may have been gained from this brief review. Firstly, that the expression 'computer', however convenient, is rather misleading in that most 'computers' are configurations of interlinked devices. Secondly, that far from being some monolithic miracle-worker the equipment has some paradoxical weaknesses – the relative smallness of immediate-access storage, for example, or the gap between processor and peripheral speeds. Both of these characteristics present users of the machine with considerable practical problems. Choosing a suitable configuration of hardware becomes a decision of some complexity; getting it to work harmoniously no less taxing. However, from another point of view, the variety and range of individual devices does allow a very welcome flexibility in selection and strategies of operation. Flexibility is permitted not only by the variety of communication and filing devices but also by a feature of modern central processors which has not so far been mentioned – their *modularity*.

Computer manufacturers have always offered a selection of machines ranked by their speed and capacity. However, until quite recently the user wishing to extend his range of applications often found that changing to a larger machine would give him more capacity than he needed (and at more cost than he could afford). As often as not, too, a manufacturer's machines were program-incompatible (see Chapter 3): that is, the programs written for his small models could not be run on his larger ones. The user's considerable investment in tried and tested software might suddenly become worthless.

The practice nowadays is for the manufacturer to produce a series, or 'family', of compatible machines. Each central processor can be upgraded simply and cheaply by fitting additional modules (e.g. of core storage) when need occurs. Adding or removing peripheral devices has also been greatly facilitated by the development of the *standard interface* (in effect a refined plugboard). Thus the user can graduate from a modest initial configuration to a very large one in convenient steps without the need to change his supplier or face the cost of complete re-programming.

From the foregoing it is clear that the question 'how much does a computer cost?' is almost impossible to answer. It depends very much on the volume and type of work to be done, and on the chosen methods of organizing the different computer jobs, what equipment any one user will require at any one time. But a modest basic system capable of handling, say, the routine office chores of a firm of one or two thousand employees, could be had for something between £50,000 and £60,000. A medium system, for the routine data-processing of a firm up to ten thousand employees or for a smaller firm attempting more ambitious applications, would be at least double this price. Large systems, incorporating a hierarchy of central processors, multiprogramming, large random-access stores, and data-transmission links, will cost anything from half a million to several million pounds in hardware alone.

The qualification 'in hardware alone' is important. The physical equipment represents on average only half the costs of entry to computerized operations. The 'software' – systems design, programming, and staff-training work – essential to a successful changeover costs at least as much as the machine itself in most cases. The reasons why will be discussed in the next chapter.

The difficulty of choosing an appropriate system; its cost; and the numerous other problems of introducing a computer are genuine deterrents for many potential users. Not surprisingly, a large number prefer to rent their equipment, a practice which insures them against sudden obsolescence as well as giving them a sanction against poor service or support from their supplier; a further substantial minority play it still safer by buying time from a computer bureau.

Yet despite all the genuine risks and difficulties of computerization, and the remaining inadequacies of the hardware, it is striking how unadventurous potential users have been in their approach to the machine beside their counterparts abroad (for whom the obstacles are similar). Over the last ten years the cost of a unit of computing power has fallen much more rapidly than utilization has grown. Admittedly, there are signs that this pussy-footed approach may be to some extent reversed in the next few years. No one seriously questions that the machine will eventually be regarded as an essential administrative tool, like the telephone or typewriter. Unlike the telephone or typewriter, however, skilful and productive use depends a good deal on the user's length of experience with it. Organizations which use computers can take up to ten years to find out how to exploit it profitably and for their members to accept the machine as a partner. The experience which so many future users have already lost by their reluctance to take the plunge is a handicap which will be with them individually, and the British economy as a whole, for many years to come.

Further Reading

The number of technical descriptions of computer hardware is immense, as are the variations in quality and difficulty between them. The pace of development in the technology also ensures that no account is ever fully up-to-date. Certain constants, however, do remain. The following three recommendations are ranked roughly in ascending order of detail and readability:

Laver, F. J. M., *Introducing Computers*, HMSO, 1965.

Scientific American, September 1966 ('Information' issue), especially the articles by D. C. Evans, Ivan Sutherland, R. M. Fano and F. J. Corbato, J. R. Pierce, B.-A. Lipetz, and Marvin Minsky.

Hollingdale, S. H., and Tootill, G. C., *Electronic Computers*, Penguin, 1965.

For the technical enthusiast some of the introductions prepared by the computer manufacturers themselves, though less readily available, are outstandingly useful: *Introduction to Computer Systems* by the Technical Publications Department of International Computers and Tabulators Ltd (ICT Technical Publication 3312), for example, is remarkably clear and readable considering the level of detail pursued.

For those interested in the computer-versus-brain issue the standard texts are von Neumann, J., *The Computer and the Brain*, Yale University Press, New Haven, Conn., 1958, and Walter, W. G., *The Living Brain*, W. W. Norton & Co., New York, 1953.

A more advanced, mathematical treatment by a theoretical pioneer of modern computing is A. M. Turing's article 'Can a Machine Think?' in von Neumann, J. (ed.), *The World of Mathematics*, Vol. 4, Simon & Schuster, New York, 1956.

CHAPTER 3

The Software Problem

'SOFTWARE'

MANY computer users dislike the expression 'software', not so much because it has an ugly sound but because in practice it has ugly associations. In its broadest sense software denotes the intellectual investment of a computer system which is the counterpart of the investment in equipment, or hardware. In more concrete terms it refers to the products, especially the *programs*, derived from systems design and programming work. The development of his software presents the user with considerable expense and difficulty. There are two closely related reasons for this. Firstly, systems design and programming are inherently time-consuming and intellectually demanding activities; and secondly, there is a considerable and increasing shortage of people qualified to undertake them.

SOFTWARE DEVELOPMENT

It is platitudinous, but it cannot be repeated often enough, that the benefits of computerization cannot be grasped merely by installing the machine. The user must decide where and how it will fit in with his overall data-processing and information system. When he has decided what jobs he wants it to do, how often, and in what order, he is still faced with the equally sobering problem of providing it with sets of instructions to exploit its prodigious, but stupid, logicality. Once it has been told what to do, step by step in logically precise sequence, it will do it fast and faultlessly. But telling it right in the first place is no mean task.

There is no evasion of this need for systems design and programming. True enough, some programs, or sections of them (*subroutines*), covering standard mathematical or data-processing operations such as the evaluation of square roots, the vetting of input, or the tabulation of results, are available off-the-peg from computer suppliers (see *standard software packages*, page 63). Others can be bought or hired from other users (the National Computer Centre, for example, assists such transactions through its National Program Index). But the great majority of programs and subroutines in the average commercial system, usually running into several hundred, must be developed by the user himself. As noted already the cost of development can equal that of the hardware. For this reason no less than the literal-mindedness of the computer itself it is evident that the process of development must be carefully planned and controlled and pay meticulous attention to detail.

There are three main phases in this program development process : systems analysis and design; program flowcharting; and program coding. (Before a system becomes fully operational there are the additional phases of program proving, or 'de-bugging', and the parallel running of the former 'manual' system with the new computer system.)

Systems analysis is an overall study of how a job which may be worth computerizing is presently done: how data are collected and collated; what operations are performed on them; what personnel are involved and at what stages; what use is made of the information generated; and who uses it. It is important that the systems analyst should not prejudge that the job is worth computerizing. Even superficial systems study often reveals inadequacies in the manual system – discontinuities in the flows of data, work duplication, imprecise lines of communication, vague boundaries of responsibility, and any number of other 'old Spanish customs' – which can be rectified by conventional work reorganization. Sometimes the manual system can be sufficiently streamlined to remove the economic justification for a computer. The first stage of systems work is concerned more with whether the job can be computerized and is worth computerizing than with how it should be computerized.

But if preliminary study indicates definite advantages from computerization the systems man adopts a more creative role – the design of a new information system oriented towards the computer. Because they will commit the concern to a given basis of operation, and probably influence what type and configuration of hardware is acquired, his findings and recommendations must be convincingly documented. In his report (usually called a *statement of requirements*) he contrasts the previous manual system with the new one he proposes. A *systems flowchart* specifies what data are to be supplied to the computer, what operations are to be carried out on them, and the form of the information to be output. It also lays down the media (e.g. punched cards or magnetic tape) to be used to transfer information from one part of the computer system to another and the peripheral devices to be called into play.

He may also – though this is more usually a job for a senior programmer – prepare a *job plan*. This document details how the job can be tackled from a programming point of view, and estimates the costs in programming man-hours and in machine-time for program testing and normal running. Later the senior programmer will prepare two further pieces of documentation. Firstly, a *program organization chart* specifying the exact programs and subroutines needed for the job (together they are known as the *program suite*) and presenting their interrelations in diagrammatic form. And secondly, a *job specification*, which, complementary to the program organization chart, is an exhaustive verbal account of the requirements of each program. During the preparation of these documents there should be continuous liaison between the user, the systems man and the senior programmer. This exchange obviously helps to pin down errors and oversights, and it is essential that there should be complete mutual understanding between the parties. Revision of the system once programming has commenced can be punitively expensive – some users even prefer to persist with an inadequate system rather than start again.

Once agreement is reached on this first major stage the job of preparing individual programs can begin. In this *program flow-charting* phase the same principle of proceeding from the general to the particular is observed. As noted, the steps in which a program is executed in the machine are individually very simple and restricted. Each instruction triggers only two or three phases of circuit activity on entering the control unit. A program for a task of any complexity requires several thousand such instructions, all logically interrelated and fully consistent with each other. Obviously the task of listing these instructions in correct order can only begin when the overall form of the total set of instructions has been determined. For this purpose the technique of flowcharting is the most illuminating and helpful.

Flowcharts are logical models in a diagrammatical form of the whole job to be carried out. The operations to be performed are listed in order from top to bottom of the page and joined by arrows indicating lines of progression from one step to another. Some of these arrows form loops back from later to earlier steps, others indicate 'jumps' where it may be possible to omit certain steps, both types of operation being dependent on the results of some kind of test. The level of detail in the flowchart can be successively increased, but at all stages the steps specified must be unambiguous and consistent. The detailed logical structure which emerges is illustrative of two things; firstly, that even trivial activities and tasks have a surprisingly complex structure; and secondly, that the computer's supposed intelligence is an absurd myth.

The tests built into flowcharts (and hence into the final machine-coded program) enable the machine to vary the sequence of operations to deal with varying cases and to proceed automatically from one case to the next. Individually these tests must be of the most rudimentary 'yes–no' form. To simulate more complex tests whole strings of such simpler tests must be strung together. Flowcharting is in fact the briefing of an obedient moron, and to illustrate the kind of expansion of a flowchart needed for programming a brief analogy is illuminating.

Suppose we had to give precise, logically watertight instructions to a dim-witted but co-operative human for a simple processing task – for example checking a deck of playing cards for missing cards. First we have to make sure that the main stages in the task follow in a logical sequence. If we want to know how many cards are missing from each suit we obviously must give instructions for sorting before instructions for counting. For complete clarity too we must indicate where the job begins and ends. Our outline flowchart might be written as in Figure 2.

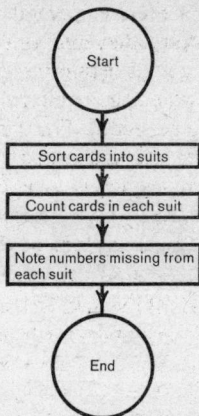

Figure 2.

But each of these instructions is too elliptical as it stands. How exactly does one go about sorting the cards into suits? How does one know when to proceed to the next instruction? We can expand the first section ('Sort cards') of the flowchart as in Figure 3.

Several features of this sorting subroutine stand out. Firstly, the single instruction 'Sort cards into suits' breaks down into eleven minor instructions and tests. (Even so the chart is still not quite a *reductio ad absurdum*: we assume for instance that no further instructions are required for recognizing the different suits.) Secondly, the tests provided are of the simplest yes–no kind and permit no ambiguity. Thirdly, the steps are arranged in such a way that every card must be allocated to a suit no matter what its position in the original unsorted pack. Finally, the eleventh step serves a critical function, preventing any escape from the loop of instructions until all cards are sorted, but then ensuring that escape is duly made.

This example need not detain us any longer. The reader is invited to devise for himself suitable subroutines for counting and writing the totals of cards in each suit, or alternative ones for sorting. Many solutions are possible, some more economical, or

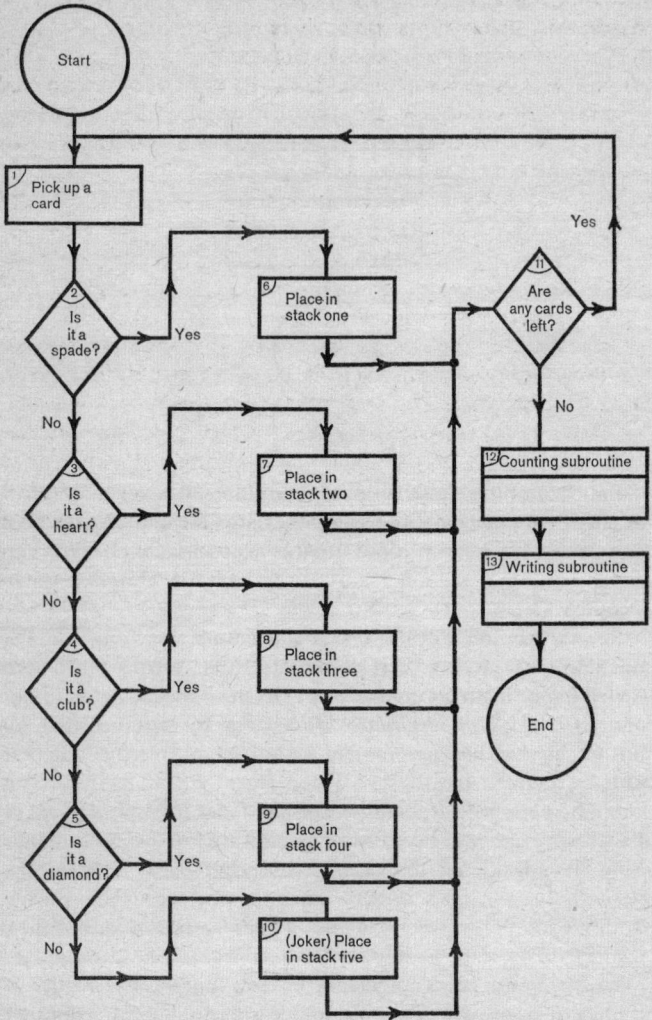

Figure 3.

58

'elegant', than others. Such exercises certainly give valuable insight into the problems and skills of programming.

Flowcharting can be broken down into a number of individual assignments for junior programmers, the overall strategy being supervised by an experienced senior. While it is important for systems men to be conversant with the affairs of the computerizing concern, this phase of the work can proceed almost in abstraction from it. The programmers work from relevant sections of the program organization chart and job specification. They need not even be members of the concern (though accuracy and ingenuity sometimes fall off if they aren't) and can be located at a distance from the factory or office being computerized.

The final stage in program writing, *coding*, is the translation of detailed flowcharts into machine instructions. Each flowchart statement, or instruction, is equivalent to about three machine instructions, which must be written down on a standard coding sheet. For ease of reference and logical ordering each flowchart instruction is allocated a number and the instructions in code are carefully related to each one. The instructions used must be drawn from the limited number available on the machine. (Their range and type will also have influenced in some measure the design of the flowchart itself.)

The coding activity is a routine and tedious business. Instructions in code take the form of numbers punctuated by commas, semi-colons and asterisks, for example: 002, 3892;. The first part of such an instruction (002,) is usually kn own as the 'operation number' and specifies what operation is to be performed, e.g. 'subtract'. The comma indicates a disjunction between it and the following number, which indicates the storage address of the item to be subtracted. The final semi-colon indicates disjunction between the instruction as a whole and the next. Translating the instructions into machine language is achieved by punching cards or paper type and feeding them into the input device, as outlined in Chapter 2.

Programming in machine code is not just tedious. Clearly transcription errors are likely to occur when so many numbers are being handled. But to write 001 for 002 will probably be the difference between addition and subtraction. Again, the coder has to keep a highly exact tally of the memory addresses he has used, thus running further risks of omission or duplication. Not surprisingly the errors which creep in, as well as logical errors stemming from flowcharting slips, make it very rare for a program to work satisfactorily the first time. The ensuing program-proving (or 'debugging') phase, far from being a mere routine check, often becomes as lengthy and expensive (additionally so, because it requires the purchase of computer time) as writing the program in the first instance.

Because of the mass of detailed work involved it is hardly surprising that developing software for even a modest set of applications takes a time measured in systems and programming man-years. Other difficulties, especially finding, training, and above all retaining staff for the work, add to the time and cost. (These latter problems will be discussed shortly.)

Is there much hope of streamlining the punctilious ritual of software preparation itself? The necessarily simplified description of programming given above can be qualified at this point, since over recent years the increasing sophistication and wider use of higher-level programming languages has certainly helped to reduce the programming burden.

Higher-level languages (HLL) pursue two main objectives: firstly, to make it possible to write program instructions in a form more convenient to the programmer than the machine; secondly, to permit the interchange of programs between machines of different make, size, and internal organization. (Programming languages directed primarily at this second objective are generally called *universal* higher-level languages). The first move came with the invention of *autocodes*. The simplest autocodes merely replace numbers with easily memorizable mnemonics: for example, ADD instead of 002. They are usually designed for specific makes of machine and for specialized rather than general purposes. More ambitious autocodes may however offer a fairly wide range of instructions and help the programmer with the task of memory-address allocation. Some instructions for commonly repeated operations may replace hundreds of machine-coded instructions – for example, for output printing operations.

Programs written in a higher-level language (*source programs*) cannot in themselves trigger the machine into action. Only programs in the machine's own code (*object programs*) can do that. The autocoded source program in fact must be regarded as itself a batch of input data to be processed into machine code. This translation is achieved by using a special *assembler program*. Once the autocoded source program has been assembled the machine-coded object program can be used in exactly the same way as one written in machine code in the first place. The only disadvantages are that it may be slightly less economical of storage space and more 'long-winded' than a directly coded program, leading to an increase in running time. On the other hand the computer relieves the programmer of the most tedious part of his job. An example of such a source program appears at the end of this chapter.

Despite their considerable usefulness autocodes have a number of inadequacies. Although they remove the need to remember a large number of machine codes they are still appreciably 'machine-oriented' in that source programs written in them are not immediately intelligible to the non-expert. Furthermore they tend to be specific to particular types of program, and, equally inconvenient, to the machines of a single manufacturer.

The sometimes desultory and sometimes eager quest for universal higher-level languages is an answer to these deficiencies. An obvious difficulty in devising such advanced programming aids is that development demands a substantial measure of co-operation between programmers, computer designers, users, and manufacturers. So far varying design philosophies in computer hardware and commercial rivalries between manufacturers have made such co-operation variable and elusive. External pressure for collaboration has been imposed to some extent on American manufacturers by federal departments. There has been conspicuously less willingness to knock the parties' heads together on this side of the Atlantic.

Nonetheless three major, internationally used universal HLL have been established: ALGOL 60, COBOL, and FORTRAN. Of these ALGOL 60 (*Algo*rithmic *L*anguage), whose use extends to eastern bloc countries, perhaps enjoys the most widespread acceptance. Designed specifically for scientific, mathematical and technical programs, it is easily learned in its simplest forms by non-specialists, and its structure and format permit ease of communication within the worldwide scientific community. Programs can in fact be written in something close to standard mathematical notation. For example, the equation:

$$x = \left\{ 1.0 + \frac{(a + b)(c + d)}{(a + d)(b + c)} \right\}^2$$

can be written

$$x := (1.0 + ((a + b) \times (c + d))/((a + d) \times (b + c))) \uparrow 2.$$

(The specimen program at the end of the chapter is also written in a variant of ALGOL.)

FORTRAN (*For*mula *Tran*slation) too is a scientific-mathematical HLL enjoying wide international support, not merely because of its unquestionable merits but also because it is sponsored by International Business Machines, whose dominance of the world computer market provides it with a unique backing.

COBOL (*Com*mon *B*usiness *O*riented *L*anguage) is designed specifically for commercial programming, and programs in it contain a high proportion of 'operations' (i.e. instructions) which not only act as a kind of shorthand for a multitude of machine instructions but are readily intelligible to the average manager: for example, 'ADD OVERTIME PAY TO STRAIGHT-TIME PAY'.

As with autocoded programs, programs in universal HLL must be translated by the computer itself into a set of machine instructions, the translating program in this case being known as a *compiler*. Because of their variations in internal organization each type of machine must have its own set of compilers for ALGOL, COBOL, etc. However, in theory a single program written in (for example) COBOL is compatible between different machines since it can be compiled separately for each. And if theory and practice did not diverge much of the effort which goes into training programmers would be unnecessary, and the mobility of programmers between assignments greatly eased.

Unfortunately, however, theory and practice do diverge, sometimes at an angle approaching a hundred and eighty degrees. As noted already a source program in any HLL will, when compiled into an object program, contain more instructions than a program written initially in direct machine code. In this sense all HLL are wasteful of the computer's storage capacity and take longer to run. By and large the growth in central processing speed and capacity have made these penalties worth accepting, however, especially when the saving in programming effort and the gain in compatibility are borne in mind. But an inefficient compiler can create such an unwieldy object program that all savings are lost.

Some COBOL compilers in particular are exceptionally inefficient. Not, it is sometimes suggested, by accident, since once a user has borne the cost of programming in a manufacturer's own autocode he will be effectively tied to one supplier. Again, it is unconventional for a manufacturer to offer a compiler which can translate all the instructions available in the official COBOL vocabulary. Clearly this may be quite impracticable for his smaller machines, given the best intentions. But with the bigger models such inadequacy is less easy to explain or excuse. (The excuse sometimes given that users do not want to program in COBOL anyway – because it is so clumsy – has a rather self-fulfilling ring.)

STANDARD SOFTWARE PACKAGES

The other main hope for cutting the programming cost is by increasing the availability and exchange of proved items. As the quality of their hardware has become more standardized, competition between manufacturers has tended to shift towards the software they offer their users either free of charge or below market rates. Each manufacturer amasses an increasingly varied stock of programs and routines for his own machine which can be used as they stand, modified for, or inserted in programs catering for the user's special circumstances. Such 'library subroutines' would include items for data vetting and sorting, output printing, calculating PAYE or pension contributions, and evaluating standard mathematical functions such as square roots, logarithms, exponentials, etc.

The 'standard software package' will also include assemblers for the supplier's own autocodes and compilers for COBOL, ALGOL and FORTRAN; a 'consolidator program' which compiles a full object program from a number of 'semi-compiled' routines written in a variety of source languages, as well as library subroutines; 'housekeeping' programs which supervise the transfer of data between different categories of storage in the most economical manner; and 'supervisor' and 'executive' programs for orchestrating peripherals and permitting multi-programmed operation.

In addition, manufacturers sponsor users' associations for pooling experience and software for a common machine. Suitable items may be borrowed, bought, or hired in this way. As noted, the National Computing Centre, through its National Program Index, has also taken a close interest in this kind of exchange. The NPI contains programs for all makes of machine, not just those of a single supplier. Contributors to the scheme specify the type of program required and one of the Centre's own computers searches its files for the closest match. The contributor must then make his own approach to the program's owner and arrange terms.

STAFFING PROBLEMS

The difficulties which stem from the intrinsic complexities of software development and the imperfections of programming aids are compounded by the shortage of systems and programming personnel of high calibre – the so-called 'liveware gap'. This additional problem will be looked at in more detail in Chapter 7. At this point it is mentioned only in passing.

From the point of view of the user the liveware gap has two main consequences. Firstly, it makes high-calibre 'datacrats' very difficult to come by. In absolute terms, of course, even the British computerization rate has been rapid, and the rise in the number of installations and extended scope of applications, taken with the generally inadequate training facilities available, have inevitably produced a shortage of personnel. Salaries have tended to spiral, and users almost always have to pay a good deal more than they expect or like to get a good man.

Often, however, the complaint is less against the 'exorbitant' salaries that this situation produces than against its effect on the datacrat's approach to company discipline. Because so many people are clamouring for his services the datacrat can adopt a more cavalier approach to superiors and company rules – or so it is suggested. In fact, as will be argued later, the position is a little more complicated than that. The datacrat's unquestionably high mobility between appointments is only in part a pure market phenomenon. And his supposed 'lack of discipline' can be interpreted just as much as an aspect of his occupational style as a product of the same market forces.

'Push' as well as 'pull' factors lead to his movement from one job to another. His ultimate career success depends a good deal on the amount of experience he accumulates of varied computer applications. In an industry where everyone is learning he cannot afford to stay with a company which botches its computer scheme or sticks to humdrum applications. The high proportion of installations which show either, or both, of these inadequacies adds considerably to his inter-firm movement. The dissatisfaction which lies behind these fickle loyalties can also stem from numerous other causes, particularly strained relations with other management staff (see Chapter 7).

Even relatively successful and ambitious computer users often overlook the need to cater for their datacrats' career development needs. Lines of progression from one computer function to another and the qualifications for each type of post need to be specified. If the datacrat cannot see his way ahead in the firm, he will leave. Large organizations such as Rolls Royce and BEA which have taken the trouble to devise a realistic staff structure for DP personnel have had far fewer difficulties over retaining staff than firms which ignore the need. It is even claimed that by so doing they can get away with paying less than the highest market rates. It may be so. But in the case of such organizations (and both those mentioned are engaged in developing very advanced applications) lower salary scales could be less a product of the datacrat's desire for security than of his eagerness to stretch the muscles of his professional expertise.

Although it can be argued that the datacrat's high mobility is beneficial to industry as a whole since it produces a kind of 'stage army' effect whereby limited manpower resources are speedily directed to where the need (and hence the cash) is greatest, from the point of view of the individual enterprise it remains a real problem. The loss of key personnel at a critical moment can set a scheme back by months. But so far it is illuminating to what extent users have tended to place responsibility for such risks on the individual cupidity of the DP man himself, rather than directing attention to increasing the overall supply of trained staff on one hand and to simplifying software development on the other. They can hardly be expected to carry out the necessary changes themselves. But they could put more pressure than they do on those – computer manufacturers and the relevant official bodies – who are in a position to take the necessary steps.

SOLVING SOFTWARE PROBLEMS

The fact has to be faced that no one is going to find a quick and simple solution to the main problems of software preparation. On the staffing side especially the liveware gap will persist and probably widen over the next five or six years.

This is especially so for systems analysis and design personnel. The systems man must have a certain maturity as well as a high educational achievement. Desirably he should have had a period of functional management experience. The number of potential recruits with such attributes is small in relation to the demand. A comparable difficulty is the lack of an established body of agreed systems design theory, and an even more severe one the absence of experienced and practising systems men willing to teach the subject to trainees. If they are good enough to teach they can earn too much in industry for educational bodies to compete.

Here again the National Computing Centre has done useful work, producing a packaged systems design course in 1967 which is currently in wide use in technical colleges and other bodies. It is still too early to say whether it will in fact appreciably improve the proficiency of new systems recruits. Even if it meets most expectations the quality of trainees would certainly be improved by more contact with high-calibre practitioners both during and in the months immediately following their formal course. In view of the urgent need the Ministry of Technology and the Department of Education and Science could perhaps give more thought to promoting the temporary release or part-time participation of such practitioners by offering suitable incentives.

The training of programmers presents fewer problems. For the present the computer manufacturers, who themselves undertake the bulk of the training effort, seem able to cope. It is rather the programming activity itself which needs to be streamlined and simplified. Here the absence of a firmer official lead is surprising.

Any such lead would be concerned above all with the future of universal higher-level programming languages. Left to itself the computer industry has developed a mass of private programming languages and 'dialects' of universal HLL. Some of these languages have an unquestioned quality, but their very excellence can be seen as an obstacle to change. It is also unrealistic to expect bodies otherwise in intense commercial competition to take steps which would undermine a quasi-monopolistic position with their established customers.

Two types of rationalization are possible with regard to universal HLL: either to secure the wider acceptance of those already existing (particularly COBOL) or to promote the development of a new, definitive language. In both cases – but especially in the second, which would require a measure of international colla boration – action at government level would be necessary.

With regard to the first alternative, American experience is instructive. COBOL was originally promoted by the US Navy, which became alarmed at the incompatibility of the software being produced for the large numbers of machines it procures annually. The official COBOL vocabulary is still administered by the American Department of Defense. Initially manufacturers were reluctant to repudiate their private programming languages and produce comprehensive and efficient COBOL compilers. But in 1964 the Department of Defense warned its suppliers that computer procurements (which run at over a thousand a year) would be related more closely to a machine's efficiency in executing COBOL-written programs. The renewed enthusiasm for the language which followed this step has to some extent reappeared in this country, thanks in part to the size of the American stake in the British computer industry.

British government purchases of computing equipment do not compare with those of the US federal government. They are, however, substantial and growing, and indicative powers with regard to the nationalized industries extend official influence in this respect. If it so wished the government could exercise this influence decisively. Whether it should be exercised in favour of COBOL is, however, a suggestion with which many would argue. In some respects the language is rather inadequate. The second alternative, however, presents considerable difficulties. Not the least would be securing the measure of international agreement close to government level which any attempt to establish an entirely novel universal HLL would require to be effective. Experience with previous international technical pacts has been far from uniformly happy, the squabbles over the SECAM colour television system being a notable reminder. (The small scale of the French industry is, however, something of an insulation against one possible source of intransigence in this case.)

Between 1964 and 1967 it almost appeared that the problem might solve itself. International Business Machines, who it will be recalled pioneered the FORTRAN HLL, had developed a new universal HLL, PL-1, in association with some of its largest customers at a cost running into several million dollars. The attractive feature of PL-1 is its provision for both commercial and technical applications. Because of IBM's dominance of the international computing scene none of its rivals, whose overriding preoccupation is with stripping IBM of its established customers, can afford to ignore its programming languages. If PL-1 had enjoyed a more enthusiastic welcome from its users

```
GR0005300APU→
begin library A6,A7,A12,A18,A23,A30;
      integer b,c,f,i,j,n,p,q,s,v,w,x;
      integer array name[1:2];
      open(20);  open(30);  f:=format([s-nddd]);  b:=read(20);
      if b≠0 then begin find(100,[20]);  c:=read(20);
                       if c≠0 then dataskip(100);
                       interchange(100);  v:=0;  w:=10;
                       instring(20,name,v,w);
                  end;
      n:=read(20);  x:=read(20);  s:=read(20);
      begin array a[1:x];
CHECK:      for i:= 1 step 1 until n do
            begin for j:= 1 step 1 until s do a[j]:=read(20);
                 p:=a[1];  q:=a[s]; if q≠1000 and q≠-1000 then goto FAIL;
                 if b≠0 then begin v:=0;  swritebinary(100,a,name,v);  end;
PRINT:      write(30,f,p); write(30,f,q);
            end;
            if b=0 then goto FAIL;
            writetext(30,[[cc]TAPE⍽COMPLETE]);
FAIL:       writetext(30,[[cc]END⍽AT⍽NUMBER]); write(30,f,p); newline(30,2);
            if q=-1000 then goto LAST;
LOOP:       p:=read(20); if p≠1000 and p≠-1000 then goto LOOP;
            if p=-1000 then goto LAST; n:=n-1-1; goto CHECK;
LAST:       writetext(30,[[cc]END⍽OF⍽RUN]);
            close(20);close(30);if b=0 then goto DONE;interchange(100);close(100);
DONE:end;.
end→
```

Figure 4. Specimen program in ALGOL for the English Electric LEO Marconi KDF9 computer for data checking and transferring.

This is an example of a program written in a higher-level programming language. Forming the first stage of the University of Salford General Social Survey Data processing Package, it is designed to check paper-tape input for punching errors and for transferring data from paper tape to magnetic tape in preparation for the tabulation and statistical analysis performed in the remainder of the package.

IBM's competitors might have accepted the language as the definitive universal HLL. However, considerable criticisms of it have been raised and some manufacturers are still unsure how much effort they should put into producing their own PL-1 compilers.

It is still possible that PL-1 may be sufficiently revised and developed to become the single major international programming language, or that IBM may come up with something better. But the need for simplification and standardization is too pressing to trust in such possibilities. This is surely one field where the present (1969) government's pretensions to technological modernity and leadership could be matched by more decisive action.

Further Reading

'System Analysis and Programming' in *Scientific American*, September 1966 ('Information' issue), is a highly readable introduction by Professor Christopher Strachey, the inventor of multiprogramming. 'Computer Programming Today', Chapter 9 of *Electronic Computers* by S. H. Hollingdale and G. C. Tootill, Penguin, 1965, is a little more technical but still quite easy going for the non-mathematician.

For more commercially oriented introductions the training manuals of computer suppliers are hard to better; see, for example, *System 4: Introduction to Programming*, English Electric Computers Ltd (Technical Publications 1054).

To learn programming it is essential to join an appropriate course, but *Teach Yourself Computer Programming* by R. Murray-Shelley, EUP, 1967, is quite useful.

CHAPTER 4

Applying Computer Technology: Competing Strategies

THE RANGE OF COMPUTER APPLICATIONS

MOST people are aware of the fact that computers are already performing an impressive number and variety of jobs in industry, commerce and official administration. While one would not expect the man in the street to recite a representative inventory of these jobs, he would hardly be surprised to learn that they include tasks as various as planning the siting of electricity sub-stations, generating insurance policy renewal notices, estimating the cost of civil engineering projects, controlling the stocks of public houses, blending margarine, administering television rental accounts, or tracking the manufacture of assemblies in engineering factories. We have, in fact, got rather used to the idea that the computer can do just about everything, that it is almost doing it already, and that any activity which has so far escaped its attentions will soon be brought under its wing.

This imprecise impression is understandable. Over the last fifteen years the mass media have provided us with a blow-by-blow account of the computer's entry into the economy which has concentrated heavily on its successively more impressive feats. We hear rather less about the important distinctions which in practice exist between what has been computerized, and what is merely forecast for computerization. There is a comparable lack of information about the important differences in the degree to which the machine is exploited in different industries, or about the varying levels at which it may be used by firms within a single industry.

But such distinctions become important when we raise the question of how computers *should* be exploited if we are to secure their greatest contribution to economic welfare. The answer is not, except in the crudest sense, simply to have more of what has been done up to now. Successful exploitation of the computer is not the same thing as simply installing it. Nor is it a necessary consequence of attempting to use it for particular 'revolutionary' individual jobs. What counts much more is the 'philosophy', the rationale, underlying its use.

As we shall see, the key distinction here is between a view of the computer which pictures it as a handy, but limited, tool for tackling particular business problems, and one which regards it – sometimes rather fancifully, but not altogether wrongly – as a backbone of administrative and business control, a complete 'nervous system' around which the whole organization can and *should* be remodelled.

The following account, then, will not take the form of an inventory of computer applications. Such lists are nowadays interminably long, somewhat repetitive, and in an important sense unilluminating. Rather it will try to describe different philosophies of computer use, some typical applications associated with each one, the likely advantages for organizations which adopt them, and some of the practical problems likely to be encountered.

THREE APPROACHES TO COMPUTER USAGE

Three major philosophies of business and administrative computerization can be identified. To a large extent they have paced the development of computing equipment itself. The 'first-generation' computer, dependent on valves, comparatively slow in operation and with rather ungainly facilities for filing information in bulk, was conceived either as a 'glorified adding machine' or, more graphically, as the 'electronic clerk', which would automate the routine chores of the large office.

The evolution of the 'second-generation', transistorized computer, with its more rapid processing and massive magnetic-tape filing capacity, led to the concept of *integrated data-processing* – that is, the articulation of (still mainly 'clerical') computerized tasks via the machine system. Thus information generated in the course of a particular batch of processing would be used directly – that is, without human intervention – to form part of the data to be processed in another computer job. For example, cost information derived from preparing a payroll would be automatically transferred to magnetic-tape files from which it would be withdrawn in another run to help compile general cost statistics.

More recently, the arrival of 'third-generation' equipment – microminiaturized central processors capable of performing several jobs simultaneously, massive random-access disc storage, and data-transmission devices – has been accompanied by the notion of the fully computerized *management information and control system*, or *total system*. In the total system, integrated data-processing would be extended to cover a much broader spectrum of jobs and occur more or less continuously: information would be tapped at its source, whether in the factory or board room, and fed directly into the computer files; many managerial decisions would be automated, and others refined by the readier availability of accurate information. But more of this later.

'THIRD-GENERATION MACHINES: FIRST-GENERATION APPLICATIONS'

It is true that these approaches to computer usage, partly suggested by and partly stimulating each major extension of the speed and capacity of computing equipment, have been developed very largely by professional computer applications theorists and the manufacturers of equipment, both of whom have a very intimate interest in the range and sophistication of the typical computer installation. It is equally true that at each stage these parties have tended to underplay the obvious practical difficulties, particularly the absence of appropriate systems design and programming experience, which stand in the way of realizing the currently *avant-garde* level of usage. Managements considering the use of the machine are certainly aware of these facts, and they undoubtedly add to the pause which one would always expect between the availability of any new machine or technique and its widespread adoption.

However, it is striking to what extent users' conceptions of the machine's utility and relevance have become fixated upon approaches outmoded by the march of technology. This has been a universal phenomenon. Even that dogged innovator the American executive, apparently nonplussed by the bewildering pace of developments, seems to have opted frequently for a range of applications four or five years behind the available technology. In this country the complaint of the computer specialist – and it is not altogether self-interested – has until recently been that in the face of third-generation equipment users adopt a philosophy of application not appropriate to the second generation but to the first.

In other words, users' evaluations of the machine have been dominated by the notion of the 'glorified adding machine', the 'electronic clerk', and the 'automated office'. And when the necessary question of what gains will be made from installing a computer has come up for discussion, management has tended to skip over the fine words about enhanced operating efficiency through improved and faster information services to the bald inquiry: how many clerks will it get rid of?

PAPERWORK THROMBOSIS

This concern with the rising administrative overheads of the modern business is, as far as it goes, valid enough. The growing scale of the modern firm's activities, the complexity of its products and technology, its ramifying marketing and supply networks, and its numerous transactions with government departments have all helped to increase its corps of routine administrative workers. To maintain rational control and to plan its future in an increasingly complex economic environment the firm has been obliged to recruit a growing army of clerical assistants to collect facts, document, interpret, and file them.

In manufacturing industry this bureaucratic efflorescence is impressive enough. In service industries such as banking, insurance, and government, which revolve almost entirely around the processing of documents, and whose services we have increasingly demanded over the last forty years, the growth of clerical employment has been not far short of astonishing. In the economy as a whole we are approaching the point when the number of routine administrative and technical workers outstrips that of manual workers employed directly on the manufacture of goods. The multi-storey office block has already replaced the factory as the characteristic industrial building of the modern city. And the language itself has been enriched by the wider currency of the terminology – ledger, invoice, roll, docket, work ticket, return, payslip – of bureaucratic administration.

To counter the growth in government bureaucracies the manager has often applied lavish admonition, to counter that of his own clerical departments he has prescribed rationalization of work tasks and – until the advent of the computer – a limited degree of mechanization. Both remedies have been relatively modest in their success.

Rationalization of office work, the counterpart of rationalization in the factory, introduces a work system based upon the factory's own batch and flow mass-production techniques, formerly complex individual tasks demanding a relatively high level of personal skill or experience being subdivided into simpler, more repetitive components. Methods of performing these new tasks are standardized and recorded in the offic manual. Lines of responsibility and authority are made more precise and explicit. Individual performance and productivity have been made more susceptible to accurate measurement. This greater systematization has often sharpened operating efficiency quite dramatically. (Though not infrequently this gain has been offset by the drop in morale which follows the arrival of the organization and methods men who plan the change, and by the lower calibre of the staff who are prepared to accept a highly rationalized office environment.)

Mechanization, however, generally has had less striking effects on the productivity of the office than on that of the factory. This is largely because the devices in most common use – the typewriter, the desk calculator, or the duplicating machine – are directly under the control of their operator and do not set the pace of his – or, more likely, her – work. In this respect they contrast sharply with much factory-floor machinery, which is capable of dictating an increase in the amount of work performed. Only with the arrival of punched-card tabulators and ancillary equipment – or with that of a computer – is such machine pacing reproduced.

Despite the palliatives of rationalization and mechanization office employment has continued its long-term expansion, both in the economy as a whole and in individual organizations, steadily adding to administrative costs – not merely in the direct form of salaries, but in overheads for accommodation, amenities, and recruitment services.

THE 'ELECTRONIC CLERK' APPROACH

To many employers, the appearance of commercially oriented computers a dozen years ago seemed to offer an escape from these swelling overheads. Here was a tireless slave accounts-clerk: reliable, accurate, an administrative automaton. The comparison, all too easily made, between a computer and a clerk, and highly invidious to the clerk, was eagerly pushed home by the computer manufacturers themselves. And it received further picturesque reinforcement in popular journalism and broadcasting.

When the clerk works on a specialized routine chore he certainly does amount to little more than a human data-processing machine. For example, when he prepares a payroll he first marshals a number of documents, such as workers' time sheets and pay records, which carry the source data requiring treatment. In each case he applies appropriate rules, makes minor calculations, and writes a summary of his operations on another document (the payslip). From each time sheet he derives a variable (hours worked) and multiplies it by a constant (rate of pay) from the associated pay record for the employee. Certain deductions, some constant (e.g. National Health Insurance, works' social club contribution) and some variable (e.g. PAYE, Graduated Pension), are then computed and subtracted from the gross pay. A summary of these calculations is recorded on the payslip, the pay record for the individual is updated, and the clerk turns his attention to the next case.

It is meaningful to describe the clerk's behaviour as highly programmed. In each case he follows a broadly similar routine, applying rules which either are known to him through practice or can be consulted in manuals or the pay records. His only major area of discretion is over the rate at which he works and the degree of concentration he devotes to the job. No other kind of judgement is demanded. In fact, it may be positively discouraged.

Because of its highly programmed nature this kind of task is in principle relatively easy to flowchart for the computer. Like the clerk the machine will deal with each case in turn, consulting appropriate records, performing arithmetic, amending records and preparing a summary. However, in this case the input data are held on magnetic tape and can be read into the machine's immediate-access store with electronic speed. The appropriate rules to apply in each case are embodied in the stored program. The movement and arithmetic treatment of data are virtually immediate. However complex the rules to be applied – for example, to allow for bonus or overtime payments, absences, holidays, transfers between departments or variations in tax liability – the machine will be beset by none of the hesitation which may sometimes overcome the clerk. There will be no pause in turning from one case to the next. It cannot – given accurate input data – overlook important facts or muddle individual cases. Its arithmetic is faultless. And while one part of the machine prints payslips (and perhaps a cheque for the payment itself) another part proceeds with new cases.

Consequently while an expert clerk takes an average of several minutes for each case the computer may take under a second with a notable increase in accuracy.

The image of the computer as an electronic clerk – not without its illustrative value – rapidly captured the imagination, and the approval, of potential users confronted with the alarming and apparently irreversible rise in their administrative overheads. It automatically defined the kinds of task eligible for administrative automation. Any office job of a relatively routine, or programmed, nature, occupying a large number of clerks, and repeated at regular intervals – jobs such as payroll preparation, cost or financial accounting, or compiling sales statistics – was viewed as a legitimate and worthwhile target for computerization.

In a sense there can be no argument with these conclusions. It is perfectly true that computers can successfully absorb the tasks of the large office and perform them at less cost and with greater reliability than a team of clerks. What is more disturbing is the extent to which users' evaluations of the machine have remained fixated on the advantages of office automation in the face of accumulating evidence that the really significant gains from computerization derive from a more adventurous use of the machine.

Yet probably the majority of computer installations in the United Kingdom still set their sights no higher than this level of use. Some of the people who originally endorsed the image of the 'electronic clerk', especially computer manufacturers themselves, must often regret the durability of what should have been no more than a temporarily useful figure of speech. Its very vividness, and its partial truth, have blocked the diffusion of a more valid conception of the machine. At present a major campaign is being waged by all those with a professional interest in the computer's wider use to convince users, and potential users, that it is every bit as much an electronic draftsman, electronic engineer and electronic manager. But the notion that its main value is in the role of a minor white-collar, or white-bloused, assistant is dying hard.

Failure to promote the machine to more advanced duties would perhaps be understandable if the general gains from clerical automation were more evident. But they are far from evident. It cannot be denied that particular organizations have cut their total administrative costs quite substantially, but it is likely that those organizations which use their machines for routine data-processing alone, taken together, have made only marginal gains. Some would deny that as a body they have made any gains at all. There are certainly many firms which because of their restricted outlook now possess computerized offices a good deal more expensive to operate than their former 'manual' ones. Not surprisingly, the resulting disillusion has reinforced the scepticism of those users who were always unsure of the machine's usefulness.

One does not have to look very far to find the reasons why

simple clerical automation seldom justifies itself economically. Initial feasibility studies have often been carried out either at a break-neck pace or at no pace at all, and by underqualified personnel. Again, some computer manufacturers – or rather their salesmen, who are usually paid on a commission basis – have sometimes pursued a somewhat short-sighted sales policy which pays too little attention to tailoring a customer's equipment to his needs. A substantial minority of users have certainly been oversold. (One can argue, however, that an excessively powerful machine is just as much an opportunity as an embarrassment.) Too often the oversold customer has been content to pour odium on the manufacturer rather than force solvency on his installation by extending his original applications.

The costs of systems studies and programming, too, have usually been poorly estimated, sometimes in the face of explicit warnings of likely problems and delays. Computer schemes are often the brainchild of a single individual in the organization, or a small group, and once he has been given the go-ahead by senior management his own reputation and judgement are at stake. Above all he is impatient to see the machine in and working. In a hurry to prove his case, he is tempted to minimize obstacles, especially those of cost and control, and other, apparently minor, practicalities.

A practicality which has been consistently waved aside, for example, is the cost of a computer centre itself. Unlike traditional office machinery the computer cannot be installed in any room which happens to be available, and connected to the nearest power point. It is a complex and delicate box of electronics, and requires appropriate treatment. It demands a dust-free, air-conditioned environment with controlled temperature. The jungle of cables between its various units must be buried under an expensive false floor. A whole sub-industry has sprung up to cater for these requirements. Inevitably they add considerably to the investment outlay. Sometimes no available accommodation is suitable for conversion and the company must build an entirely new centre. Occasionally this has been realized only when a sales or leasing contract has already been signed.

But above all, users have been far too sanguine about expected reductions in staff. Clerical automation may indeed cut a swathe through densely populated accounts or wages departments, though surprisingly often it is a rather narrow swathe. But data does not feed itself into the machine. Cards and tapes have to be coded and punched, and a new army of data preparation staff merely takes over the empty desks vacated by more senior male clerks. The computer is automatic but it still needs operating staff. It is highly reliable mechanically, but only if it receives regular maintenance by skilled engineers. To administer the computer installation and supervise its staff an appropriately qualified, and appropriately remunerated, computer manager must be appointed. Old office empires may disappear, or, more likely, marginally contract, but a new data-processing empire springs up to inherit the charge on the concern's overheads. Visitors to computer centres are often struck by the apparent scarcity of workers amongst the shining enamel cabinets of the machine: they would be equally, though otherwise, impressed if their itinerary were allowed to include a tour of the crowded card-punching and verifying rooms.

In other words an automated office is often little more than a glamorous luxury, a public-relations rather than an economic asset. Few users can hope to show an overall profit on such a restricted use of the machine, and few have. The payroll may indeed be prepared in two hours of machine-time but it is senseless to invest in an expensive machine-tool like the computer if it is to stand idle most of the working week. And for a computer the working week is, or should be, something approaching seven days of twenty-four hours each. If an organization does not envisage a range of applications which will fill this week it can always buy a parcel of computer time from an outside data-processing bureau, or from another user with spare capacity. But surprisingly few organizations have preferred this alternative to the status-conferring possession of their own machine.

Interestingly enough, organizations which claim to have benefited from clerical automation often hasten to point out that their real economies have stemmed from quite unexpected sources. For example, computerized payroll preparation may result in a measurable rise in the productivity not of the office but of the factory. This is especially likely to occur in factories which operate complex piece-rate or bonus systems. Production workers, once they have become accustomed to the computerized payslip, come to recognize the machine's superior reliability, or, as they see it, superior trustworthiness. Consequently less time is absorbed in raising queries about payments and agitating for redress. The computer can be recognized as reasonably objective and impartial, while a wages-clerk is not infrequently the object of shop-floor suspicion.

When a firm is committed to installing the machine it can often use the experience gained in systems analysis to rationalize the work of other departments which are not scheduled for computerization. Computers, in other words, can stimulate users into a review of efficiency as a whole; and not only the efficiency of clerical workers but of managers too. Managerial efficiency is what business computing is about. One of the most commonly reported 'invisible' gains from routine clerical automation is the improved supply of management information. Managerial activity is characterized largely by the making of significant decisions. The quality of these decisions is directly related to the adequacy and timeliness of information about fast-moving events. Because of its ability to marshal and sift a vast number of individual items of data, and to do so extremely rapidly, the computer can provide the manager with information which was previously unavailable, not available quickly enough to be useful, or too expensive to collect. Even cast in the modest role of electronic clerk the computer can supply information of this kind; for example, illuminating labour cost and utilization data as a by-product of payroll preparation, or surprising correlations from accumulated sales statistics.

Some of this information appears largely by chance, in the sense that no one originally visualized that it would be generated as a natural result of programming a job in a particular way. It may then be realized that if other programs had been written differently, or more closely related to each other, further substantial 'fall-out' would have been available. This realization can be rather depressing. A proven program represents a considerable capital investment with no second-hand value. If a firm buys a lorry and later finds it needed a different type of vehicle for the job it can modify it, or, failing that, cut its losses by reselling it. But most programs are tailored to the unique requirements of a particular concern and can seldom find a market. They are, however, sometimes capable of revision. But the firm that wishes to adapt a whole suite of programs to seize previously unseen opportunities will usually have no alternative but to start again from scratch.

An important aspect of the reorientation towards the computer which occurs when management begin to appreciate its powers as an information tool is a fuller recognition of the interdependence of information channels in the firm.

Awareness of this interdependence and its implications is often inhibited in the non-computerized firm by the wide measure of functional autonomy which is either bestowed upon, or arrogated by, particular departments. Departments of a firm usually develop a good deal of independence of each other, which may be displayed in the growth of departmental styles, or subcultures, and in a certain amount of rivalry, friendly or otherwise, between their respective members. But this growth of departmental individualism also tends to reduce the freedom with which information crosses their boundaries. Information is vital for decision, and if its movement is blocked by departmental walls the overall operating efficiency of both the departments themselves and the concern as a whole is reduced.

Departments may attempt to solve the problems which this reduction in communication poses by attempting themselves to collect the information which others should send them. Thus files are unnecessarily duplicated, and often may be inconsistent between departments. And the additional independence which a department acquires from its 'private' information, by removing the sanction of retaliation, permits it to reduce still further its transmission of information to rival departments. An obvious consequence of this increasing secretiveness is that the flow of information to senior managers, who rely upon it for co-ordinating and planning the activities of the concern as a whole, will also seriously diminish.

The logic of computerized administration has scant regard for departmental boundaries. Even the establishment of a relatively restricted office automation scheme can oblige departments to supply information in greater detail and more highly standardized form than they have been accustomed to. In effect, the computer recentralizes the flows of information. Facts and figures run increasingly into a central pool – the machine's own files – from which they can be redirected (as reports and summaries) to those managers whose decision-making will most benefit from them.

Moreover, individual streams of information usually possess value for decision-making only when they are merged or reconciled with others. This reconciliation in the non-computerized concern is undertaken by clerks and managers, and as we have seen is often hampered by departmental walls. But once information starts flowing into the computer system from a number of quarters and in a more disciplined manner, reconciliation can often be effected by the machine itself. Recognition of these possibilities often encourages the concern to consider the establishment of some form of integrated data-processing system.

THE 'INTEGRATED SYSTEM' APPROACH

Although there is some disagreement about the precise nature of an *integrated system* the essential notion is that of using the computer as the clearing house for all the routine information flows of a firm. The focus of attention shifts from individual, relatively isolated clerical jobs like payroll preparation to the interlocking via the computer of numerous essentially related jobs. One computer job will be articulated carefully with others and all will together form an extensive and coherent whole.

Wherever possible, data for processing will be captured at source and fed directly into the computer system. (For example, in a retail business a special cash register generating punched paper tape would be installed at each sales point, and the tapes fed into the computer each evening.) And comprehensive files for the whole organization will be built up centrally as the keystone of the computer system. To achieve all this clearly requires a fairly high level of systems analysis and programming skill. It also demands, in view of the volume of processing likely to be called for, a fairly substantial computing capacity. As we have noted, this kind of capacity became commercially available at economic prices only with the arrival of second-generation, transistorized computers.

The relationships between one computer job and others in an integrated system are necessarily complex, and the sort of operations which might occur can be described here only in outline.

Let us take the case of a manufacturing concern. Orders from customers, if possible submitted in a precoded form on standardized documents, and written in magnetic ink to permit direct input to the computer by way of an automatic character-reading device, are fed into the machine in batches. This, depending on the nature of the business and the design of the system, could occur each week, each day, or at even more frequent intervals. The computer will arrange this incoming data in an appropriate manner and record it on magnetic tape. If orders are usually met from stock the machine can generate invoices for each order and prepare picking lists for the warehouse staff.

First, however, it will consult its stock files to ensure that the goods are available, and check its customer accounts files to ascertain the customer's credit position. If both are in order it will prepare the appropriate invoices, automatically update the customer's account, and alter the stock files by subtracting the amounts earmarked for each order. If an order cannot be met, either through lack of stock or because the customer has exceeded an agreed credit limit, the machine will print out 'exception reports' for management, i.e. a list of cases which require special handling.

Copies of customer invoices record dispatches of goods from the warehouse in any chosen period, and can be fed back into the machine system to produce a statement of the value of sales in this period, which, compared with information about costs, provides a picture of the firm's profitability. They also provide the data for a comprehensive sales analysis, which indicates in detail which products have sold best where and to whom, and which are lagging behind. This sales data can be reconciled with the findings of market research to prepare a sales plan for the next month or quarter, which indicates the total numbers of each product the firm will need either to manufacture or to provide from finished stock.

The firm can now work out the implications of these production targets. Each manufactured item will consist of a number of components or ingredients, which themselves must either be manufactured or purchased from outside suppliers. On file in the computer system will be data on the components required for each assembled item. The total number of components which need to be manufactured, a complex piece of multiplication, can then easily be calculated by the machine.

The components required for any assembly will of course change regularly as a result of research and development. Feeding these modifications into the centralized computer files avoids the danger that management in different parts of the firm will miscalculate the work to be done as a result of working from out-of-date or otherwise inconsistent separate departmental files.

When the component requirements have been calculated they can be compared with the computer's records of completed components in stock. Management needs to prevent finished stocks from rising too high, because they tie up large sums of working capital. Comparison of stocks with customer requirements may result in the downward adjustment of production requirements. It will certainly enable the evening-out of stock levels in the longer period, avoiding over-production at one time and sudden rushes at others (which often involve expensive overtime working). This comparison will also assist in the planning of purchases of components and raw materials from outside suppliers, to avoid the expense of buying in at short notice and the risk that the articles required may be unavailable when the need for them suddenly becomes apparent.

Once the adjusted list of parts to be manufactured has been prepared, work loads for the factory can be calculated by reference to work-content files which store information on the time and labour needed to produce an item or given amount of finished product. It will also enable the generation of requisition orders to the stores for the supply of raw materials to make the given number of items. The machine may also go on to produce schedules for weekly production in the various factory departments; and as items are manufactured this information is fed into the computer system to update the finished stock files.

Underlying this kind of computer system is a philosophy of application which contrasts sharply with that of clerical automation. Much clerical work is of course removed by the integrated data-processing system, but any reductions in staff are regarded more as a benefit incidental to the provision of better information than as an end in themselves. A vast amount of paperwork disappears into the machine system, but the predominant gain from this is that files become fully centralized and more up-to-date. The 'one-shot' approach by which a single stream of input updates numerous records eliminates the delays and inconsistencies which are an inevitable accompaniment of a purely manual system.

Management is in a far stronger position to achieve an optimum blend of resources at any one time and a more rapid adjustment to changes. Control of the organization can become more rational and better planned. Individuals have a greater awareness of their objectives and their level of performance at any time, with a consequent boost to their morale. Pressure on managers is reduced, enabling them to concentrate more on long-range planning and personnel problems. Customers receive a better service because orders can be processed and dispatched more rapidly, and the centralization of information allows their queries to be answered more promptly and fully.

These are attractive advantages and one might expect a large number of concerns to be pursuing them. In fact, only a minority are doing so, and until recently a very small minority at that. Probably no more than 400 of the near-3,000 computers presently (1968) installed in Britain are involved in attempts to establish true integrated systems.

Many schemes are proudly labelled 'integrated systems'. The phrase has become a catchword. Admittedly many of the projects so termed go beyond '*ad hoc*' clerical automation. But not far. The great majority of self-announced integrated systems are in fact no more than integrated financial accounting systems.

There are indeed good reasons for this preoccupation with computerized accounting. Firstly, those concerns first to show interest in the wider possibilities of the computer were largely in service industries like banking and insurance whose own business control information is almost exclusively financial in character. Expertise in designing and programming more advanced computer jobs consequently became largely oriented towards their needs. Secondly, in establishing any computer system attention must be paid to the availability and ease of collection of input data, and in most firms the most highly systematized channels of data acquisition are for the collection and transmission of accounting and cost information. Finally, the impetus to install a computer has frequently come from a firm's chief accountant, whose own professional perspectives are bound to influence his conception of valid applications.

No one would minimize the importance of accurate, up-to-date financial information in any type of business or administrative machine. The ultimate yardstick of success in business is the balance between income and expenditure, and the efficiency of individual operations becomes plain only when they are clothed in their costs. But in manufacturing industry in particular, day-to-day managerial activity depends just as much upon information about quantities as about costs. Quantities which immediately spring to mind here are, for example, the level of stocks, the number of assemblies at a particular stage of production, absenteeism in the labour force, or sales to particular customers or markets.

Integrated accounting subsystems will of course form an essential part of a truly integrated computer system, mirroring the manufacture of products, the efficiency of labour, dispatches to customers, and the arrival of raw materials in the warehouse. The automatic generation of financial information about the physical transactions it reflects is obviously a great advantage to higher management. On the other hand the restriction of the computer to the sophisticated manipulation of accounting data whose main message may often be the inefficiency of functional management seems a particularly frustrating exercise; computerized proof of their managerial shortcomings may give managers a spur to improvement but it hardly provides them with the means to achieve it.

But the obstacles to more advanced use of the computer amount to more than the continuing power of the traditionally-minded accountant in British industry. One powerful deterrent has been the relative failure, in terms of cost savings, of clerical automation. Higher management, faced with a proposal to extend a computer system, needs more bait than the promise of better control information, especially when it considers the indifferent gains from its automated offices.

Because users have employed computers at a low level – where they seldom pay – they are shy to employ them at a higher level – where they do pay. Furthermore, doubts about likely benefits are reinforced by more practical and quite genuine worries. A definite brake on the rate of computerization in the United Kingdom has been the critical scarcity of systems and programming personnel, and also, to some extent, friction between these highly paid, highly mobile specialists and the managers with whom they must collaborate. It is of course reckless to embark upon a change as extensive and complex as integrated data-processing without the technical know-how to make it a success. However, the personnel who possess this know-how are expensive to employ, sometimes (as many managers see it) temperamental, and they are always likely to move without much ado to other organizations in pursuit of rapidly escalating rewards.

Another barrier to integrated computing, though it is a hazy one which is rarely admitted by those accused of raising it, has been managerial opposition to the computer. Integration reduces departmental and individual managerial autonomy. Managers, or, as will be argued in Chapter 7, certain types of manager, are not always so easily convinced that this organizational change will bring the forecast benefits to their efficiency. By losing his private files of control information the department manager forfeits a good deal of his former independence. He becomes more reliant on the machine and more subject to its discipline. It opens a window on his performance for higher management.

These prospects are unnerving and will often overshadow the manager's appreciation of the computer as a tool for refining his own operating efficiency. Some managers may even view it in much the same light, and with far less justification, as the clerical worker usually pictures office automation, or the production worker factory automation; that is, as a direct threat to the security of his job itself. Opposition will not of course be presented in such bald terms. Rather it typically manifests itself in an intense scepticism about the machine's supposed benefits or the feasibility of applying it usefully to any major aspect of an individual's own work. A group in a firm pressing for more advanced applications must take cognizance of these objections. Often they are strong enough to seriously retard computer plans, to modify them into triviality, or to blight them altogether.

THE 'TOTAL SYSTEM' APPROACH

The reluctance that many users who could profitably exploit more advanced computing have shown in adopting the philosophy of integrated data-processing has not deterred the formulation by applications theorists of an even more radical approach towards computerization. Their objective, the fully computerized *management information and control*, or *total*, *system*, can be described only in outline because no such system has yet been established, though a handful are at present under development in Britain.

There is also a lack of complete agreement between computing specialists as to what exactly a 'total system' implies, and even over the usefulness of the term itself. Several key features which recur in differing technical descriptions or strategies of implementation can however be distinguished. And there is no question that the underlying rationale of the sometimes conflicting accounts is basically similar.[1] It is equally certain that the total systems approach will be the dominant computer philosophy of the future.

1. For example, Greenburger, M., 'The Uses of Computers in Organizations', *Scientific American*, September 1966 ('Information' issue); Beckett, J. A., 'The Total-Systems Concept: Its Implications for Management', in Myers, C. A. (ed.), *The Impact of Computers on Management*, MIT Press, Cambridge, Mass., 1967; Simon, H. A., *The Shape of Automation for Men and Management*, Harper Torchbooks, New York, 1965.

Themes which predominate in any discussion of total systems are the extension of integrated data-processing to cover as many of the concern's flows of information as technically feasible; the capture of this information at source and its transmission by electronic communications links to the computer centre; the establishment of massive random-access computer stores to provide an 'information bank' for immediate *ad hoc* interrogation; the automation of many managerial decisions; and, in appropriate cases, the direct control of machines and men by the computer itself.

What is envisaged is the extension of on-line and in-real-time, multiprogrammed computing to weld man – whether he be manager, engineer, clerk or production worker – and computer into an intimately interacting whole: the exploitation of the powers of computing and data-transmission equipment to provide the organization with the analogue of a biological nervous system, making the control of operations and adaptation to environmental changes rapid, sensitive and close.

The 'brain' of the system would be the computer itself (or more likely a hierarchy of computers providing higher and lower 'nervous centres' linked to functional areas of administration, or geographical subdivisions, of the overall organization) backed by massive storage or 'memory' devices; its 'nerves' would be its data-transmission links; and its 'sensory' and 'effector' organs its input terminals, its human partners – one hopes they would be nothing less than partners – and directly linked machines on the factory floor.

Two features besides the sheer pervasiveness of its information-handling operations distinguish the total system from conventional integrated data-processing. In the first place there are its on-line and in-real-time characteristics. Most conventional integrated systems process data in batches. Work is carefully scheduled over the week or month and each processing job occurs at its appointed time. Some rescheduling is of course possible, and time can usually be found for special jobs such as tests of new programs (though often the time may be on the night shift). But because of the restricted capacity of the second-generation equipment typically available the system is rather inflexible and demands an organized queue for jobs. Further-more, data have usually to be brought to the computer centre for input, and processed information must be conveyed from the centre to its users by human messenger.

These limitations are overcome by on-line and in-real-time multiprogrammed computing. Because the computer can tackle several programs simultaneously and arrangements can be made for certain types of work to receive priority, processing of data for particular jobs can occur whenever there is a need. With on-line facilities, moreover, there is no need to carry data to the computer centre for input: it can be fed in directly from a 'remote' terminal connected to the centre by transmission lines. Processing can therefore occur at intervals appropriate to the nature of activities rather than those dictated by the machine's availability.

For example, stock movements can be filed as they actually occur rather than at daily or weekly intervals. File updating as a whole can become continuous rather than periodic and some information in the computer system is always literally up-to-the-minute. Conversely, information can be captured from the system on an *ad hoc* basis by users far removed from the machine itself. The very latest in users' status symbols is the office cathode display screen which in response to dialled requests withdraws information from the computer's files and presents it as a table, a graph or a bar chart.

The second key difference between the integrated data-processing and the total systems concepts revolves around the implications of the latter for managerial decision-making. Integrated computing itself is chiefly justified on the grounds that it rationalizes and accelerates the flows of information upon which advantageous decision and sensitive control are based. Total systems would apply this rationale in the most rigorous, thorough-going and radical manner. The computer would become the manager's natural partner in the control of the enterprise. All decisions would be much better informed. Often they would be the product of 'dialogues' between man and machine. In many cases they would be generated by the machine itself.

The contention that a computer can produce the analogue of a human decision is notoriously liable to provoke indignant disbelief. But resistance of this kind is usually based on an imperfect appreciation of the nature of decision-making itself. Decisions are acts of choice between alternative courses of action designed to produce a specified result, and are made on a review of relevant information guided by explicit criteria. When the grounds upon which a decision is made can be stated precisely and the data which will inform our choice can be obtained and arranged meaningfully we can say the decision is 'well structured'. If, for example, we need to decide whether to make a certain journey by bus, train or private car we might establish the requirements that the journey should take no longer than an hour and that its direct money costs should be minimized. Applying these rules to our information about the costs and times for each means of transport would lead us automatically to the correct decision.

(It is very important to note in passing that 'correct' does not of course mean 'universally correct', but merely 'correct in terms of stated criteria'. There is a vital distinction between the two which is often lost sight of in discussions of mathematical and computerized decision-making. The criteria, or 'decision rules', are always to some extent coloured by certain assumptions which derive eventually from social and individual values. Thus no decision or decision-making process, however highly formalized or quantifiable, is absolutely objective in some idealized sense. Nonetheless there are people who seem ready to believe that such perfect, abstract objectivity is possible, and that, particularly with regard to economic matters and governmental administration, it will be more closely approached with each new breakthrough in mathematical model building and computer software. Adherents to this viewpoint, their critical ability impaired by their enthusiasm for these new and undeniably valuable techniques, must surely either hold naïve assumptions about the degree of consensus behind prevalent values or be too ready to assume that the values which they themselves possess, or represent, are those which everyone else *ought* to have. This question will be taken up again in Chapter 10.)

In many instances, of course, the grounds for a decision are less open to formal specification. The information on which they are based is incomplete, and qualitative rather than quantitative. In these 'ill structured' decisions choice becomes less rational in the sense that being less formalized it is less accessible to review and criticism. It results more from evaluations which cannot be written down as a series of facts, figures, and relationships. The success of the decision therefore depends heavily on the judgement and experience of the decision-maker.

In business, the division of decision-making labour places the responsibility for the most important ill structured decisions in the hands of higher management. With each step downwards in the chain of command decisions become better structured, narrower in scope and more 'highly programmed' in the sense that the criteria on which they are based become increasingly laid down by the policies and operating rules determined by higher management. The intervals at which they are made also grow more frequent.

Well structured, highly programmed decisions are in principle ripe for computerization, translating readily into flowcharts and computer programs. We have already seen how this is done for many clerical operations. Most clerical decisions are arrived at virtually automatically: the rules of choice are explicit, the data exact and quantified, and the clerk has virtually no room to exercise personal initiative or judgement.

However, the association of ill structured, non-programmed decisions with higher management, and consequently with high personal status, may sometimes invite lower and middle organization members to deny the routine nature of much of their decision-making. By representing what are in fact relatively well structured, repetitive decisions as unique and dependent on personal attributes of experience and intuition, the middle manager bids for some of the prestige attaching to the highest decision-making positions. He has something to gain by surrounding his behaviour with a certain amount of mystery. This tendency to mystify routine decision-making may be to some extent unconscious, and it leads to deep emotional resistance to the suggestion that, besides its usefulness in the automation of clerical decisions, the computer has comparable relevance to his own work. The response is understandable but unjustifiable.

In many advanced integrated systems the computer is already producing decisions which were regarded formerly as a managerial prerogative. A common example is the reordering of raw-material stocks. Once reorder levels have been determined they are held in the machine's files and checked periodically against the levels of stock actually remaining in the warehouse. Items below or close to their predetermined reorder levels are listed by the machine on a printed 'exception report' for managerial attention.

Further integration would permit the computer to consult its stored information on suppliers, and, after matching their prices, product quality, and delivery performance with the urgency of the need for resupply and the quantities required, specify which supplier should be given a particular order. An impressive real-time system already providing this service is operated by the American Lockheed Aircraft Corporation in its Marietta, Georgia, factory.[2] Another American company, the Westinghouse Electric Corporation, which probably possesses the nearest approach to a genuine total system in the world, processes incoming customers' orders in real time and leaves the computer to decide which branch warehouse stocking requested items shall make the delivery.[3]

The main obstacle to the computerization of these and more sophisticated managerial decisions, besides the human one, is the difficulty of specifying the grounds on which the decision is made. Sometimes this is a genuine impossibility – because the information or the criteria either cannot be translated into a quantifiable form for the computer or could be only at prohibitive expense. Some managers make great play on these obstacles yet often they are more imaginary than real. The trouble may be less that criteria and information cannot be specified in principle than that they have never been in practice. When the manager claims, for example, that the computer cannot decide which supplier shall receive an order because such a

2. As described in 'Super-Management by Machine', *Management Today*, September 1966.

3. Greenburger, M., op. cit.

decision must depend on his personal judgement, what he is often saying in effect is that he has never been troubled to draw up his own criteria of choice or consult all available information in making a choice. His decisions have been personal guesses.

Sometimes managers readily admit the element of guesswork in some decisions and are prepared to agree that in principle all the factors bearing on it could be specified and quantified. But, they quickly point out, the complex interaction of these factors in practice precludes any attempt to reconcile them fully in the urgent atmosphere in which decisions usually have to be made.

There is, for example, the recurring general problem in a manufacturing concern of how much of what to make and when. The decision-maker must compromise between numerous interacting and to some extent irreconcilable factors such as the need to keep stocks low, the need to satisfy customers promptly, the need to keep the factory busy and to produce articles in economically sized batches. If stocks are minimized some customers may have to be turned away. If they are too high they freeze large sums of cash. Products manufactured in one order may secure the most economic use of machinery but be very expensive in terms of labour. A different strategy might reverse these relationships. Both might be operable only if very high stocks of raw materials were held. The maze of variables and constraints amount to a vast puzzle which for its best solution – and the best solution will vary from one time to another and always involve some compromise – demands extensive mathematical manipulation.

It is upon problems such as this that the business scientist – the operations researcher – and the computer specialists are increasingly concentrating their fire. Operations research covers a group of decision-optimizing and activity-scheduling techniques – network analysis, simulation, queueing, renewal and games theories – which the operations researcher can draw upon to construct computable mathematical models of business decision-making and planning situations, and even of the activities of a whole company. After study of the variables and constraints involved in a situation the OR man plots their intricate inter-dependencies as a series of mathematical expressions usually running into many hundreds, and sometimes thousands. The equations can then be clothed in numbers and the consequences of adopting alternative policies calculated on the computer.[4]

It is not uncommon for companies which have exploited these techniques to achieve a fifty-per-cent overall reduction in their inventory levels, representing sometimes annual savings running into several hundred thousand pounds, while providing a better customer service and a more economic use of machines and men. A particularly spectacular use of them has been made by the large international oil companies in planning their production, refining and distribution operations.

The complexity of these operations is illustrated by the case of British Petroleum, who produce crude oil in fifteen countries, carry it to forty refineries in 300 tankers and sell a vast range of finished products in seventy-five national markets. Needless to add, productivity and type of oil vary from one oilfield to another. So do the capacity and economics of individual ships and refineries, and the pattern of demand and profitability of markets. To orchestrate its worldwide activities and cope with their intricacies of cost and mutual influence BP relies heavily upon operations research and massive computing, spending upwards of one and a half million pounds a year on computer time alone. Although it is impossible to determine the exact extent of the savings from allowing these computers not merely to produce information but to use it, they are believed to run into several millions per year.[5]

Computerized decision-making is a fact of modern industrial life and as the operations researcher gains skill in unveiling the subtle structure often underlying apparently ill structured problems it must necessarily devalue the 'judgement' and 'intuition' which still receive so much emphasis in managerial self-conceptions. A start has even been made on the computerized assistance of the most ill structured, unprogrammed

4. For a straightforward description of many standard operations research techniques see Battersby, A., *Mathematics in Management*, Penguin, 1966. For a longer and more argumentative statement see Beer, S., *Decision and Control*, John Wiley, New York, 1965.

5. See 'Experience: The Computer behind the Oil Supply', in *The Gentle Computer*, *New Scientist* Publications, Harrison Raison & Co., 1965.

decision-making of all, that is in planning the future growth of the concern. Such simulation with the computer of the results of adopting different investment policies, which incorporates probabilistic forecasting of the outcome of research and development programmes and changes in the economy as a whole, cannot be expected to provide the board of directors with a precise blueprint for expansion but it does enable a broad evaluation of different growth strategies.

It should be emphasized, however, that the marriage of automated decision and real-time computing remains for the present largely unconsummated. The nearest approach to the total systems theorist's ideal of the continuous two-way communication and control between the computer and factory floor of the big engineering plant, as far as the United Kingdom goes, is the shop-control system currently being developed by Rolls Royce's Aero Engines Division at Derby.

Rolls Royce's investment in computer hardware and software is currently worth something of the order of £10 million, and its annual expenditure on running and developing its impressive aero-engines computer installation is around £2 million per annum. It handles the storage and updating of engine specifications and parts lists, running dossiers on every engine the company makes while it remains in service, research and design calculations for engineers, and a striking variety of other more routine data-processing jobs including the servicing of share and dividend records.

But these jobs are secondary to the real-time production control applications which are being pressed forward. Because any number of unforeseen eventualities can undermine a production schedule in a large advanced technology engineering factory – and Rolls Royce employs nearly 80,000 factory staff alone – and management only gradually obtains information about these disturbances which enables it to make rational rescheduling decisions, human control is at the best of times partial and uncertain. The aim is to get the computer to constantly reschedule the work taking account of these disturbances to plan. Each time an operative completes a job he will dial a message to the computer from an input terminal close at hand. The machine will digest this information and immediately issue any necessary instructions for rescheduling, taking account of the latest order and stock situation. So far the computer has been doing this only once a fortnight on a batch-processing basis, though at the time of writing the firm is in the throes of installing shop-floor terminals which will generate punched cards for batch processing as an intermediate step before the final direct linkage of shop floor and computer.[6]

Still further away is the direct linkage of automatic machines to the main computer system – at any rate in the mass production of discrete products such as engineering assemblies. The direct control of oil refineries, power stations and chemical plants is a much easier proposition, thanks to the nature of their products, which lend themselves to continuous process techniques of manufacture. Nonetheless, the numerically controlled automatic machine-tool has already made some impact upon engineering work. These machines, in which human control is replaced by a small computer on the machine itself interpreting control instructions from specially prepared paper or magnetic tapes, at present operate largely in isolation.

In a true total system they too would be linked to the main computers. This integration of information systems and machine control is another objective of the Rolls Royce scheme described above. In the words of the company's Chief Computing Engineer:

These systems will involve the direct coupling of a computer to complete lines of numerically-controlled machine tools, to transfer mechanisms, and to inbuilt inspection processes. In this case, data collection of shop floor movements is automatic and provides possibilities of direct integration with the shop control and other management systems. These developments offer the possibility of significantly reducing the appreciable time and cost spent between actual machine operations.[7]

The facilities which would appear together in a true total system have as yet done so only severally in individual highly integrated on-line and real-time systems, contradicting some

6. 'The Hard Road to Real-Time', *Management Today*, September 1967.
7. *The Times* Business News Special Survey of Computers, 15 September 1967.

optimistic forecasts of a few years ago which predicted a number of operational total systems by the present time. These setbacks have stimulated doubts about the realism of the total systems concept even amongst systems theorists themselves.

There is of course little argument that the computer hardware is already available to handle the prodigious volumes of data-processing demanded. Where a single large machine operating in the multiprogrammed mode is inadequate it can be partnered by another, or a whole hierarchy of processors can be linked to form a structure reflecting that of the organization itself. Automatic data acquisition and transmission can ensure the ongoing capture and immediate handling of information from a large number of scattered input points; and batteries of output devices operating simultaneously ensure the immediate transmission of results or control signals to human users and machines. Libraries of current and historical business information can be amassed in random-access memories for 'conversational' machine systems. The equipment is there already and will become steadily more sophisticated. It will also become cheaper. But will it become cheap enough to tickle the user's innovatory palate?

It is the soaring costs of the software which blunt most appetites. Few specialists would deny that the increasingly sophisticated tools of the operations researcher, systems analyst and programmer are becoming capable of fashioning the necessary operating systems. But the intricacy of the problems they attack is such that solving them may be quite uneconomic. One such problem is the organization of the random-access memories essential to any real-time system, especially one providing manager–computer conversational facilities.

Even the airline booking systems already referred to (see Chapter 2), in which a booking clerk captures information on seat availability direct from a distant computer's files, despite their highly specialized nature, have presented problems of file organization solved only at a quite alarming programming cost. And these information banks do not store anything like the volume and variety of information which would be necessary to establish comparable facilities for the management of large, multi-product manufacturing concerns. The problems of structuring such stores to cater for the pattern and timing of calls on them – and, no less important, ensuring the security of their contents from accidental destruction, deliberate sabotage, or unauthorized inspection – have not been squarely faced until recently.

But these checks have not obliged the hard core of total systems advocates to lower their sights. Rather they have revised their time-scales. Sooner or later, they argue, the establishment of total systems, like lunar expeditions, will become a more routine affair. What is needed is a wider acceptance amongst potential users of the philosophy, a greater willingness to experiment, and sometimes to experiment expensively, in order to build up the fund of systems and programming experience which is demanded. Some users recoil sharply from the visions of automated management which are conjured up. Others, perhaps the majority, are simply baffled. But a growing number are ready to give them a hearing, and at least to begin speculating on the probable costs and benefits. It is a reasonably safe prediction that over the next fifteen years this is a trickle that will become a tide.

Further Reading

General descriptions of the varying types of computer applications appear in Hollingdale, S. H., and Tootill, G. C., *Electronic Computers*, Penguin, 1965, and in Laver, F. J. M., *Introducing Computers*, HMSO, 1965. See also:

'Advanced Management Information Systems', *Management Accounting*, December 1966.

Dearden, J., and McFarlan, F. W., *Management Information Systems*, Irwin, Homewood, Illinois, 1966.

Department of Scientific and Industrial Research, *Automatic Data Processing*, HMSO, 1961.

Kantor, J., *The Computer and the Executive*, Prentice-Hall, New York, 1967.

'Managing to Manage the Computer', *Harvard Business Review*, September–October 1966.

'Top Management and Computer Profits', *Harvard Business Review*, July–August 1963.

CHAPTER 5

The Computerization Process:
Problems and Pitfalls

As Machiavelli wrote: 'It must be considered that there is nothing more difficult to carry out, nor more doubtful of success, nor more dangerous to handle, than to initiate a new order of things.' Few people, and certainly no one who has experienced a changeover, would dispute that computerized operations are very much a new order of things. Upset and frustration typically accompany the establishment of the new system. In the words of a sales manager interviewed by the writer, 'It was a very exciting and turbulent period for us all . . . thank God it's over.'

The kind of experiences which computerization provides for middle managers and clerical workers, and their responses to them, will be reviewed later. For the present we shall concentrate upon the particular problems with which the change presents that group – senior management – which alone can initiate innovation of this scale and cost, and which ultimately must bear responsibility for its success or failure. A responsibility, it would be fair to add, which is owed not only to the staff and shareholders of particular establishments but also, in so far as computerization contributes to general economic vitality, to society as a whole.

MOTIVES FOR COMPUTERIZATION

A wide body of opinion inclines to the view that as a whole British higher administrators and business leaders have tended to fight shy of the uncertainties of computerization – indeed, from the exploitation of advanced technology as a whole. Even when changeover to the machine has been decided on, it is suggested, the motives behind the decision have often been inappropriate, and the management of the ensuing change patchy, uncertain and slack.

There is a good deal of evidence to support these strictures. But in some ways they are unjust. Would some kind of reckless determination to innovate for innovation's sake be preferable? In America constant technical innovation is an accepted managerial obligation. As a result innovatory activity sometimes appears to take on the form of an unconscious and uncontrollable mannerism, a sort of occupational tic. Rushing into computer schemes as though they were a high-pressure product launch, many American users have later found themselves in a good deal of expensive trouble. In fact some computer specialists on this side of the Atlantic believe that British industrial competitiveness has so far suffered comparatively lightly from the less impressive penetration of the machine in this country. Because British users failed to embark on *clerical automation* on the same massive scale as their American counterparts, it is argued, British industry is not burdened with so many dead-end, marginally economic systems. Consequently it is in a strong position to exploit computers *en masse* at a higher, more worthwhile level of application. It is necessary to add, however, that those who adhere to this view sometimes go on to express doubts about whether such a 'great leap forward' will in fact occur.

Maintaining proper control over the changeover to computers, and there can be no such control if the motivation for change is not carefully examined, is a universal problem. It relates just as much to the inherent nature of computing technology itself as to any international distribution of managerial skills. It is something of a paradox that the computer, which has to do with enhancing communication and control, is typically attended during its introduction by serious problems which are themselves largely the product of communication and control problems attributable to the characteristics of the computer as a novel and unique technological phenomenon. One illustration of what is meant here will be provided shortly.

THE PROBLEM OF CONTROL

The need for controlling every stage in the acquisition and installation of a computer can hardly be overstressed. The prospective user is making a major capital investment not only with great cost but with great organizational and human implications. He must ensure that he buys the right machine for the jobs he proposes, designs the best operating systems for performing them, recruits and trains properly qualified staff, and devises equitable and acceptable personnel policies. These requirements generate a host of practical problems and opportunities for disaster. Once change has begun it often proves irreversible. Unless events are planned and controlled with the utmost foresight and sensitivity they will take their own shambolic course.

All too often this is precisely what does happen. Senior management, its ability to exert control over the mounting chaos forfeited with its failure to maintain control over the earlier and more manageable stages of the process, is relegated to the position of a virtually impotent witness to a mystifying and alarming succession of events seeming to possess their own inscrutable momentum. Sometimes a rescue operation is possible. Occasionally everything turns out more or less all right in the end, thanks to luck more than anything else.

But more often than not the end result is an expensive state of near-chaos; the wrong machine for the job, delivered late and of variable reliability; a collection of long-winded, Heath Robinson programs; a ramifying, self-sufficient computer empire; staff from copy typists to senior managers themselves in revolt against the work-duplicating, overtime-producing nonsensicalities of the new 'system'.

Senior management, at the apex of the concern's pyramid of power and communication, is alone able to exert the kind of control which will avert this common outcome of a computerization scheme. And it must exert it from the moment the scheme is conceived. Control need not be direct, of course. In fact it seldom can be, and for the same reason that it is sometimes effectively surrendered altogether.

THE NOVELTY OF COMPUTING CONCEPTS

When a concern, for example a firm in manufacturing industry, is considering the adoption of a new machine or production process, it is usually possible to relate its novel features to the basic concepts of one or another established branch of technology. Members of higher management may not include a qualified engineer or technologist to carry out an appraisal, but there will often be a number of people in the firm well able to give advice. This advice, together with the experience of board members, will generally make it possible either to accept or to reject the innovation on rational grounds. Practical problems occurring during its acquisition and installation can be foreseen and provided for. Its contribution to productivity and its costs are usually open to objective calculation, albeit a rough one.

But the *information technology* of the computer is unique, original and rapidly evolving. Even the qualified engineer may have difficulty in grasping its concepts and mode of employment. To the normal director of an industrial firm the machine is an absolute novelty. To senior managers in non-industrial concerns, to whom even ordinary engineering concepts are a closed book, it is if anything more mysterious. It is of course not necessary to understand exactly how the machine works to make use of it. But some knowledge of its general mechanical features is a great advantage in those people who have to decide whether to get a computer, and, if so, which computer.

There have been any number of attempts to explain and educate potential users in basic computing concepts. Some of these efforts are in fact highly successful as far as they go. But the very complexity of the equipment and operating techniques, and their rapid evolution, put a limit on what can be done. An unfortunate consequence of this is that simplistic concepts like the 'glorified adding machine' or the 'electronic clerk', which tend to direct attention away from the more valuable sorts of job a computer will do, have gained too wide a currency. All managers face these conceptual difficulties in grasping the essential features of the technology. But they are especially severe for those who have reached a certain age or a position in the firm where it is not conventional to admit incomprehension gracefully. Unfortunately these attributes are not infrequently associated with board membership.

COMPUTER JARGON

The difficulties surrounding the concepts of information technology are increased by the somewhat mystifying science-fiction terminology in which they are expressed. Computing is undeniably jargon-ridden. Some computer specialists seem to take almost as much pleasure in the development of a neologism or acronym as they do in the invention of the component or operation it describes. But much of computing terminology is legitimate and necessary. To try to reject it makes as much sense as insisting on saying 'device for transmitting sound between two speakers placed at a distance from each other' rather than 'telephone'. Nonetheless it certainly makes for sometimes fatal difficulties of communication between the layman and the specialist. The following exchange is imaginary but far from unimaginable:

COMPUTER SALES CONSULTANT: The *immediate-access store* on this machine consists of 32K *bytes*, each of eight *bits*.

MANAGING DIRECTOR: But these 'kay-bites' are actually connected together – by wire, I mean?

COMPUTER SALES CONSULTANT: 'Kay-bites'? Sorry. . .?

MANAGING DIRECTOR: You referred to 'kay-bites'. You said they came in eight bits, and there were thirty-two of them. I'm asking if they're actually joined together. . . .

COMPUTER SALES CONSULTANT: I'm with you! I'm with you now. Yes, that's right, there's thirty-two of them. But they're not called 'kay-bites'. Just bytes.

MANAGING DIRECTOR: You definitely said thirty-two 'kay-bites'.

COMPUTER SALES CONSULTANT: I'm sorry, no. Thirty-two K – letter K – bytes. B–Y–T–E–S.

MANAGING DIRECTOR: Ah I see . . . bytes.

COMPUTER SALES CONSULTANT: The 'K' stands for a thousand, of course. When I say 'K' I really mean a thousand of something. Sorry about that.

MANAGING DIRECTOR (*eagerly*): A thousand bits?

CONSULTANT: No, actually. Bytes of eight bits here.

MANAGING DIRECTOR: Just eight bits?

CONSULTANT: That's it. Eight bits. . . . No! no! I tell a lie! There's a *parity bit* too with each byte. . . . We call that one a 'parity bit'.

MANAGING DIRECTOR: An extra one? That's good. That's very handy. It must be handy if you have extra work. This sounds a very good machine.

Severe problems of communication inevitably accompany any attempt to adopt the machine. To some extent they can be reduced, though rarely entirely resolved, by education. All members of a firm intending to introduce a computer should receive some appreciatory training in computing and data-processing concepts and terminology. A large number of introductory courses, many of the best being operated by computer manufacturers themselves, are nowadays available.

Although the vast majority of computerizing concerns do take advantage of these facilities it is clear that for a number of reasons it is unrealistic to expect too much from them. Largely because of the short time most people can spend away from their normal work they are not designed to provide an advanced grasp of the subject. Senior managers, whose need for computer education is the most urgent of all, are usually the people who are most short of time. A week's crash course may do wonders for their personal morale, but it cannot provide anything like the degree of fluency necessary to talk on equal terms with computer salesmen.

THE COMPUTER 'OVERLORD'

One solution to this kind of problem is to select one member of the higher management team to specialize in the subject and acquire the necessary familiarity. It is extremely desirable anyway that someone at this level should be given special responsibility for overseeing the computer scheme. In family firms in industry it is becoming a pattern for the 'Crown Prince' to acquire this expertise or adopt this 'overlord' role for the changeover. The trouble is that in some concerns no director may possess either the aptitude or the inclination to become fully conversant with commercial and industrial computing. In others, the suspicion sometimes arises that whoever is chosen for the job will gain unduly in personal influence and authority as the scheme progresses. As a result no one individual gets the responsibility, and the scheme soon gets bogged down. Nothing is slower than computerization by committee, and nothing riskier if the committee is unqualified.

If no one at this level is prepared or encouraged to take on the job a workable compromise is to delegate a senior manager to take full responsibility for the success of the scheme and to appoint under him an appropriately qualified data-processing manager. Whatever the arrangement, it is vital that senior managers should involve themselves and their reputations in an intimate way with the success of the scheme. Of course, the selection of a data-processing manager itself demands some knowledge of practical computing. It is, however, possible to hand over the selection to a specialized management selection bureau.

Often in the past data-processing managers, or less specialized overlords for the scheme, have 'emerged' rather than been selected in an objective way. This was perhaps inevitable in the early days of commercial computing when the various data-processing occupations had not appeared in their present form. The impetus towards computerization typically originated – as it still often does – with a middle-level departmental manager, most commonly one in the accounting function. The reasons why this function should so often have been the source of enthusiasm, hinging on the idea that the computer was first and foremost an accountancy tool, have already been dealt with elsewhere. Many such individuals have now successfully overcome their former specialist outlook in line with their absorption into a new occupation and are now conversant with and enthusiastic about the more advanced approaches to computer application. But others have blossomed less readily, and in view of current thinking about the real value of the machine they would be best passed over.

Nowadays it is unlikely that a suitable candidate for the job of data-processing manager will exist within a non-computerized concern, though sometimes an enthusiast may be doing his best to 'emerge'. Better qualified individuals will be available on the open market either amongst the ranks of experienced data-processing managers or of the more senior systems and programming practitioners.

There is a further argument in favour of an outsider for this appointment. Such an individual lacks a prior involvement in the political and status struggles of the concern. Although the newly appointed data-processing manager will soon become embroiled in these inescapable processes, his unpopular actions – and the majority of his actions certainly fall in this category in the earlier stages of a changeover – can less easily be interpreted as the settlement of old scores. It is likely that there will be considerable disapproval of what other managers regard as his undue authority and reward (particularly in terms of his age). But it will be much less of an obstacle to collaboration in the case of an outsider than in that of a promoted insider, whose humbler days are not easily forgotten or forgiven.

CLARIFYING OBJECTIVES

The first task of the newly appointed DP manager, in association with his board-member overlord, will usually consist of an attempt to persuade senior management to clarify and explicate its motives for, and main objectives in, the switch to computers. Achieving this is made up of two distinct phases.

The first phase revolves around the question 'Why do you want a computer?' Many firms who now possess an uneconomical computer installation would have done well to press this question on themselves. Computers may be widely feared for their disruptive potential, but this attitude often alternates with an equally uncritical veneration of them as the symbol *par excellence* of administrative modernity, something with which to dazzle customers, competitors, staff and shareholders. While never the sole motive for computerization, this urge towards 'conspicuous investment' has often prevailed when other and more rational things have been equal.

Frequently, too, the acquisition of a machine seems to have resulted less from a precise calculation of expected benefits than from the feeling that use of the machine had become in one way or another inevitable. Forty per cent of those users replying to an official questionnaire in 1964 mentioned 'Compulsion' of one form or another – for example, the need to save manpower and office space or to replace outworn accounting or tabulating equipment – as their prime reason for acquiring a computer.[1] As these users saw it, change had been dictated by external pressures rather than suggested itself as the result of a voluntary and searching study of the information-generating qualities of the machine. Such motives are not necessarily invalid, of course. But they do tend to restrict attention to those tasks from which 'compulsion' appears to derive, while other inherently more worthwhile jobs may be ignored.

From what has been said about approaches to computer usage in the previous chapter it may be accepted that the most appropriate underlying motive for computerization should have to do with a concern with administrative efficiency as a whole, and the appreciation that as an advanced information-generating tool the comparative advantage of a computer lies in its contribution towards more precise managerial decision and control. Yet at the time of the survey referred to above only a minority of users replied in terms which suggested the acceptance of this viewpoint. Only 24 per cent stated that their aim had been a 'better service to management'; 5 per cent referred to 'quicker processing' (and hence more timely control information); and 3 per cent talked about a 'better service to customers'.

Commenting on these figures the report remarked

It has sometimes been said that users are now motivated by the desire to 'run the business better' (by which is usually meant the provision of better management information) rather than the desire, as previously, to save data-processing costs, including staff costs. Study of this aspect of the matter during the present survey led to the conclusion that there had in fact been no significant change over recent years in the reasons for acquiring [computers].[2]

The first few months of the DP manager's appointment may well be largely absorbed in shifting the attention of higher management from the status-conferring and electronically-clerical to the information-providing powers of the machine. One of his

1. Ministry of Labour, *Computers in Offices* (Manpower Studies No. 4), HMSO, 1965, pp. 11–12.
2. Ministry of Labour, op. cit., p. 12.

greatest difficulties will be to persuade his bosses that it is some-times virtually impossible to make any precise prior calculation of the benefits to be gained from this level of usage. The salary of a redundant clerk is much easier to visualize than the vaguer fruits of faster growth or greater competitiveness.

To a large extent he must argue from the first principles of the nature of decision and control itself. Frequently this educational effort may bring him into conflict with received ideas about the virtues of intuition and experience in administration and management. But he does have at least one trump card to play. This is the ability of the computer to strengthen or reassert central control of the enterprise and to reduce departmental empire-building. Naturally, prospects such as these have a strong appeal to the top brass.

When agreement on overall objectives is finally reached they should be carefully recorded. This gives an essential point of reference should future dispute about them occur – and such an eventuality is highly probable. It is then possible to proceed to the drafting of an outline master-plan for applications, procuring equipment and personnel, and phasing activities.

PLANNING THE CHANGEOVER

It is naturally impossible to establish something so complex as an advanced integrated computer system – and we will imagine this is the final objective – at one bold sweep. The overall change-over must be broken down into stages which form a logical and as far as possible a smooth progression. Full benefits from the system will only appear when the later stages are reached but there should be some attempt to ensure that each major step forward brings definite advantages.

The reason for this requirement is not merely to derive some financial return on a sizeable investment as soon as possible, but also to retain the interest and support of the user's staff. Computer changeovers typically take a number of years to bear fruit, and unless the intervening dislocation is periodically relieved by tangible benefits disillusion rapidly sets in. This will obviously reinforce the scepticism which many staff members are likely to feel anyway, and lower the morale of the mobile systems specialists.

Even the establishment of the first phase of a typical scheme is likely to take a period measured in years rather than months. Official calculations show that even a modest computerization project takes an average of four years to complete, and the larger schemes around seven years. The average for all schemes at the time when the survey which throws up these figures was conducted was marginally under five years. The time-scale in Figure 5 is illuminating. It should be remembered that it is based on averages. Even the shortest changeover reported took over a year. The longest took sixteen.

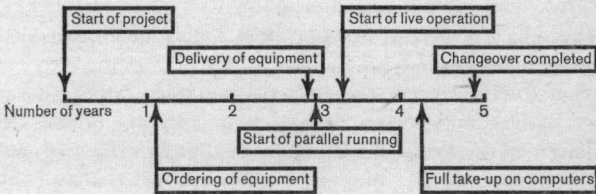

Figure 5. Average time taken to set up a computer system (for advanced data-processing). (Adapted from Ministry of Labour, *Computers in Offices*, Manpower Studies No. 4, H M S O, 1965, p. 16.)

These hold-ups, a constant irritation to senior management impatient for financial returns and to functional management and clerical workers anxious to discover their precise roles in the future organization, are largely inevitable. They derive from the need for careful planning; the difficulty of recruiting and training systems and programming staff; the need for great care in redesigning systems and writing programs; the preparation, perhaps the building, of a computer centre; and staff education and relocation. However strong the temptation, these activities must not be rushed; though this is not to deny the need for a steady momentum to be maintained. The user must be properly forewarned of likely delays and the reasons for them.

SELECTING THE EQUIPMENT

It is particularly unwise to demand undue hurry over the next most important step – the choice of an appropriate model and configuration of computing equipment.

The hardware must fit the proposed system rather than the system the hardware. To enable the preparation of specifications for the machine a feasibility study must be carried out. This study should show how the scheme can be implemented most conveniently from a technical point of view. Since it will probably commit the user to a particular make and model of computer, which if it later proves inadequate may be changed for another only at considerable cost and dislocation of plans, it is essential that this study should be conducted by well qualified personnel.

The difficulty here is not only that highly qualified systems men are in very scarce supply but that they often prefer to work on the more advanced stages of systems design rather than the early. Attracting systems analysts and designers of the right calibre may itself run into a number of months. The alternative of subcontracting this stage of the work to external computer consultants, and its hazards, will be discussed later.

When the preliminary feasibility study has been completed a 'statement of requirements' which itemizes the equipment likely to be needed can be prepared and circulated to those computer manufacturers from whom it has been decided to invite tenders. The DP manager should be seasoned enough to know roughly which ones are likely to be able to supply the equipment envisaged. For reasons to be outlined shortly it is unwise to invite more than four or five suppliers to place bids. The manufacturers on this preliminary short-list are then permitted to carry out their own feasibility studies. These can be completed quite quickly if the customer's own study has been sufficiently searching. Each manufacturer then devises a basic system best adapted to his own range of equipment. His recommendations are then submitted in a lengthy report to the customer.

Experienced DP managers command very high salaries but at this point they are in a position, if they really know the computing business, to save the user sums of money representing many times their own annual salary. They can do so only if they are given sufficient time to carry out a thorough assessment of the manufacturers' reports and to subject their salesmen, where necessary, to cross-examination.

David Shirley, a well-informed business computing practitioner and writer, estimates that the number of defective computer systems in the United Kingdom whose weaknesses can be ascribed to careless, hurried, or inexpert scrutiny of manufacturers' reports runs into several hundred. In an extremely useful guide-book for intending computer users,[3] he points out that the main source of delay at this stage is the length and complexity of the reports themselves. They often run to several loose-leaf volumes, and are packed with charts, arrow-diagrams, and tables of figures. This mass of detail not only confuses the non-expert, but can stimulate the presumption that its quantity reflects the care with which the manufacturers' representatives have carried out their study.

But of course quantity and quality are by no means necessarily so simply related. In fact much of each report may be largely irrelevant, inserted as a matter of course into every report the manufacturer issues, and conveying little of direct importance to the matter in hand. Sandwiched between the wodges of verbal expanded polystyrene are the sometimes quite brief sections which actually describe the proposed system, estimate its likely costs and delivery-dates for the machine, and which are thus of primary relevance to the aspirant user's decision.

Even the best-prepared report is likely to contain some important omissions, errors or oversights, owing, for example, to the scarcity of expert systems personnel – a problem for manufacturers no less than for users – and to shortage of time for conducting the study – for which the prospective user himself may be partly to blame. Many of these slips will immediately be nailed by an expert DP manager. Equally important, he will recognize his own limitations, which prevent him recognizing every important mistake.

He may therefore decide to recommend a check by a specialist computer consultant. This, however, will be an always expensive

3. Shirley, D., *Choosing a Computer*, Business Books, 1966.

and, for reasons to be mentioned subsequently, a sometimes less than reliable recourse. A cheap and very effective alternative – though it is often explicitly forbidden by caveats of problematic legal standing in the manufacturers' reports themselves – is to show rival reports to each representative, 'whose zeal', in the words of Mr Shirley, 'in finding flaws will be remarkable.'[4]

Although these tactics might seem ethically questionable their prime objective is not, or should not be, merely to find ammunition to justify rejecting a report altogether, but to enable its rectification. Clearly it would be foolish to exclude a manufacturer who might ultimately prove to have the best equipment for the work merely because some of his less able personnel had been allocated the job of preparing the report. (Though obviously the fact that he had not ensured, or been able to supply, more skilled attention might, whatever the virtues of his hardware, be allowed to count fatally against him in the last analysis: the prospective user will require further systems support in the future from his chosen supplier and must therefore take into account the distribution of systems skills between manufacturers.)

After opportunity for revising the reports has been provided, the DP manager is in a position to make his final recommendation to the user. Several of the proposed systems can be eliminated more or less immediately on the grounds of cost or technical adequacy, and usually the final choice will lie between two, or possibly three, more or less equally matched contenders. To adjudicate between them can be extremely difficult. The factors which will enter into the final choice will be largely technical, upon which the DP manager is competent to advise. But there may be others to which only higher management, with its knowledge of the concern's future plans or confidential involvements, may be capable of giving a weighting.

For a full discussion of the factors which usually are assessed the reader is referred again to David Shirley's guide. They can be outlined only very briefly here. First, of course, there is the cost. The cost of the equipment is, however, rarely a sufficient yardstick in itself. Because the hardware of a proven and functioning computer system represents on average only half its total costs,

4. Shirley, op. cit., p. 69.

even a machine which is ten per cent more expensive than a rival will add only five per cent to total costs if programming costs are the same for both machines. It might be much easier to program for the work required and thus offset this margin or even give it an advantage over its rival. It might have a slightly larger capacity or higher speed, thus cutting actual operating costs and providing the opportunity to use it more intensively or to sell some of its spare capacity to small outside users.

Comparisons between machines in their speed and capacity are, however, sometimes difficult to make in advance, and they depend to some extent on the type and pattern of work actually to be done, not merely in the earlier stages of a changeover but in its final version. This is because machines vary so much in basic internal organization and mode of operation. Individual units of core storage, for example, in one machine may be comparatively wasteful of space when they are storing numbers but extremely economical when they are storing alphabetic characters. In a second machine the reverse could hold true.

Straight comparisons of addition and subtraction times for a given piece of processing may be completely deceptive of the relative speeds of two machines in practice, which will vary with the nature of the arithmetic likely to be demanded. The prospective user must estimate what amounts of which kind of work he will need to do both initially and in future. Complex formulae are provided by manufacturers to permit such comparison. But to apply them a great deal of laborious calculation by a specialist assessor is usually required. (Computers themselves are coming into use for this kind of work.)

Advantages of speed or capacity may anyway themselves be outweighed by the degree of flexibility which a machine offers. If the user proposes to make numerous future additions to his installation he will obviously be extremely inquisitive about the degree of modularity (see Chapter 2) the machines offer. How much additional central processor capacity will he be able to plug in? How easy will this upgrading be from a technical point of view? What will it cost? How many additional peripheral devices can be connected? Will it be possible to run them on-line simultaneously? Answers to such questions may completely

alter initial disparities of speed and capacity between basic
models.

Closely related to the question of modularity is that of *program-
compatibility*. It is clearly important that programs written for an
initial configuration of equipment should be readily transferable
to a later, more expanded range without the need for costly and
time-consuming program revision. One serious risk in the past,
not altogether removed today, was that the manufacturer of a
chosen machine might introduce a new series of machines which
while not entirely incompatible with his previous machines
would execute programs written for them only very wastefully of
time. Again, the customer will probably consider the degree of
compatibility of a machine with those of other manufacturers.
A user can effectively be tied to one supplier if this facility is not
available. A chosen supplier's service might prove unreliable or
his future machines inadequate. Competition between suppliers
is intense and there is always the possibility that a supplier, like
many predecessors, may be forced out of business. These risks must
be borne in mind. More important, the knowledge that his users
can switch without too much disruption to the machines of a
rival is a powerful incentive to the supplier to ensure efficient
maintenance and installation support services.

These services, anyway, must be assessed. Modern computers
are certainly highly reliable mechanically but naturally they
require regular maintenance if they are not to break down.
Break-downs do occur occasionally anyway. The risk of break-
down is often higher in the early production models of a new
machine, especially if it embodies some 'revolutionary' new
component. Will the reduction in processing times have to
be repaid in the form of sudden break-downs at critical
moments?

Reliability is also related to the manufacturer's standard of
workmanship, which itself may be connected to the length of his
order book. A long order book may also be a deterrent because
it can delay delivery-dates for equipment. The reliability of early
models of a series may have contributed to the manufacturer's
success in securing large numbers of orders. So favourable
reports about his standard of workmanship from long-standing

customers may be a poor guide to his present production standards.

But doubts on these scores may be offset by the quality of the maintenance service offered. The prospective user should attempt to discover whether the manufacturer's service staff have a good reputation for their training and ready appearance when things go wrong. Will the supplier provide a resident service engineer of his own for the proposed installation, or will he merely offer to train a member of the customer's own staff for the job?

Though not directly related to the technical qualities of the machines under consideration the calibre of the manufacturer's other systems support services must be evaluated. Undoubtedly the most important of these is the quality of his standard software (see Chapter 3), in particular what programs are available and how many are available free of charge in his 'standard software package'. There are also the questions of how efficient his own higher-level programming languages are; how effective his compiling programs for universal higher-level languages are; how wide a range of instructions written in them can be compiled. The quality of his software determines very largely the ease of program writing, and hence its cost in programmer man-years, as well as the operating efficiency, especially the time of processing runs, of the established system. Answers to these questions consequently have a critical bearing on the capital and running costs of the system.

Related to the question of software costs is the standard of the manufacturer's educational and training services. While some systems and programming people for the scheme will have to be recruited on the open market, it will greatly ease problems of recruitment, and to some extent problems of systems study itself, if some of them can be found internally. And more junior grades of computer staff – coders, data-preparation personnel, and machine operators – must be found almost entirely from the user's own staff.

These people must be selected and trained for their new tasks. All manufacturers undertake psychological aptitude testing and run appropriate courses. But the quality of these services does vary somewhat. So, too, do arrangements over payment:

better-heeled or more competitive suppliers may offer them virtually free of charge. They may also back up this formal training by loaning the customer a number of their own programming staff both to assist with software preparation and to help the newly trained systems personnel settle into their new skills. Computer appreciation courses must also be provided for members of the firm less directly involved in the scheme. Since their perspectives on computing in general have important implications for the success of the changeover the standard of the courses they attend should be as high as possible. In view of the numbers of individuals to be handled in most cases, whether a manufacturer makes a charge or not for this service is an important consideration.

The quality of these services and the open-handedness or otherwise of the supplier in providing them will depend to a great extent on his general position in the market. The larger his share of the market the greater his opportunities to achieve economies of scale in the provision of support services no less than in the production of equipment. Another important factor relating to the supplier's share of the market is the influence of the latter on the size of the general fund of programming experience for his machines. Despite the growing importance of universal higher-level languages the bulk of programming is carried out in manufacturers' own autocodes (see Chapter 3). Programmers tend to specialize in one manufacturer's programming languages, and the more of these machines in use the wider the pool of expertise from which the user can recruit or replace software staff.

Furthermore, there is some interchange of programs, experience and technical assistance between common customers of a manufacturer. The larger his market share the bigger the opportunities for mutual co-operation via these users' associations. The scale of the supplier's operations, together with his growth-rate, also gives some indication of his ability to finance the continuous research and development which will maintain and improve the quality of his products, and in the last analysis ensure his survival in a highly competitive, advanced technology industry.

This evaluation process cannot be skimped or hurried if the

user is to choose the machine best adapted to his plans. Necessarily it absorbs a great deal of time and prevents the DP manager or whoever is responsible for assessing the manufacturers' reports from planning other aspects of the changeover. If he delegates the selection procedure, and perhaps the preparation of the initial statement of requirements also, to an outside specialist the length of the changeover can sometimes be reduced by several months. Although the cost of these services – usually amounting to several thousand pounds – adds somewhat to the total costs of the changeover this extra expenditure can be partly recouped in terms of saved time. And they are invaluable if they succeed in preventing the acquisition of the wrong equipment for the job. Even a well qualified internal assessor may welcome the chance of an independent check on his findings. For these reasons there is considerable demand for the services of computer consultants.

Nor is there any shortage of supply. The abundance of consulting firms and partnerships creates almost as many difficulties in the selection of a consultant as in the selection of the machine itself. Much comment has been made on the increasing use made by management in Britain of specialist consultants as a whole. Surprise is, however, sometimes expressed at the willingness of some managements, otherwise well known for their business acumen, to place themselves so readily in the hands of members of an occupation which lacks agreed standards of training, qualification and competence, and which has no controlling body capable of regulating admission, policing standards of practice, or enforcing a code of professional ethics.

This freedom of entry to the occupation, which is of course a great embarrassment to the genuinely expert and ethical consultant, allied to the fashionability of computers, the impressiveness of computer jargon and its lack of meaning to the average prospective user, and the urgency of the need for advice on business computing problems, has provided the bland, semi-competent adventurer with golden opportunities. There is no simple, fool-proof method for detecting the quack computer consultant. But David Shirley has suggested various criteria which are useful guides to his likely competence and honesty.

Probably the most important is that he should be able to claim (and, if necessary, prove) a number of years' direct experience of routine systems work and programming, preferably on more than one make of computer. Shirley stresses that the consultant should be asked to authenticate his claimed experience. A prospective client should carefully check at least one of his references.[5]

ADMINISTERING THE CHANGEOVER

The tight control which can only be guaranteed when senior management are prepared to identify themselves closely with the success of the scheme and to appoint a qualified DP overlord must not be relaxed after the choice of the computer. Up to this point, management of the changeover will have been largely a matter of acquiring and interpreting technical information with the purpose of making a rational investment decision. There has been a single broad problem: which computer to buy. The user must now switch to a more detailed form of control and planning, and a more active one.

Before the delivery of the machine a host of events and activities must occur. These revolve around the preparation of a computer centre; recruitment of systems and programming staff; software development; and consultation with and staff planning for personnel affected by the scheme. The sequence of these events and activities, and their interrelationships, must be carefully set out, together with estimates of their demands on resources like time, money, personnel and accommodation. One method of clarifying the sequence of events and their complex inter-connexions is to prepare *network diagrams* of the type commonly associated with civil engineering projects. Some computer suppliers are prepared to assist with their design.

The details about the numerous events need not delay us, nor the precise form of the networks which may be prepared. Three generalizations can, however, be made about them. Firstly, they call for a good deal of active participation on the part of middle and junior management staff. Computer enthusiasts at these

5. See Mr Shirley's article 'Choosing a Consultant', *Data Systems*, June 1967.

levels have the chance to contribute more actively to the progress of the changeover than is possible during the tedious ritual of selecting a computer. For example, whoever is delegated the task of preparing the computer centre must select and obtain approval for an appropriate site, seek planning permission for any necessary structural alterations, ensure the connexion of all necessary services, and oversee the purchase and installation of furniture and fittings. All these jobs must be finished in time for the delivery of the machine.

Secondly, the critical path through the network of activities as a whole is likely to run through those which have to do with software preparation. (A *critical path* is that logically necessary sequence of activities whose total time for completion determines the length of a project as a whole: in the 'project' of cooking a meal the critical path runs through those activities to do with the roasting of the joint.) We have seen that the average period between the ordering of the machine and the first dummy runs on it is around two years. This is the virtually irreducible minimum for the preparation of adequate software for a scheme with any serious information-providing objectives.

For a start there is the problem of recruiting systems staff. As we have noted, securing the right people may take several months in itself. Furthermore, these people, who generally will be allocated the more senior positions in the data-processing department and are consequently of strategic importance to the progress of the scheme, tend to move very readily from one concern to another. If a key systems man leaves in the middle of a scheme it can be back-dated by several months. External programmers must also be secured and they too present similar problems in recruitment and retaining. Junior systems men and programmers must be recruited internally and sent to the computer supplier for training. All this takes time, and the delay is often unnecessarily increased because users fail to book aptitude tests and course places at the earliest opportunity.

But the main source of delay is the meticulous, time-consuming nature of systems and programming work itself. The perfection of computer-based work systems and their associated programs only results from the most careful study of the foregoing 'manual' work systems, revision of them into a logically consistent structure oriented to the machine, the drafting of job organization and increasingly detailed programming flowcharts, and the exact documentation in both verbal and graphical form of each of these stages.

The information the systems man requires initially does not come ready-made. He needs the skills of the historian, the anthropologist and the detective for a good deal of his work. His work is complicated by the requirement that he participate to some extent in the very system which he is trying to document and understand, and his presence may introduce certain distortions to the system. He has to support his findings with considerable amounts of exact and wherever possible quantified information. This information will often be initially unavailable or cast in an inconvenient form. Occasionally it is deliberately withheld or doctored by individuals who regard his presence as a personal threat.

The work system which he studies also possesses social-system characteristics related importantly to the structure of tasks and authority. No anthropologist is called upon to remodel the social relationships that his fieldwork uncovers into a new, more rational, completely consistent form. He would no doubt regard even a partial attempt at any such redesign as beyond his competence. But the systems man must undertake such a restructuring. Although the relationships which have to be realigned relate mainly to specialized work tasks rather than to complete social roles they do possess important social-system characteristics. The systems man should bear in mind the consequences which his work may have for the social organization of the work unit.

The technical basis of the work is to be transformed. Any technical work system has a range of associated in practice typical and in theory possible forms of social organization. The characteristic social organization accompanying a specific technical arrangement of work will sometimes of itself produce human pressures which lower the morale of the people manning the technical system. With any change in the technical basis – and a drastic one is signified by the arrival of a computer – there will almost certainly follow a corresponding shift in the accompanying 'socio-technical' relationships of the personnel. This may be such as to produce interpersonal tensions offsetting the purely technical virtues, the drawing-board 'rationality', of the formal work system.

A systems designer must produce not merely a *viable* man-machine system – a tough enough proposition in itself – but one in which the rationale of the technology does not blight and sour the social relationships which inevitably spring up around it. It is regrettable that in practice systems designers, whether through lack of time or of awareness of the social-system implications of their work, do not seem to give full weight to these considerations. Ideally, too, one would wish to see some participation in the redesign of the system on the part of the affected workers.

Systems work results in a plan for achieving the proposed tasks on the computer which specifies how and when, by whom, and in what form data will be supplied to the computer; what processing operations will be undertaken by the machine; and what will happen to various categories of processed information – what reports, for example, will be generated for which individuals. It will indicate what programs are demanded to enable the computer to play its full part in bringing the new system to life. Programming cannot begin before systems design has reached an advanced stage of development. Once, however, the new system and its requirements have been fully documented, flowcharting can go ahead. As was pointed out in Chapter 3, if documentation is adequate the preparation of programs can actually occur outside the computerizing organization.

Some users attempt to speed up their program writing by subcontracting the job to specialist software bureaux. Similar comments to those which have already been made about computer consultants are often heard about these bodies. Even if the user engages one of the many perfectly competent bureaux there is a risk that the break in communication between programmers and systems analysts and designers may result in serious flaws in the finished programs. This removes any apparent savings in time. The programmer may detect faults in systems design which are easily rectified if the systems staff can be readily contacted.

Likewise, systems staff will wish to review the progress of program preparation.

The intricate logical structure of a program and the limitations of most compiling and assembly languages stand in the way of rapid preparation. So too do the human qualities of the programmer. However carefully he takes thought, however carefully he checks and double-checks the logic of his flowcharts, mistakes and omissions creep in. Thus a substantial part of the total time for software preparation is absorbed in program proving, or debugging. The revision to which these tests give rise can sometimes take as long as the initial writing of the program. Clearly it is extremely wasteful to await delivery of the user's own machine for debugging if other arrangements can be made. Time can always be booked on a machine reserved especially for this purpose at the supplier's headquarters.

While programs are being debugged the user's own machine should be undergoing its installation and acceptance tests. A team of card punchers and verifiers will be under training. Files of information will be undergoing conversion from their paper form to magnetic tape in readiness for the start of live operation. If scheduling has been tidy and each phase of the changeover well regulated live runs on the computer can begin as soon as the proved programs are passed ready for use.

At first, live running is likely to cover only parts of the full system because it takes some time to translate everything from its form on paper to everyday practice, and many unforeseen difficulties have to be dealt with on an *ad hoc* basis. Staff will be unused to the new rhythms of work and changed standards of performance, particularly the demand for much greater care and accuracy in the preparation of documents and strict adherence to set time limits. The machine itself may occasionally give trouble, especially if it is in the hands of newly trained operators. Consequently the new computer system has to be run in parallel with the old 'manual' system of work for a time. This way of meeting the problem of adapting to the new methods and the risk of occasional break-downs – perhaps even of complete failure – is the only real insurance against disaster. It can last for as long as a year.

The extra work involved is inevitably unpopular with staff, and temporary workers are often engaged to minimize overtime working. Eventually, however, the changeover to an all-computer system will be completed. Before this event is reached, in order to maintain momentum and to retain the interest of valuable systems staff, planning for the next set of applications should have begun. Computerization in organizations which have properly understood the use of the machine is a continuous process.

CONSULTATION WITH STAFF

It may seem a little out of sequence to revert to it at this point but it is now necessary to say something more about what should be the very first event after ordering the computer. This is the public announcement of the fact to all the staff. The light in which staff at all levels perceive the events and aims of the changeover has a direct bearing on its eventual success. If severe ho stility to the whole idea is aroused, many members of the staff are in a position to jeopardize its progress (by refusing to co-operate with systems personnel for example).

A second danger is that key clerical or middle management personnel, doubtful about their future roles in the reorganized system and its possible effects on their seniority, chances of promotion, or the size of their personal 'empires', may decide to seek posts in other organizations where prospects and security are less cloudy. Such 'anticipatory redundancy' can denude a prospective computer user of the experience and expertise he needs to keep current operations running smoothly. Suspicion about the likely consequences for them of the change in those staff who stay on can make for a very tense industrial relations atmosphere.

The writer cannot claim to believe, as many appear to, that the solution of practically all industrial relations problems, and those of technical and organizational change in particular, is merely a question of fostering 'good communications' – however defined – or that other and equally mysterious process, 'consultation'. The fact has probably to be faced that, however adroitly the user communicates his intentions to staff, however many provisions he makes to shield employees from any harmful effects to their security or prospects, whatever practical or public-relations steps are taken to smooth its introduction, computerization, or practically any other form of automation, will inevitably arouse a good measure of personal anxiety and uncertainty.

Computers, like it or not, are now unambiguously linked to fears of down-grading and dismissal, even on the part of individuals who have heard of relatively straightforward change-overs or who are quite unable to cite a single genuine instance of redundancy. These worries naturally vary from one individual to another and there is evidence that the degree of anxiety manifested is connected to characteristics such as age, sex and personal qualifications. This is not to say that such fears are irrational and groundless. Some staff-saving objectives are embodied in nearly all computer schemes. This is public knowledge. Staff fears stem from a legitimate form of self-interest, just as one can argue the user's decision to computerize does. It is ludicrous to suppose that this concern of the individual with his own future can somehow be 'communicated' or 'consulted' away.

While an active programme of communication and consultation with staff is most unlikely to remove their anxieties altogether, it is, however, safe to say that they will be artificially inflamed in the absence of such measures. Some prospective users are genuinely puzzled, and others outraged, by the suggestion that staff have a right to know at the earliest moment of the plan to computerize, or that such notification is at least judicious. Such important matters they regard as their own affair, not that of the staff, and the less 'interference' the better. Sometimes they rationalize this kind of approach by explaining that a 'premature' announcement might panic staff into unnecessary resignations, thereby creating severe dislocation of normal business. In many cases failure to make an official announcement does not result from any conscious policy but simply from oversight.

Perhaps the most curious feature of a policy of deliberate secrecy is the belief that it is operable. But to suppose so runs completely contrary to everyday industrial experience. A major decision affecting the whole future of a concern has an uncanny knack of finding its way into the grape-vine of informal communication. Suitably edited and embellished at each telling it soon becomes common knowledge, usually in a thoroughly garbled and alarming form. Once such rumours are current it is often difficult to put a stop to them by coming out with the truth itself. A belated official announcement, forced on the user by the general disquiet, is quite likely to be regarded merely as a mollifying exercise in propaganda. The assumption usually prompted by original 'secrecy' and strengthened by profuse official denials is that higher management wanted to keep everyone in the dark because massive redundancies were envisaged. Sometimes this assumption has in fact been correct. (That the machine eventually displaces far fewer people than was originally planned is of course a fact that no one can take account of at this stage.)

An early announcement may stimulate undesired resignations, though it is safe to say that the extent to which this happens will vary with the previous climate and history of industrial relations in each individual business, and also with the detail that is volunteered or later provided on request. The more enlightened users have generally followed a written communication to each employee with a programme of explanatory talks and the offer to discuss any personal doubts privately with individuals.

Where a clerical trades union or staff association exists its local officials have often been notified immediately and sometimes asked to divulge the information to their membership on behalf of the concern. Where such representation exists it obviously forms a convenient body through which continuous consultation can occur throughout the changeover. Needless to say, the user should not try to disguise any likely employment problems while going through the motions of consultation. Again, such secrecy must eventually be uncovered and the loss of confidence which ensues may have worse repercussions than no communication at all.

Further Reading

'Crisis in Giant Computers', *Management Today*, August 1967.
'Managing to Manage the Computer', *Harvard Business Review*, September–October 1966.

Mann, F. C., and Williams, L. K., 'Observations on the Dynamics of a Change to Electronic Data-Processing Equipment', *Administrative Science Quarterly*, 5, 1960.

Mumford, E., and Banks, O., *The Computer and the Clerk*, Routledge, 1967.

Scott, W. H. (ed.), *Office Automation: Administrative and Human Problems*, OECD, Paris, 1965.

'Top Management and Computer Profits', *Harvard Business Review*, July–August 1963.

CHAPTER 6

Office Automation: Clerk versus Computer?

INTRODUCTION

THE previous chapter was concluded with some remarks about the treatment of workers affected by a computerization scheme, and it was noted that the manner of this treatment can have important effects upon the ease and pace with which such a scheme can be introduced and upon its final operational success. Reference to these issues brings up the whole question of the effects of computerization on the employment and work of those categories of staff who have so far, contrary to many expectations of a few years ago, borne the brunt of automation.

These groups are predominantly the routine clerical and administrative workers of business, industry and government, the so-called 'white-collar', 'white-bloused' and 'black-coated' workers in banks, insurance companies, the Civil Service, and manufacturing industry. They are groups which have steadily grown in both absolute and relative strength in the labour force as a whole in line with the increasing scale and technical complexity of industry, the growth of official administration and the general secular expansion of the tertiary, or service, sector of an industrially advanced economy.

It has been largely to counter the growth of its private bureaucracy, its army of paper-handlers, and the increasing charge on its payroll that the individual concern has resorted to computerization in recent years. The claim is often made that success in cutting office costs by these means has been elusive. Nonetheless, some savings in administrative costs are a normal feature of any well devised computerization scheme, though the main benefits may accrue from elsewhere. Nearly all schemes absorb some office jobs – though these may be those which would have appeared only with a growth in business if computerization had not been attempted, and they may be too few in number to offset the additional costs of the computer.

THREE PROBLEM AREAS

The general issue of the employment and manpower effects of the computer divides into three main composite questions. Firstly, how severe have its effects been, not only on the total number of jobs available to clerical workers, and how severe will they be in the future? Furthermore, what does it do to the content of clerical jobs which remain; and how does it affect the clerk's prospects of promotion? Secondly, how are its effects seen and interpreted by clerical workers themselves? Is there in fact any important difference between what the computer actually does to employment and work themselves, and what it is perceived to do, or thought to threaten, by those individuals who encounter it? Thirdly, what results follow from the actual and perceived consequences of computerization from an industrial relations point of view? Do affected workers welcome or resist the change, and does resistance take an individualistic or a collective form?

It is this last question which is perhaps most interesting of all. Since the term, 'automation', itself was coined (in 1947 by D. S. Horder of the American Ford Motor Company) it has been recognized both by those who are optimistic and by those who are pessimistic about the long-term employment implications of the process that during its introduction some measure of technological unemployment is more or less inevitable and that the scale on which it occurs will be important, quite apart from the issues of relocation, retraining and compensation it will raise, in that it may itself act as a kind of automatic regulator of the rate at which automation can be introduced.

If the pool of technologically unemployed in any occupation grows rapidly, it is argued, the threat of individual displacement will become more readily visible to those who remain in employment. Though previously they may have avoided collective organization they may now embrace it with enthusiasm and the resulting organized worker resistance will bid up the price to be

paid for a faster rate of change, possibly making further automation temporarily uneconomic.

It is sometimes conjectured that the cumulative effects of
computerization on clerical work, in the sense of adverse changes
in career prospects, in methods of work and in the typical content
and rhythm of clerical duties, no less than in the total number of
clerical posts available, combined with and intensified by a much
faster rate of administrative automation in the next few years,
will eventually – 'eventually' here implies a time within the next
fifteen or even the next ten years – galvanize the members of
many white-collar occupations in a type of collective resistance
to further automation one would more readily associate with
manual workers.

Though this resistance would not halt the progress of administrative automation it would inevitably retard it substantially and
would bid up the asking price in terms of redundancy and
severance payments and provisions for retraining and relocation
which individual establishments and government agencies would
be expected to pay for a more rapid rate of change.

We shall consider such an eventuality later. For the moment
it is worth commenting that there are no unmistakable signs that
such a show-down is an immediate prospect. It would depend on
a wide measure of technological unemployment amongst white-
collar workers, and such conditions, as we shall see, by no means
appear likely for the present. In Britain at least, most recent
large-scale displacements of office staff have resulted less from
computer automation than from conventional organization and
methods (O and M) studies or reorganization following the
rationalization of the structure of certain industries in the wake
of take-over bids and mergers.

INDIVIDUAL CHANGEOVERS: CLERICAL REACTIONS

Individual resistance at the level of the work unit itself is another
matter. Here the reaction of the clerk is not necessarily governed
by what he sees computers doing to clerical occupations as a
whole, though his experiences in a changeover may sensitize him
to such a concern. He may be presented with evidence that shows

the relatively minor impact so far of computers on office employment and conditions and be urged to draw the inference that his security with his present computerizing employer is not seriously at risk. In the great majority of cases he is likely to find that such reassurances turn out to be quite genuine. But how is he to be sure of this happy outcome before the changeover is carried out? It is far too well known that staff savings are the major justification for most schemes. Often, too, as noted before, the bungling manner in which management may go about announcing a scheme and administering necessary staff changes is sufficient to provoke the suspicions of all but the most steely-nerved individuals.

We can in fact answer the second major question at this point. There is often a very big gap between the actual and the perceived employment effects of the office computer, both before, during, and to some extent after its introduction.

Partly, the anxiety which typically accompanies the introduction of a computer results from a failure to present the known employment facts to affected staff. Providing such information is seldom likely to ensure favourable acceptance of the scheme, however. After all, what the clerk is mainly concerned about is not whether other clerks have been made redundant or turned into a 'rubber-stamp' by the machine but whether he will be. The facts may assure him that such results are rare elsewhere but they hardly guarantee his personal immunity from them. Besides, the facts must contend with all the blood-curdling forecasts of the job-destroying and work-trivializing powers of the computer which since its discovery have monopolized popular conceptions of the machine. Computers tend to be seen in this light and it is very doubtful whether there is much prospect of implanting a different view. After all, it is only honest to admit the possibility that in the long run the computer could in fact turn out to produce some of its most feared consequences.

By no means all clerks are moved to pessimistic resistance or fatalistic resignation by the arrival of the machine. A good many are quite indifferent, and some see the changeover as an opportunity to transfer to better rewarded and more interesting computer jobs. Nor should the prevailing pessimism and sceptical imperviousness to reassuring information be taken to contradict what has already been said about the desirability from the standpoint of both industrial relations and ethical personnel practice of giving early notice to affected workers of a proposed computerization project, of encouraging a free two-way exchange of information and opinion, and of laying on computer appreciation courses.

Such ventilation of plans is more than a routine courtesy. The opposite policy, that of secrecy, is not merely unethical and arrogant but invariably impracticable. When the secret is leaked it is likely to generate more hostility and suspicion than would otherwise have existed, and to slow up the rate at which the scheme can progress. Contributors to a report of a number of case studies of office automation concerned mainly with its administrative and human problems, undertaken a few years ago in four European countries, made this point very plain, and the editor of the report, Professor W. H. Scott, commented:

Overall there was a tendency towards secrecy and a lack of con-sultation. This seemed to be due partly to higher management's own uncertainty about the precise course of future events, but also to the absence of any tradition of negotiation and consultation with clerical and administrative employees within the enterprise. On the one hand, this uncertainty led to caution and gradualism on management's part, but the lack of adequate information and consultation seems to have led to a good deal of anxiety amongst employees.[1]

On the other hand, nowhere do the writers of this report suggest, as sometimes do spokesmen more directly concerned with the manufacture or installation of computers, that com-munication of managerial intentions and the offer to discuss the implementation of the scheme will of itself guarantee rapid acceptance to the changeover. Secrecy usually results in serious friction. But frankness does not necessarily avoid it. As two of the report's contributors, Enid Mumford and Olive Banks, remind us in a later publication, studies of staff opposition to change in industry as a whole seem to show fairly clearly that, while proper communication to workers of plans for change and

1. Scott, W. H. (ed.), *Office Automation: Administrative and Human Problems*, OECD, Paris, 1965, p. 91.

encouragement to participate in implementing them may on occasion produce a very smooth transition, such techniques, however well intentioned and liberally administered, are generally compromised by offsetting factors.[2]

In some cases staff may simply not wish to be consulted – though it would be misleading to suggest this applies very often to office automation schemes: clerical workers usually believe themselves to have a close relationship with management, and anything which appears to go against this will be resented. Again, the actual business of participating in the planning of change may overstretch the individual's social and intellectual skills and be unwelcome for these reasons. But above all, the proposed change may be, or may be perceived to be, of such a radical and pervasive nature that the benefits of communication and participation are all inevitably outweighed by the individual's estimation of the likely effects on his position.

Such frequently seems to be the case with office automation. Frankness on the part of management may marginally reduce these anxieties and hence head off some forms of practical resistance, but it can rarely be expected to remove them altogether.

We do not have to search very far for the reasons why the administrative worker is alarmed by the computer, and why techniques for securing approval of technical and organizational change which have often proved effective in the factory are sometimes less successful in the office. Above all he, or, less often, she, is afraid of personal redundancy. Most office workers are no less aware than management that office staffs have been increasing rapidly in recent years (specifically clerical workers now form something like fifteen per cent of the total working population against five per cent in 1914), that they represent an increasingly heavy charge on a concern's administrative overheads, and that the computer has been advertised, promoted, and extolled as a device for reversing this trend.

The great expense of the machine is well known and it is only common sense to conclude that it must be offset by economies

2. Mumford, E., and Banks, O., *The Computer and the Clerk*, Routledge, 1967, p. 221.

elsewhere. Where else but in the removal of a large body of staff? The computer is brought in to save labour and the saved labour must prepare to go. Assurances that displaced individuals will be found work in other departments or branches of the firm may be treated with scepticism. Equally they may lead to worries about what such transfers will imply in terms of lost seniority, and the handicap the worker may suffer in another department by inexperience in its work and methods.

Strikingly often, and in the face of assurances to the contrary, office workers report that their immediate response to the news of computerization has been that 'practically everyone's for the sack'. True enough, such reactions are less likely in establishments such as banks and government departments where high job security is a contractual or traditionally well-respected feature of employment. Yet even here there will usually be substantial qualms about the possible consequences of computerization upon the structure of promotion ladders. In establishments where job security is regarded less as a 'constitutional right', or is less frequently written into the contract of employment, to these lesser – though potentially explosive – apprehensions will be added the felt threat of dismissal itself.

It is worth noting too that this fear of redundancy is not simply that of the loss of a convenient, well paid, or previously promising appointment, nor the worry of finding another to replace it, with the accompanying possibility of a period of unemployment, the need to move house perhaps, and other dislocations. The indignity of severance itself, its assault upon individual feelings of self-esteem, even sometimes of indispensability, is no less repellent than these mundane practicalities. Even if he did not do so before he perceived the threat, the individual may now begin to identify with his present post and to view it as a symbol of his individual worth. His determination to cling on to it grows accordingly, though sometimes prior to the threat of computerization he had held a low estimation of it, an unflattering opinion of his employer, or had even been contemplating a voluntary move to another concern.

White-collar workers, then, frequently assume that large-scale redundancy is the inevitable result of computerization; or that the concern's organization will be transformed to such an extent, in order to meet the technical needs of the proposed computer system, that personal skills, status and prospects will be seriously undermined. They are either for the sack or on the way to becoming a rubber-stamp.

These reactions are all the more pronounced because technical and organizational change has traditionally been only a minor feature of office work. The clerical worker still retains something of the outlook of his Victorian and Edwardian predecessor in his view of the significance of his work to management and his relationship with the boss. He – and she too, to some degree – still thinks of himself as something of a personal aide to management, fulfilling uniquely duties which are vital to the firm and require the personal, experienced touch. Mechanization, large-scale organization, the rationalization and subdivision of work tasks, have certainly had their 'manualizing' effects on the nature and status of office duties. But they have occurred slowly and on a relatively narrow front, and both their immediate and their longer-term effects have been far milder than comparable changes in the latter part of the last century and the early part of this on the factory floor.

The office worker's traditional immunity from the twin scourges of redundancy and rationalized work is swept away with the decision to computerize. Gone is his envied security and the basis of his belief that his work is a unique contribution to the life of the concern. Suddenly the office is to be treated just as if it were the factory.

The suddenness and potential scope of office automation strikes him all the harder because technical change has formed so small a part of his occupational culture, or has occurred too haltingly to come to constitute an obvious intrusion on his responsible autonomy.

What follows when office workers feel themselves threatened by the loss of their security or prospects thanks to the computer? Gradually fear and resentment of the change may become transformed into practical resistance, though the forms which this resistance takes are in line with the standards of decorum which one would expect from staff who lay claim to a certain standing in society. Perhaps its most common form is anticipatory resignation. Assuming, usually against managerial assurances to the contrary, that he is in for the eventual chop the worker 'sacks himself' by taking the first opportunity of an alternative appointment. This step solves both the presumed future practical problem of securing another post and the psychological crisis of facing the affront to personal dignity which involuntary severance would occasion. It also deals a minor retaliatory blow to an 'ungrateful' employer, whose assurances about the future are viewed as the shallowest hypocrisy.

If the worker stays, his resistance rarely takes the form of concrete steps to sabotage the scheme. But his resentful and anxious frame of mind often results in behaviour having the same practical consequences as more explicit, calculated opposition. One aspect of this syndrome is a refusal to accept that the machine will be able to absorb work of any degree of refinement. This is by no means a denial of the computer's usefulness altogether. Rather it derives from the reassuring conviction that a machine – even the 'mighty electronic brain' – can be capable of no more than very low-grade work. No one is eager to have it thought that his own work meets this definition. It follows that an individual must reject the machine's applicability to it and condemn any attempt to absorb it in the new computer system as misguided nonsense.

This intense scepticism about the machine's relevance to the individual's own work is likely to be supported and reinforced by similar sentiments on the part of his colleagues. The probable consequence is a refusal to co-operate with systems analysts and designers. To the individual they may appear to be doing something which inherently cannot be done – devise a machine-oriented system of work which will automate away the personal touch and the call for experience, including, perhaps, the individual's own personal touch and experience.

It goes without saying that no commercial computer system can be devised without the assistance and advice of those individuals operating its manual predecessor. The analyst must obtain a picture of its workings from interview, observation and a study of documents. The consciously or unconsciously resistant clerk (or manager) can all too easily obstruct and delay this work. There may be no need even to prevaricate or withhold information deliberately to sabotage the work effectively. All that may be required is a refusal to volunteer anything or to correct misunderstandings. Where only a few workers are resistant to systems work, heavier reliance on those well disposed to the change will of course easily solve the problem of a few recalcitrants. Where the majority are minded to obstruct the systems studies, non-co-operation may result in a completely botched system.

Systems men usually have personal experience or knowledge of whole strings of cases where such resistance occurred. When resistance of any kind appears to be hampering their work they have little alternative but to request the superiors of resistant individuals to put pressure on their unhelpful subordinates. Friction with systems staff intensifies as a result, and much of the hostility which workers initially felt against management for deciding to introduce the machine is redirected on to the emerging system itself and its designers.

The belief that the new system is inoperable is often partly justified when the computer actually comes into commission. It is very rare to attempt to achieve the switchover from a manual to a new computer system in one step. However well it has been designed, some time will be required to acclimatize to the new methods of work. Numerous unforeseen inadequacies must be purged. Consequently many hold-ups and errors must always be expected in the first few months of computer operation, during which it is necessary to operate the old manual system in parallel. During this period every mistake the computer appears to make (for example, as a result of faulty programming or careless input coding) will be seized upon with relish and paraded as evidence of the folly of trying to use it at all.

These teething troubles, however, may cause less jubilation if they become so serious as to necessitate the working of overtime. Sometimes the work of the newly computerized office becomes so completely disorganized that this step is inevitable. Overtime working is not regarded as a normal feature of clerical work and the affected personnel will see it as further cause to denigrate the computer. Ironically, the necessity for overtime work may itself result from carelessness in preparing input documents and so forth – which is itself partly the product of opposition. As disillusionment grows so does the propensity for error. So too does the attitude that 'they' – management and computer specialists – wanted the system so let them make it work. It may take anything up to several years to break out of this particular vicious cycle.

At the level of the individual, then, there is often considerable fear of and hostility towards the machine and its masters which seriously impedes the changeover process and the achievement of operating efficiency in the individual concern. Unfortunately much of this response is inevitable and could not be removed by any amount of reassurance or careful provision for personal job security and prospects. We have to remember too, that careless systems work, or tactless investigations of individual work duties, can do much to stimulate a latent hostility into active opposition.

Nevertheless, it would be wrong to exaggerate the extent of the office worker's resistance to the computer. The term 'office worker' is itself an omnibus expression masking great differences of function between different grades of worker, and equally important variations of age, sex and seniority.

Unquestionably some categories of office worker positively welcome the introduction of the machine, regarding it as a means to mobility in the firm, to acquiring valuable qualifications, or as offering them the chance of interesting or prestigious work in the computer centre. For example, a small but important minority can expect to secure selection as junior systems analysts and programmers. Usually the younger male worker is most eligible for these roles. And some young female clerks and machine operators are enthusiastic about what they regard as the high-status, even glamorous, function of computer operator.

Other workers are indifferent, particularly those – and today they form a large minority of all clerical workers – who are anyway already engaged in highly routine, machine-oriented duties, and who entertain few illusions that their present post is a stepping-stone to higher things. For them computerization is of little importance one way or the other.

It is those workers who see themselves as having least to gain and much to lose from computerization who fear it most and whose open or tacit opposition is consequently the most pronounced. Most indications are that these individuals are likely to be the more senior male clerks, especially those who have held hopes of rising eventually to executive positions. Their value to the firm rests largely upon their long experience of departmental affairs, and to a lesser extent on their acquired adroitness in handling individuals whose personalities they have come to understand. Their skills are largely specific to one aspect of the firm's affairs, and it is as a repository of this expertise that they may hope to qualify for advancement.

The computer – which partly because of their age they find more difficult to understand – is easily seen as a threat to this unique position in the firm. Skill and experience are to be captured and codified in the new impersonal machine system, depriving the individual of his capital value to management. Opportunities for departmental advancement may be radically altered because the machine system redistributes the numbers and type of junior posts. An individual who has set his sights on the leading post in a section may see the section disappear altogether. Younger workers can face the need to transfer to a new section or department with most of their career before them. The older worker is less ready or able to adapt.

Again it must be stressed that responses to the changeover may depend less upon what changes are actually to occur than upon what the individual's general impressions of the computer lead him to expect. These expectations seem to be related to personality factors to some extent, but more often to attributes such as sex, age and position in the office hierarchy. Pep-talks and reassurances about the new system will have only a marginal effect on reducing anxieties when these attributes coincide. This does not mean that the responses of office staff to computerization can simply be written off as 'emotional' or 'irrational'. Such terms do not help much with explanation. All the same it can be argued that there is occasionally a tendency to over-reaction – at least if we can be perfectly sure that staff are indeed acquainted with the known facts about the effects of the machine.

What, briefly, are these facts as they apply in this country? Without going into such factual information as is presently available about the employment effects of the computer in any detail at this stage, it is worth pointing out that up to 1965 the Ministry of Labour could find no evidence for large-scale redundancies as a result of computerization. Only four per cent of organizations which replied to its queries on this score reported that they had dismissed workers and the total numbers involved amounted to less than two hundred. Nearly all of these individuals were married women or part-time workers, and the concerns in question appear to have been fairly generous in providing compensation for displacement and free time to search for other employment.[3]

Again, with regard to effects of computerization on the structure of job opportunities in the office it commented:

One of the fears sometimes expressed about A.D.P. (advanced data-processing) is that it will alter the structure of office staff in such a way that, while there will be an increase in the number of machine operators in the lower levels of the hierarchy and to a lesser extent of executives in the upper levels, the number in the grades in the middle will sharply decrease. This, it is supposed, would create an awkward blockage to promotion between the lower and the upper levels of the hierarchy. Although the survey confirmed that there had been some movement of this kind in the numbers of staff, it was not so large in the office as a whole as to create much difficulty. In fact, diagrams constructed to show the position in the average office before and after the event were almost indistinguishable. Moreover, there are two factors which tend to prevent serious trouble. First, the status of machine operators has risen with the installation of A.D.P., particularly in the computer room; and secondly, the turnover rate among machine operators is very high and only a few of them look for a career in the office. It would, perhaps, be a fair statement to say that, while there might conceivably be isolated cases of difficulty where blocks of routine clerical work undergo a large amount of conversion to A.D.P., in the great majority of organisations in this country there are not likely to be any appreciable problems in the foreseeable future.[4]

3. Ministry of Labour, *Computers in Offices* (Manpower Studies No. 4), HMSO, 1965.
4. Ministry of Labour, op. cit., pp. 25–6.

These conclusions, though it will be noted they are fairly well hedged, accord well with those of nearly all published case studies of particular computerization schemes in the office. So to a large extent do the report's statements about working procedures and general conditions in the automated office. The organizations which replied claimed they had come across little trouble over such factors as shift-work, noise and heat from computing equipment, the discipline of the computer-oriented working procedures, monotony and fatigue. Most individuals exposed to such possible conditions are anyway full-time computer personnel, who seem to accept them, where they occur, as part of the normal conditions of their work. We have seen that even relatively low-skilled tasks associated with the operation of the computer are frequently regarded as relatively prestigious by the workers who perform them, and the physical environment of the computer centre, with its sound-proofing, controlled temperature, and air-conditioning is in many ways superior to that of the average office.

In fact, the only quibble that one might make about these findings (apart of course from the general one that they are based upon reports from managerial staff responsible for the success of the computer installation and its smooth operation rather than upon direct observation and interviews with the personnel concerned) is over their optimism about workers' acceptance of the discipline and monotony of some computer-oriented clerical tasks.

True enough, the staff engaged on many of the most dreary of these duties, such as card punching and verifying, are young female workers with foreshortened career horizons and little expectation of more challenging work who do not readily voice their dissatisfactions. But other studies show that these workers often suffer considerable stress and frustration. Merely because complaint about these rigours is inarticulate does not mean they do not exist. It is also known that more elevated clerical workers whose work is affected by the computer's demand for accuracy and the provision of information exactly on schedule often resent this discipline. However, by and large, the conclusions of the report on these questions may for the present be taken as broadly valid.

ORGANIZED CLERICAL RESISTANCE
TO THE COMPUTER

One must always bear in mind, however, that the penetration of the computer is at present still modest, and that the schemes which have been devised for the automation of office work often represent little more than a more fully mechanized form of the old manual system. The work of more senior grades of office staff has, therefore, been left virtually intact, and they remain largely untouched by the computer's discipline.

Yet, despite these marginal effects on the security, content and rhythm of work, there has been considerable fear and opposition to the machine. One is bound to ask whether the further spread of office automation, as part of a general wider use of the machine, may not in fact bring the severe and widespread disturbance which has so far been feared but has not materialized. Could such disturbances lead to the crystallization of a more formidable and collectively organized opposition of white-collar groups to the machine? If white-collar workers have sometimes opposed computerization apparently without what many people would regard as just cause, what might this opposition be if just cause did appear?

Such an eventuality is certainly real enough to merit discussion, and this being so it becomes worthwhile to consider the possibility that opposition might be collectively organized, that is, channelled and promoted by trade unions.

While many people may be prepared to accept that more rapid administrative automation may provoke more active resistance by clerical workers at the level of the individual or the work unit, the suggestion that it might be organized collectively tends to be discounted. It runs against the stereotype most of us cling to of the clerk as a lower-middle-class individualist who identifies with the aims of management (including the aim of higher efficiency via mechanization), who strikes a personal bargain over his rewards and conditions of work, and whose world-view and occupational ideology runs counter to the values and objectives of trade unionism.

It even comes as something of a surprise to many people

143

(despite the widely reported militancy of important white-collar groups during the economic troubles of recent years) to discover that some administrative workers are already fairly highly unionized, for reasons which have very little to do with administrative automation but which can be traced to the progressive invalidation over the last fifty years of the very stereotype of the clerk to which we still find it convenient to adhere. Major social and economic forces have transformed the industrial and occupational position of the clerk himself. Broadly in line with – though sometimes a half-step behind – the changing realities of his situation the clerk has tended to modify and redirect his values and loyalties, so that today many of the necessary conditions for the type of collective resistance to administration automation which is hypothesized for the future are unquestionably fulfilled.[5]

Since this suggestion may not be accepted automatically it is worthwhile to summarize the important changes of the last half-century which have so altered the position, outlook and allegiances of the administrative worker, concentrating in particular on those processes which have made him increasingly ripe for unionization, and, equally important, those which have facilitated the practical business of organizing him. For if unionization is to occur the members of an occupation must not merely share certain major objective economic interests but subjectively recognize these congruences: identity of interest must not only exist but be perceived to exist. Further, individuals who recognize a community of interest must believe in the efficacy of a common representative body to protect and advance common aims.

Equally important, they must believe in the legitimacy, the social propriety, of this type of representation. No worker will voluntarily join a trade union, or comparable body, if he questions its ability to secure significant advantages for him or if he doubts the rightness of securing them by these means. Even if he arrives at a high estimation of the potential value of union representation and of its social appropriateness his wish for

5. The discussion of this issue has leaned heavily on David Lockwood's celebrated analysis of white-collar unionization. See Lockwood, D., *The Blackcoated Worker*, Allen & Unwin, 1958.

membership may be frustrated by constraints in his industrial situation – if, for example, he tends to find himself isolated in a small work unit, inaccessible to union organizers, and in continuous close contact with superiors antagonistic to trade-union objectives.

Such isolation of itself will in fact operate to reduce the visibility to him of shared occupational interest. Under such conditions, if his pay is low, if his hours are long, if his surroundings are cold and cramped, and if his prospects of promotion are problematic, it is easier to place responsibility upon himself for choosing the particular job or failing to negotiate directly with superiors for improvements. If others are seen to be sharing his difficulties the arguments for seeking joint rectification become more acceptable. The growth of larger work units consequently becomes at once an important precondition both for the stimulation and for the marshalling of collective sentiments.

Even as recently as Edwardian days practically every feature of the administrative worker's economic position and working environment, and, by derivation, of his relationship with management and of his perceived situation in the industrial and social structure as a whole, militated against the growth of an interest and involvement in trade-union affairs.

The typical office was minute, rarely containing more than a handful of clerks. Each was something of a specialist, holding his position by virtue of his superior education and a progressively deepening experience in one or another important aspect of the firm's affairs. Distinctions of age and length of service to the firm were scrupulously observed, and advancing years and dutiful stewardship brought their own rewards. Promotion to managerial status was common enough to be recognized as a realistic objective, and relationships with management were sufficiently close and intense to ensure a thorough identification with its values. Employment with the firm, too, seen as the result of a personal bargain, was viewed very much as a life-long commitment. Clerks did not have jobs. They had situations.

Personal job satisfaction and personal economic well-being were seen as a product of individualistic effort in an atmosphere of fiduciary understanding between employer and employee.

Whatever grievances the individual might feel about his rewards, prospects or working conditions, these were thought to be entirely a matter for personal negotiation and adjustment. Thus although objectively the majority of clerks certainly shared common economic and working problems the extent of this community of interest was almost completely obscured from the individual's view. In a sense common interests were defined away: the only interests which could exist were individual interests, and their only means of protection and advancement individual negotiation and loyal, conscientious service. The clerk was the manager's personal assistant and identified with him. Since he was an extension of management there could be no question of conflict with management, any more than the hand can defy the brain.

Even where collective interests were identified, and trade unionism perceived as a relevant and effective vehicle for furthering them, the clerk's social philosophy and his sense of his own social status operated against their development. Unionism was viewed as the (rather questionable) industrial weapon of the manual worker, and hence that of the working classes. Most emphatically the clerk did not wish to sacrifice the higher social prestige to which, by virtue of his superior education, his marginally higher rewards, his greater job security, his proximity to management, his neat dress and appearance, and his residence in 'respectable' areas, he laid claim, and was to a large extent awarded, by embracing solutions which were so indivisibly associated with his social inferiors.

Thus such white-collar trade unions as existed up to the First World War (and some white-collar unions have no less lengthy a history than their manual counterparts) remained weak in membership and industrially ineffective, for the most part rejected by a potential membership who denied their relevance and legitimacy, or trembled before the social penalties of affiliation. Significantly, however, they did find members in those localities or industries where the status distinctions between manual and non-manual worker at work and between the 'respectable' working class and the lower middle class in the community were not sharply drawn, and where non-manual workers were concentrated in relatively large units and could thus negotiate as a body or were subjected by a common employer to a measure of official grading on the job.

Between then and now practically every basis of the administrative worker's hostility to his own unionization has been progressively eroded. Firstly, previous economic advantages with respect to manual workers have disappeared. Although wide differences of pay between different grades of clerk and between clerks in different industries have always existed, and to some extent remain, until fairly recently the average clerk received direct financial rewards which were markedly superior to those of the average manual worker. His security, in both the short and the longer terms, was more assured: absences due to sickness or personal crisis were more likely to be permitted without loss of pay, and in many cases he could look forward to retirement secure in the knowledge that he would receive a pension from his former employer, albeit a modest one. During his working life, which significantly he could with some realism describe as a career, he could usually expect periodic increases in his pay, and his economic prospects were generally brightened by the greater likelihood of promotion to managerial rank. But during the last fifty years, and particularly the last twenty, manual earnings have steadily drawn level with and presently, on average, marginally surpass those of the routine non-manual worker.

The relative 'affluence' of the manual worker may to some extent depend on his willingness to work overtime. But the chance for regular overtime earnings is typically denied to the clerk altogether. Manual workers' relative prosperity also still depends more closely on the general buoyancy of the economy and the maintenance of recent full-employment policies. But such policies have been upheld since the war, and can be questioned or infringed only at the greatest political risk. And the comparative security the non-manual worker has always enjoyed from all but the gravest economic fluctuations has been in some measure extended to cover many manual groups, as a consequence both of official employment and redundancy policies and of collective bargaining at the industry-wide and plant levels.

As for the opportunity for promotion to managerial ranks,

which clearly must be counted as among the economic rewards of any occupation, both manual and non-manual groups have suffered as managers become increasingly recruited from the abundant supply of graduates pouring off the university production-lines. But the loss of these opportunities has perhaps been relatively more severe for clerks, and they certainly seem to feel it more bitterly since they previously entertained ambitions of such advancement more frequently than manual workers. Again, although the clerk still enjoys advantages in terms of his daily starting time and the length of his working day and working week, the standard manual working week has been falling rapidly and there are now – overtime apart – only slight differences in this respect.

The overall physical conditions and environment of factory work too have steadily improved, while those of many, especially small, offices have lagged behind. Indeed, some factories provide a physical environment and a range and standard of facilities which are on the whole superior to those of many offices. It would be idle to pretend, however, that anything like full equalization has yet been achieved in this field.

It has been in the area of task organization that some of the most impressive convergences between the work situations of the manual worker and the clerk have occurred. With some justice it has increasingly been claimed that the flows, content and tempo of work in many larger offices have gone far towards reproducing the work organization and working rhythms of the factory production-line. These changes should not be exaggerated: most office workers still enjoy considerable autonomy over their working methods and pace of work, and are allocated a sufficiently broad range of duties to provide them with the satisfactions of a whole and rounded job. But, as we have seen, the creation of larger office units has invited the application of the rationalizing techniques of mass-production whereby complex tasks are subdivided into smaller, more specialized, and repetitive units, and skill and judgement are organized out of existence.

Machinery, too, has been increasingly applied, and though until the arrival of the computer it has generally remained under the direct control of its operator its very adoption tends to blur the formerly clear boundary between the factory and office: a tabulating room, a typing pool, and a machine shop possess an obvious fundamental similarity.

Such changes in the relative economic positions and work situations of manual and office workers have inevitably undermined the clerk's own, and other people's, conception of his social status. Reluctant to forgo his traditionally superior prestige with respect to manual workers he has nonetheless witnessed the dissolution of the realities upon which it was based. As manual rewards have advanced – significantly, largely as a result of trade-union activity, a fact not lost on the clerk – so the relative desirability of clerical work has fallen, a devaluation intensified by the progressive equalization of the security of manual and non-manual work, the decline of the office as a career ladder to management, and the more sophisticated rationalization of office work itself.

Consequently, the office job is no longer the natural choice it was for the lower-middle-class school leaver, or the prize it was for the working-class entrant. The general educational, and to some extent social, qualifications which were formerly demanded of the office recruit have been relaxed in the face of a heavy demand for clerical workers and the decreasing ambition for an office career in lower-middle-class children. The social composition of the office has consequently changed in the direction of heavier representation of entrants with a working-class background – a background where trade unionism is generally regarded with more approval.

An equally dramatic change has occurred in the sexual composition of the office. To some extent, this large-scale 'feminization' of the office has protected the career-minded male clerk from many of the rigours of rationalized work since the female worker is typically allocated and retained in the more routine, undemanding office tasks. To some extent, true enough: but far from entirely. More important, however, is firstly the effect of large-scale feminization on the general conception of the nature and status of clerical work: office work is increasingly viewed as 'women's work', an evaluation which lowers its prestige as a whole. And secondly, feminization compromises to some extent

149

the ability of the careerist clerk to recoup his losses by collective action. The young female worker, who usually regards her job merely as a means to support herself until marriage, is not over-popular with union organizers.

Clerks who regard their choice of occupation as relatively permanent, and consider its long-term prospects, have therefore to face the fact that its economic advantages have diminished, that it is becoming more routine and boring, and that it is rapidly losing the former social prestige which attached to it and helped to offset its disadvantages. With the example of manual workers before them, collective solutions have gained in attractiveness at the same time that changes in social values and in the composition of office staffs have reduced emotional barriers to embracing them. Consequently there has been a steady, and impressive, rise in the membership of administrative workers' trade unions. But what has facilitated this development no less than economic pressure and changed attitudes has been the great change in the scale and structure of administrative operations and administrative units.

Offices have grown bigger and bigger, and with bigness has come the rationalization not only of work but of work relation-ships. The personal and direct responsibilities possible in the small unit cannot be maintained when offices are transformed into giant bureaux. Lines of responsibility have to be drawn up, and chains of command exactly determined. A neatness is introduced into organization – sometimes imposed on it – and this neatness includes precise scales of pay, criteria of adequate performance, and formulas for promotion to higher rank.

This new, tighter organization removes the clerical worker from that direct personal contact with management which previously he had and cherished. The boss recedes into the distance, and the worker becomes another bureaucratic cog sharing an obvious common situation with other workers – a situation which is to a large extent enshrined in the office manual and his contract of employment. Self-advancement can now come less from gaining the boss's eye or ear. The boss can hardly keep his eye on several hundred or several thousand workers. Promotion becomes a codified procedure, depending more on qualifications or length of service than on exemplary individual application or loyalty. Upward steps may be slow in coming, and eventually blocked altogether. When such a process of bureaucratization is sufficiently far advanced the only betterment to hope for is a collective betterment.

No less important than the sharper appreciation of his situation which the larger scale of office work units encourages in the clerk is its simplification of the practical task of the union organizer in signing him up. Because numerous workers are concentrated in each unit individuals become more accessible for the initial approach. This can more easily be of a face-to-face kind, and so can subsequent communication and liaison.

In some ways the organizer can come to inherit the former close relationship of boss to worker. As lengthening chains of command increase the distance between the ordinary worker and superiors with sufficient authority to handle grievances effectively, the union representative can step in as the earpiece of complaints and suggestions. And bigness increases the number of workers with a single boss. This facilitates the job of negotiation itself, and in turn promotes the further standardization of pay and conditions, thus increasing the visibility of the workers' common situation and problems.

To show the growth in trade-union membership among office workers in numbers is not easy since the relevant statistics are seldom available in full or in strictly comparable form. Fifty years ago the white-collar trade unionist was a rarity while in 1964 about one in every four (2,625,000 of 10,065,000) British trade unionists was a white-collar worker.[6] (The term 'white-collar worker', as it applies to these figures, is highly inclusive, embracing draftsmen, teachers, technicians, foremen, performers, doctors etc. However, the largest single block of white-collar workers are in clerical occupations. (It is worth noting in passing also that much of what has been said of the influences operating in favour of greater clerical unionism are equally valid for many other white-collar groups.)

More impressive than overall figures are those for individual

6. See Bain, G. S., 'The Growth of White-Collar Unionism in Great Britain', *British Journal of Industrial Relations*, 3, No. 3, 1965.

white-collar unions. The National and Local Government Officers' Association (NALGO) expanded from approximately 5,000 members in 1905 to about 360,000 in 1967. The Clerical and Administrative Workers' Union (CAWU) increased from roughly 12,000 to 76,000 members between 1914 and 1966. Between 1950 and 1966 alone the National Union of Bank Employees doubled its strength from 29,000 to 58,000.[7] These substantial rises in membership are of course closely connected also with the rapid increase in the number of workers in these occupations in recent years, though this rise can by no means explain them away. It is noteworthy too that there are big variations in the rate of growth between different unions. Significantly, growth in membership has been slower in those unions which aim at organizing workers in some branches of manufacture where the small office unit survives with its face-to-face paternalistic relationships between employer and worker. The 'density' – that is, the ratio of actual union memberships to the total theoretically possible membership – of white-collar unionization is inevitably reduced by these survivals, as it is by the increasing employment of female workers.

But failure to recruit more than a fraction of total potential membership may be no serious handicap to bargaining strength if absolute membership is high and buoyant, or if the bulk of members are concentrated in firms or industries which set the general pattern for pay and conditions. Non-unionized members eventually come to enjoy some of the benefits gained by their pace-setting unionized colleagues. Over recent years the growing absolute memberships of white-collar unions does seem to have added considerably to their militancy, partly because it provides a wider base for supporting a strong central staff of negotiators. One sign of this increasing militancy is the greater willingness of white-collar unions to affiliate to the Trade Union Congress, and another, as exemplified in the recent affairs of the draftsmen and bank clerks, the spread of the white-collar strike.

It is with these important developments in the power and militancy of the white-collar unions in mind that those who

7. These are the figures quoted in recruiting and publicity material for these unions in 1967.

predict widespread collective resistance to the computer make their speculations. Quite apart from the threat of computerization, it can be argued, the factors which have produced these developments – especially the spread of larger, more rationalized work units, and the erosion of the rewards, economic and social, of office work – will work increasingly powerfully in favour of stronger white-collar trade unionism. If, on top of this, more widespread computerization began to have a serious effect on employment, working conditions, and prospects, massive union-organized resistance to the machine could well follow – in some eyes, would needs follow.

Needs follow? Perhaps not. We should remember that the enormous contraction of employment in industries such as mining and the railways in recent years, partly as the result of technological change, has been by and large fairly smoothly achieved. One is certainly not justified in assuming that white-collar workers would prove more militant than their manual counterparts in the face of technological unemployment on a wide scale. But leaving this question aside, what signs are there that a substantial contraction of clerical employment is at hand thanks to the machine?

We have seen that up to 1965 the Ministry of Labour had been unable to find much evidence of actual redundancy following computerization. Other evidence on this score tends to show that the greatest difficulties have so far occurred in isolated cases only, in particular where a concern is so located that displaced staff have few employment alternatives locally, or where computerization was accompanied by a move of premises to a different part of the country and some staff were unable to follow. Admittedly, the 1965 Ministry report does not seem to have covered all firms who had installed office computers or all those who were intending to do so, nor those which made use of service bureaux. It does not go very far into the question of voluntary severance in the face of computerization, yet it is generally known that the proportion of workers who 'sack themselves' because they fear involuntary dismissal, or down-grading, is sometimes substantial. But these may be minor quibbles. Those who foresee a fairly imminent contraction in clerical employment as a whole would probably focus more attention on other 'invisible' effects of the machine, especially on the so-called 'silent firings' of workers who would later have been demanded if manual methods had been retained.

But discussion of this issue is clouded by uncertainty about the future underlying demand for office workers if computers could be imagined away, about the numbers of machines likely to be installed, about the scope of the work they are likely to do, and hence about the exact employment effects of the average computer installation. Demand for office workers has been growing at a yearly rate of around three per cent in recent years, and it is perhaps reasonable to expect it to continue doing so for a few years more, though maybe, computers apart, it might slacken to around two per cent.[8] If this is so, about 700,000 additional office vacancies will have been created between 1964 and 1974. During the same period, according to Ministry of Labour forecasts the number of computers 'for office work alone' should rise to 6,000. (Many people would argue that this is a very conservative estimate, and pays too little attention to the growth in speed and capacity of equipment.) To calculate how many jobs are likely to disappear because of the machine, given these figures, and therefore to assess whether their loss will be offset by those created by underlying economic forces, we need an estimate of the average number of jobs which are removed when a computer is introduced.

Such an estimate is provided in the Ministry report. When the number of jobs which were discontinued in computerized departments of the average firm are added to those which would later have become available in those departments if computerization had not occurred (fifty-eight in the first case and fifty in the second) they produce an initial total of 108 'posts taken over'. However, both kinds of displacement were offset at the level of the concern itself because the organizations introducing computers were usually expanding. In fact, many asserted that it was shortage of staff itself which impelled them to computerize, and some of the 'discontinued posts' were actually vacancies which it had been found impossible to fill. Within the computerized

8. Ministry of Labour, op. cit., p. 42.

area itself eighteen jobs created by the computer system reduced the net total of discontinued jobs from fifty-eight to forty. These new posts were for computer operators, programmers and systems analysts, etc.

The general expansion of these concerns during the changeover period resulted in the creation of 188 extra office jobs in non-computerized areas. Therefore the average concern in fact ended its computerization period with 148 *more* office staff than it had previously, sufficient explanation in itself why so little redundancy following office automation has so far been reported. The transfer of staff between departments, incidentally, seems also to have been considerably eased by the length of the changeover period, which, averaging five years, allowed ample time for relocation and, where necessary, retraining. By far the largest proportion of workers (seventy per cent) affected were female, usually young and in routine work, whose ready mobility between firms and exposure to the claims of marriage and maternity permitted the steady run-down of unrequired workers by 'natural wastage'.

Whatever the particular conditions in the average computerizing concern, however, what matters for present purposes is that there was a net reduction of ninety jobs from the total that would eventually have existed in the computerized area if the machine had not been introduced, comprised of a net forty jobs removed from the previous strength of the computerized department and an additional fifty new vacancies which would have occurred if computerization had not happened. Although the notional ninety workers who had actually filled these posts or would have filled them were provided with more than ample alternative employment opportunities in the form of the 188 extra posts created elsewhere in these firms during computerization, the fact remains that in book-keeping terms there would have been altogether 238 rather than 148 extra jobs ultimately available to other workers without the computer.

Admittedly, some of the additional jobs which did actually occur eventually may have been generated because the machine increased the firm's competitiveness, and hence its business, but it is all the same rather confusing to find the Ministry, in a later section of its report, apparently ignoring the forty jobs which were actually removed in the computerized areas when they make estimates of the effect of silent firings over the period 1964–74.[9] According to these forecasts, a stock of 6,000 office computers in 1974 will have reduced the net additional demand for office workers by 300,000 in the previous ten years. This calculation appears to be based on the figure of fifty silent firings per installation.

If we accept these figures the general employment position of office workers should remain favourable up to the mid 1970s at least, with a net additional supply of 400,000 jobs between 1964 and 1974. Even in 1973 there would still be a balance of 24,000 extra jobs for the year, and office workers would enjoy the hangover from a tight labour market for several further years. If, however, one is using the Ministry's other figures, which seem to indicate the removal of 90 jobs per installation, the picture changes a good deal. If this figure is nearer the truth, the 700,000 extra office jobs expected by 1974 will have been almost completely offset by automation, and presumably if the rate of computerization subsequently remained at a high level there would be substantial inroads into the total number of office jobs nationally available thereafter.

It should be remembered, however, that all these predictions, optimistic or pessimistic, contain a large element of guesswork and are based on imprecise information. On balance, though, it does not seem improbable that a contraction in general clerical opportunities may begin to occur within the short rather than the long period. We have no choice but to wait and see whether this does in fact happen, and, if so, whether it really does lead to greater militancy among white-collar unions. It must be said that white-collar union officials are at present for the most part far from militant in their remarks on the whole question. In the words of one:

We realize that computers are coming and we don't think we can stem the tide like King Canute. We just hope to delay it where it occurs long enough to get safeguards. Our policy is to give management one-hundred-per-cent co-operation in return for no redundancies, a ban on

9. Ministry of Labour, op. cit., p. 42.

recruiting, and no loss of pay on transfer. We also say existing staff must get priority for being programmers and what-not. Companies, we find, usually agree.

This is a far cry from the kind of tough bargaining one would expect if office workers were faced with any immediate threat of large-scale permanent redundancy. But such a stiffening could come, and it is noteworthy that the kind of concessions American white-collar unions are beginning to demand in return for collaboration in computer schemes are somewhat farther-reaching than those which, for the present anyway, are being requested in the far less heavily computerized United Kingdom.

Further Reading

Hoos, I. R., *Automation in the Office*, Public Affairs Press, Washington, 1961.

International Labour Office, *Effects of Mechanisation and Automation in Offices*, ILO, 1960.

McDonald, J. C., *The Impact and Implications of Office Automation*, Canadian Department of Labour, 1964.

Mann, F. C., and Williams, L. K., 'Observations on the Dynamics of a Change to Electronic Data-Processing Equipment', *Administrative Science Quarterly*, 5, 1960.

Ministry of Labour, *Computers in Offices* (Manpower Studies No. 4), HMSO, 1965.

Mumford, E., *Living with a Computer*, Institute of Personnel Management, 1964.

Mumford, E., and Banks, O., *The Computer and the Clerk*, Routledge, 1967.

Scott, W. H. (ed.), *Office Automation: Administrative and Human Problems*, OECD, Paris, 1965.

TUC Non-Manual Workers Committee, *In the Automated Office*, TUC, 1964.

CHAPTER 7

The 'Datacrat'

INTRODUCTION

THE slogan 'computers need people' has achieved wide currency in the conventional wisdom of data-processing. It is often paraded when some attempt is being made to further the idea that people need computers and that opposition to the machine on the grounds that its only effect on employment is to absorb brain and muscle power is uninformed and improper. Computers certainly do need people in the sense that they have created a variety of new data-processing occupations which have to some extent offset the loss of jobs which may follow upon administrative automation. But the present chapter will not be another of the many essays which set out to demonstrate that the net manpower consequences of computerization will be to stimulate the demand for labour, and labour of a very much higher calibre and training. Its purpose rather is to say something about the people computers have needed most up to the present and will continue to need into the foreseeable future.

The problem of ensuring the supply of these people is a serious practical issue which has caused concern in recent years. At present this supply is very short, and unless it can be increased may put a brake on the future rate of installation. This problem of computerization, which has obvious implications for official policy, will be dealt with in Chapter 9.

The shortage of these people creates other problems which have a more immediate bearing on successful use of the machine, and for the present it is more useful to focus attention upon them. In particular it is necessary to say something of the source and consequences of the friction which often builds up between the higher grades of computer personnel and their employing organizations. To understand this conflict we must ask who the people are that computers need, what are their functions, their rewards, and their outlook.

COMPUTER SPECIALISMS

Computing, commercial computing in particular, has thrown up at least a dozen new occupations ranging from the esoteric skills of the computer designer to the monotonous drudgery of the data-preparation girl, and the range includes such specialisms as those of the computer salesman, the computer consultant, the computer training instructor, and the computer maintenance engineer. However, the most important specialisms are those of the people who reduce the complexities of a commercial or manufacturing process to an explicit routine, who transform such routines to sets of detailed instructions to the machine, or who supervise the work of those engaged on these tasks and take general responsibility for advancing the progress of a computerization project.

It is towards these people, the operations researchers, systems analysts and designers, organization and methods men, programmers and data-processing managers – the so-called 'liveware' of computing – that we shall direct attention. For it is members of these groups who are the true 'datacrats' in the new hierarchy of computer occupations, holding the keys to effective exploitation of the machine (a fact of which they show some awareness), and who in practice are frequently the storm-centre of the organizational and human upsets which may accompany the installation and operation of the machine.

Before we examine the nature of these conflicts it is necessary to say something about the precise functions these various practitioners discharge and the relationships between functions. Doing so presents some difficulty because in practice there is a good deal of confusion both over the job titles of data-processing and over the duties which should go along with any single, commonly used title, such as 'programmer'.

Reference to press advertisements for data-processing staff yields a baffling assortment of apparent specializations with subtle implied distinctions as, for example, between 'analyst-programmers' and 'programmer-analysts'. Commercial computing, despite its intimate association with logic and economic rationality, no less than with rapid change, has been notably slow to standardize its set of constituent occupations, to modify job titles which sprang up in its early days and are now out-moded, or to decide on lines of progression from one function to another. These failures introduce a good deal of imperfection into its labour market, and although they can be partly explained by the pace of change itself there is some reason to believe that many data-processing employers would be reluctant to accept greater standardization. Experienced datacrats are in very short supply, and inflated or obscure job titles can sometimes be used as bait. Employers often complain of the datacrat's ready mobility between firms, or, as some would call it, his 'disloyalty'; but at least some of this movement seems to be a response to the mistakes of placement which occur thanks to baffling job titles and reluctance to specify job duties.

Distinctions of a general kind have, however, always been recognized between systems work and programming. Systems specialists have been broadly distributed between operations research (OR), organization and methods (O and M), and systems analysis. It is generally understood that the function of the *systems analyst* revolves around a survey of the area of the total business information system it is prepared to computerize, in which he determines the direction and volume of flows of information and their interconnexions, later going on to devise a more rational and elegant method of linking them based on the computer. 'Systems flowcharts' and a 'statement of requirements' summarizing this phase of software preparation will then be passed to a *senior programmer* who creates successively more detailed 'program flowcharts' which, with further documentation, will finally be passed to a *junior programmer*, or *coder*, for translation into sheets of detailed machine instructions in computer code ready for punching on cards or paper tape.

In practice, however, one individual has often undertaken all three phases of activity, and this absence of rigid specialization has enabled some career progression from coding to analytical work. Analysts have sometimes doubled as operations researchers too, though more frequently as organization and methods men.

But a number of forces have been working to sharpen the distinctions between these functions and to change the nature and demands of particular functions. Coding, for example, is becoming much more of a routine chore with the steady improvement of higher-level programming languages (see Chapter 3), permitting some relaxation in the qualities demanded of junior programming staff. Programmers of higher ability can therefore concentrate on the more demanding work which the growth in the variety of applications per installation and in the complexity of individual applications is producing.

Although the very volume of programming activity in the larger installation increasingly provides the programmer with a career ladder which leads to a supervisory position within the programming function itself, it does seem to be reducing the ease with which they can transfer to systems work. Programmers may double as analysts in smaller installations, and in all installations there is a case for providing them with more 'creative' systems work from time to time to relieve the comparative monotony of their work. But it appears likely that they may have increasing difficulty in crossing the border between the two specialisms in future.

Systems work itself is becoming more specialized and demanding. A proficient systems man has always been as much a designer as an analyst, not merely establishing a model of the system as it exists but reshaping it into a new and more effective, computer-oriented set of information-flows. Management, who too often in the past have insisted upon a computerized replication of the old system, are beginning to take to heart the truism that to exact the maximum value from the computer it is necessary to ask what problems the former system set out to solve and then to ask how the machine could best solve them.

Acceptance of this philosophy brings an increasing stress on the creative side of systems work. A recent official report[1] on the confusion over data-processing job titles and job duties recommends that the term *systems designer* should completely replace *systems analyst* (and its variants). The report goes on to itemize the specific duties which various grades of computer staff should assume. While these are no more than suggestions they do

1. Ministry of Technology, *Staff Titles and Job Description in Commercial Data-Processing*, H M S O, 1967.

accord with distinctions which have gradually been emerging spontaneously and will probably be fully accepted in the near future. According to the report the duties of a senior systems designer should be as follows:

1. Estimates the cost of carrying out an appraisal.
2. Appraises the organization's information needs in an area defined by management.
3. Appraises the available information, both internal and external, in relation to the needs of the organization and particularly of its management.
4. In the light of those appraisals, defines, in conjunction with management, the information required to meet the current and expected needs of the organization.
5. To meet the information needs, designs an 'information system'; provides an outline plan showing the flow of information, the processing required and the equipment which may be needed; where appropriate prepares a model or advocates a pilot scheme. The design will include block diagrams, broad flowcharts and narrative suitable for presentation to managers concerned.
6. Estimates the time required to implement and develop the proposed scheme.
7. Estimates the resources required for and the total costs of developing the systems design and related manual and other procedures, and introducing, implementing and operating the proposed scheme, based on detailed estimates prepared by systems staff.
8. Estimates in conjunction with user departments the direct savings resulting from the proposed system of processing information, assesses the value of other quantifiable benefits and describes any non-quantifiable benefits or disadvantages.
9. Submits the justification reports through the data-processing manager to obtain top management's approval to proceed with the project; conducts any formal presentation.
10. Controls the progress of projects, by regular review meetings.
11. Monitors the operation of the installed system and compares results, including costs, with justification report.
12. Keeps under continuous reappraisal the effectiveness of the information systems in relation to the changing needs of the organization and to equipment becoming available.
13. Assists in recruiting systems personnel, and their training; reviews their performance.
14. Keeps abreast of all relevant developments.

15. Lays down standards and techniques to be observed in systems work and ensures conformity to them.

For a more junior systems designer:

1. Participates in the feasibility study and in particular does any necessary fact-finding.
2. Examines the proposed information system and defines in detail the input and output requirements, the file contents and the relationship between them.
3. Prepares in a form suitable for programmers a specification of the processes to be carried out (elaborating as required the broad flow-charts) and agrees the contents with the user parties concerned.
4. Assesses the input, output and file volumes, and the frequency of each of the various processes in conjunction with programming and operating staff, so that the time and cost for complementing and operating the system can be estimated.
5. Collaborates with auditors to ensure the necessary controls are incorporated in the system.
6. In conjunction with users and other computer staff, designs the forms for input data and results.
7. Specifies any required manual or non-computer processing, the information required for it and the controls necessary to minimize and correct inaccuracies in transferring data to and from the computer.
8. Collaborates with the procedure designer[2] to ensure that instructions or a manual of the revised procedure is provided for user departments.
9. Specifies requirements of and provides test data for trying out the system and arranges trials.
10. May control or assist in the implementation of the system.
11. Checks that the system in operation meets the specification.
12. May control junior staff to assist in all or some of the above duties.
13. Devises and supervises the education and training of all user personnel concerned with the project.

Finally, for a senior programmer:

1. Works from an outline design produced by the systems designer, defines the files and programs needed and their interrelationship, estimates the preparation and running time and cost and provides such further information as may be needed to reassess the effectiveness of using the computer to do the job.

2. This individual is an organization and methods practitioner.

2. Provides a detailed plan for programming the job and agrees with the systems designer that it meets the specification. The plan includes detailed layouts of the major files and outline flowcharts of the more complicated programs. It serves as a source document for subsequent programming work.

3. Produces detailed progress schedules of subsequent programming work (flowcharting, coding and trials) and controls the work to ensure that the target date for each phase is met.

4. Codes any part of the program which is beyond his assistants and directs them in the use of software and other special facilities.

5. Keeps under review estimates of time and cost and reports significant changes.

6. Arranges for the testing, correction and linking of programs; in conjunction with systems designer, operator and users, carries out the final system test, pilot and parallel running.

7. Ensures that adequate computer operating instructions are prepared in liaison with the computer operating staff.

8. Ensures that all necessary documentation of programs is done progressively as the job develops, is kept up to date and is maintained in the form of a job manual.

9. Controls the amendment of operational programs, operating instructions and associated documentation to meet changes in requirements.

10. Allocates work to and supervises programmers, ensuring that proper standards of programming work are maintained and that manufacturer's software is fully exploited.

11. Carries out specialist programming work requiring substantial experience and high technical ability, e.g. production of special purpose software.

Again it should be emphasized that these are no more than model job descriptions which may be modified to suit individual circumstances. They do, however, underscore some of the key differences – and key interrelations – which have always existed between the systems design (or analysis) and programming functions as well as those features which may accentuate the lines of demarcation between the two specialisms in future. They indicate incipient lines of demarcation with other specialisms, particularly organization and methods ('procedure design' in the Report's terminology) and operations research.

With the arrival of computers a large number of O and M

men transferred to systems analysis and design and this (generally one-way) movement continues. The objectives of both kinds of work are in fact fundamentally similar in that each is concerned with the drafting of more effective flows of work and information, the O and M practitioner specializing in the improvement of these flows in non-computer information systems. In any new overall information system the manual and computer subsystems have a necessarily close interdependence and the main brief of the O and M specialist is to devise appropriate new clerical procedures, more convenient individual document forms, and lines of communication, to ensure that effective articulation is achieved.

Something has been said of the operations researcher's special field in Chapter 4. He is the business scientist whose analytical tool-kit enables him to construct computable mathematical models of business decision-making situations – models which aim to offer optimum solutions to particular problems because of their ability to express the complexity of a host of mutually influencing variables for which values can be provided or estimated when the need for decision arises.

While the systems designer's job consists in the reorientation of the concern's flows of information to the computer to improve the quality and availability of information for decision, that of the operations researcher is to exploit some of this information directly in the automation of decision. To automate decision is not quite the same thing as automating decision *away*, but on occasion that is how the operations researcher's brief may be viewed by middle management. Consequently he may often be involved in conflicts with management similar to those more commonly associated with systems designers, of which more presently.

Personnel filling the roles of systems designer, programmer, O and M specialist (procedure designer), and operations researcher are usually located in a data-processing department and responsible to a supremo whose title again varies considerably from firm to firm but who is most likely to be termed either the data-processing or the computer manager. If there has been uncertainty about the precise tasks which should fall to the systems and programming staff there has been even greater vagueness about the responsibilities of the DP manager and his position in the management structure of the organization.

Partly, the contradictions which have sometimes arisen in his position and functions can be ascribed to the uncertainty of the DP manager himself about what his aims should be and what powers he requires to achieve them, and to uncertainty due not only to rapid changes in the philosophy of computer applications or the reluctance of higher management to formulate a definite policy for exploitation of the machine but also to restrictions of outlook carried forward from a pre-computer specialism. For as we have noted elsewhere, a substantial minority of computer managers were until recently recruited within a concern, or 'emerged', from a specialist function, particularly accountancy.

The DP manager originally recruited from a non-computer specialism may have had a fairly clear idea of his original aims and the amount of authority and resources he required to meet them, but as objectives become more ambitious, perhaps as a result of pressure from the systems and programming team he has assembled, he can be carried out of his depth, unsure whether the new objectives are worthwhile and even less certain about the powers it would require to attain them.

Again, the task of heading an installation with an established set of applications and promoting the development of new systems at one and the same time presents the DP manager with competing demands on his time and attention which are extremely difficult to balance successfully. Day-to-day operation of the computer centre may gradually shake down into a routine, but it nonetheless demands careful supervision and administration. If the DP manager concentrates on this side of the operation he may lose his grip on systems development projects and be unable to give development personnel the leadership and support with senior management which are essential to the success of their work. If, on the other hand, he concentrates on the promotion of new projects to the neglect of routine administration, the operating efficiency of the computer centre may deteriorate with the effect of producing or reinforcing a scepticism of the machine's value on the part of the concern's members which undermines the very development work upon which he has chosen to concentrate.

But the most important source of the DP manager's often vague position in the firm has been the failure of senior management to appreciate the importance of the new data-processing function and their reluctance to agree upon the DP manager's precise responsibilities, which, it sometimes seems, must be left to emerge just as the individual himself, and the machine, may have done. Such imprecision is less of a handicap when the DP manager is supported by a board-room enthusiast for the computer, but whether this support is available or not some classification is essential if the DP manager is to do his job properly.

Sometimes an agreement is obtained only as a result of a direct confrontation. Questioning one DP manager about his job specification the writer received the following reply:

'Oh, yes, my responsibilities are very precise indeed. They have to be or I just couldn't do this job. No one could. They're very clearly laid down. I made sure of that when I wrote them.'

'You wrote them yourself?'

'I had to. When I came here, they [the board] hadn't the faintest inkling what introducing a computer meant in practical terms or what I should be doing except maybe chatting with manufacturers' reps. After a time it got impossible. So I wrote a job specification which would really allow me to do the job. I showed it to the board and they promptly turned it down flat. "*He's* getting uppity so let's tread on him quick." So I said "Right, I'll go," and they said "All right," and here we are.'

The DP manager's responsibilities, then, often depend on his own background and perspectives and how senior management are prepared to look at the computer. They are also related to the size of the data-processing department. As data-processing departments grow in size it is becoming common to appoint a computer operations manager to take charge of the detailed administration of the computer centre. Such delegation reinforces a general tendency for the DP manager to identify primarily with the development aspects of his work, an emphasis furthered by the increasing recruitment of DP managers from a systems or programming background. The need for his detailed responsibilities to be laid down precisely also receives more recognition than it did, thanks in no small measure to the lively efforts of an emerging professional organization, the Data Processing Managers' Association.

These changes are enabling the data-processing manager to assume as a right the role – professional organizational innovator – which previously he acquired more through default or personal political manoeuvre. It is a role which involves the establishment of overall objectives; the creation of practical policies for attaining them; 'selling' these objectives and policies to management; acquiring the necessary human and financial resources; and motivating subordinates to press forward with the task of systematic organizational remodelling.

It is a role of increasing importance and prestige. But it is not one which is designed to endear him to the more time-serving members of the concern, whose sense of security is not titillated by his explicit commission to transform the organization of the firm, to scrutinize and replace many of its hallowed procedures, and to impose more rigorous standards of performance – a task in which he is assisted by a corps of assistants whose rewards, background, values and manner are such that they are often construed as an offence in themselves.

TENSIONS AND CONFLICT BETWEEN DATACRAT AND MANAGER

Clashes between the data-processing department, especially its systems design wing, and middle management personnel during a computerization project are common and sometimes bitter. To quote another DP manager: 'We've been a storm-centre since we started and I'm the lightning conductor.' In part, such conflicts stem inevitably from the explicit objective of the data-processing department to bring about change. Organizational change is unwelcome to many merely because it interrupts day-to-day routine. Furthermore, to admit the need for change, which the decision to computerize amounts to, can be read as a criticism of previous performance. The reactions of those who take it this way, sometimes quite correctly, are likely to be defensive or defiant.

Tensions between 'line' management and specialist departments are a well known feature of organizational dynamics. But usually staff specialists such as economists and technologists act in a purely advisory capacity to the line manager and he is free to accept or reject their recommendations as he chooses. Even such specialist departments as research and development laboratories, which can cause considerable organizational disruption through their creation of new products or techniques, seldom have any power to interfere directly with the *status quo*. They can be located at a safe distance from the main factory or head office. Whether to accept their innovations is a decision for senior management. And contact between their personnel and functional management, often marked by friction deriving largely from differences of values and deportment, can be mediated by specialist go-betweens.

Such segregation is not possible in the case of systems personnel. The very reason for their introduction is to work directly on the firm's organization with the object of redefining it, and reorientating it to the needs of a suspiciously regarded machine. Certain organizational provisions can help to produce a satisfactory working relationship between datacrat and manager; and the composition of the management group in terms of age, education and experience has an important bearing on its acceptance of the objectives of computerization and systems men, as will be argued in Chapter 8.

Nonetheless, some strain, some overt conflict on occasion, is more or less inevitable between computer and other personnel, however favourable other factors may be. In any organization there are many individuals who have a career investment in the organizational *status quo*, or who have become habituated to particular methods of doing their work. The systems man's brief is to upset this stability. His and their interests, in the engineering of change on the one hand and in the defence of the *status quo* on the other, are in fundamental opposition. Conflict is structured into their relationship, and one of its most common manifestations is the animus and sarcasm directed by many managers against systems personnel as individuals. Resentment of the innovation is aggravated by resentment of the innovator:

resentment of his rewards, his values, his manner, his vocabulary, his prestige as change-maker, his apparent freedom from 'normal company discipline', his promotability (because of the intimacy he acquires with the concern's affairs), his dress, his fickle loyalty to the firm, and, not least, his youth.

THE DATACRAT AS AN OCCUPATIONAL TYPE

These are grave charges, but how strong are their foundations? Can any generalizations be made about data-processing practitioners as an occupational group which in any way support the sometimes bitter portraits of them that are sketched so readily by resentful middle managers and angry directors?

Perhaps the sorest point with most managers is the datacrat's earning power. Not only does he come to disrupt but he is highly paid to do so. The second part of this proposition is certainly true. Even in the United Kingdom computerization has been sufficiently rapid for the supply of properly qualified data-processing specialists always to have fallen behind demand. If anything this 'liveware gap' is widening and the likelihood that it will put a brake on the rate of computerization has been officially recognized for some time. The vast majority of systems designers and programmers receive their initial grounding in training courses operated by computer manufacturers. Good as such courses unquestionably are, they can deal only with limited numbers of students and must remain comparatively short, being supplemented by practical work on actual projects. Until recently there was virtually no provision for computer education of any kind in the general educational system.

When a concern embarks on computerization it can rely on its computer supplier to train personnel for junior posts, but vital senior staff must be recruited on the open market. As more organizations embark on computer schemes, or extend the scope of their applications, the market price of data-processing expertise has soared. In the last dozen years the average salaries of programmers and systems men have approximately doubled. Computer men are now among the highest-paid specialist groups in industry, and when age is considered they are overall the highest-paid specialist group in the under-forties.

It is unlikely that an organization could attract any but the most junior programmer for under £1,000 p.a. A school leaver with two A-levels would expect at least this much as a starting salary and within four or five years would command £1,500 p.a. Although he (or she: programming is largely free of sex barriers) would expect more competition for senior posts, he would probably think the worse of himself if he had not reached £2,000 p.a. before thirty.

Systems designers do better. A number of factors make their supply still less elastic than that of programmers. Firstly, the educational standards required are usually higher, a degree (subject immaterial) nowadays being considered a desirable sign of suitable ability. Secondly, because women are even less acceptable to managers than men as 'snoopers' there is a sex barrier. Thirdly, systems work requires a certain maturity in the individual, particularly in his handling of human relations, and its quality benefits from a period of general commercial experience, both of which requirements push up the average age of entry. Consequently, starting salaries are somewhat higher, commencing around £1,600 and rising fairly rapidly to £2,000.

If he graduates to primarily design functions the systems man should be drawing £2,500 by his later twenties, and beyond that the cream who transfer to internal or external consultancy work, or data-processing management, will usually draw very much more – for the most part, it should be said, not merely making big money but earning it. (O and M men and OR specialists seem to earn slightly less and slightly more respectively than systems designers; but their chances to transfer to data-processing management, unless they have had systems experience, are less good.)

A graphic illustration of the lively demand which has produced these buoyant earnings can be found in the appointments column of the 'quality' press, one Sunday newspaper being in the habit of running a special 'Computer Personnel' section remarkable for the scale and grandeur of its display advertisements. Advertisements? They are more like appeals, vying in their glowing descriptions of the advertiser's advantages of location and working conditions, the ambitiousness and high intrinsic interest of his project, and the prestigious nature of the team of datacrats he has assembled. Actual salary details may not always be offered because to do so helps to bid up the price which has finally to be paid, but it is conventional to hint that the outrageous demands of the exceptional applicant will be met. A typical specimen prints in bold type: 'Salary is negotiable and we are aware of current market values in data processing.'

Most datacrats are no less aware of these rates, and if they cannot be troubled to calculate the latest asking prices for their particular expertise there are sometimes others quite willing to provide such a service. For example, the magazine *Data Systems*, a well-known data-processing trade paper, used to print a weekly tabulation of the average salaries for the major grades of specialist in the industry, based on an analysis of all press advertisements which carried salary figures. Comments were offered on significant movements and any particularly interesting offers.

Previously, it went even further, its detailed market reports including much sharp, sometimes satirical, comment on the apparent meanness of some offers and even on the presentation and wording of an advertiser's copy. If this ebullient feature of *Data Systems* has now disappeared the feelings of self-confident marketability amongst data-processing men themselves which it expressed have not.

The bullish nature of the demand for data-processing skill leads to consequences which lend some support to managerial strictures of the datacrat's 'disloyalty' to the firm, and freedom from 'normal company discipline'. By 'disloyalty' is meant mobility between appointments. On average, systems men and programmers change their jobs every four years. Many threaten to leave a good deal more often, their motive being primarily (though by no means exclusively) that of a move itself, which is to say, more money. When such an ultimatum is given there is often little alternative for the paymaster than to pay up the ransom. In the words of one:

'They're just like prima donnas. If your head programmer says he'll resign in the middle of a changeover what choice have you got? You could be set back six months if a key man goes, even if you get another good man from outside, which isn't certain and costs I-don't-know-what for advertising.'

One must sympathize with senior managers who face such dilemmas, but it is only fair to remark that they stem very largely from the existence of a free market, an economic phenomenon for which senior managers otherwise express considerable enthusiasm. And many of those people who show such righteous indignation over the 'fickleness' of the datacrat's attachment to his employing organization would, given comparable inducements, show themselves hardly less footloose.

Besides, we should remember that there is a growing tendency for most kinds of more highly qualified business specialist to move frequently between firms to extend his experience before he becomes immobilized by family commitments. Because most computer men are young (at a rough estimate fifty-five per cent are in their twenties, thirty-five per cent in their thirties, and almost all the remainder in their early forties) their overall mobility is exaggerated by this unequal age distribution. From a number of aspects, too, this mobility is welcome, since by extending individual experience it adds to the overall stock of an important set of skills.

There is, in fact, much more to the datacrat's mobility than sheer acquisitiveness. A move often results less from 'pull' than 'push' factors. The datacrat's ultimate career prospects depend very largely on his continuous accumulation of experience in an industry where technological and theoretical innovation is rapid. A highly qualified man cannot afford to remain with a firm to which he may have been attracted by its claim to be embarking on higher-level applications if it turns out that no such plans exist.

Nor is it entirely reasonable to expect internally trained staff who have worked on an initial project to hang around waiting for some tormented high-level decision to go ahead with more sophisticated work. Even individuals whose natural inclination is to stay put may be panicked into a move by an employer's unwillingness to define internal career prospects and lines of progression. Finally, some employers, and this is regrettably true of academic and government work in particular, whether from choice, ignorance or external constraint, simply do not pay a market rate for the job.

Economic influences, whether 'push' or 'pull', do not by themselves adequately explain why the datacrat so easily acquires the reputation of a 'bad company man'. Intellectual and social factors lie behind some of his interorganization moves. Most data-processing specialists are of high intellectual calibre and many have received university-level education. They derive considerable personal satisfaction from exercising their trained minds and their acquired skills. Pedalling in a low mental gear creates intense frustration, and if the scheme they are working on gives few opportunities for running at full stretch they will begin to look around for more challenging work.

The other major intrinsic reward they seek in their work is contact with like-minded and comparably qualified colleagues. Such contacts certainly help to increase the individual's marketability through the free exchange of ideas but they are also sought for their own sake, for their socially pleasurable and emotionally supportive features. This is not to deny that the datacrat may often generate worthwhile contacts with other managerial specialists, but his preferences are naturally for those individuals who share with him a common occupational experience, common values and interests, a common expertise and a common language in which to express it.

Just as engineers identify themselves mainly with other engineers, industrial chemists with other industrial chemists, and economists with economists, the datacrat identifies with the skills and practitioners of data-processing rather than with the organization which employs him at any one time. His primary commitment is to data-processing or one of its constituent specialisms not to organizations which *use* data-processing. But this by no means implies – what established members of his employing organization sometimes ascribe to him – a fundamental lack of concern with the affairs or commercial success of his employing organization. For although he may not look on it as a context in which to achieve his long-term career ambitions, it should be evident that he is very intimately concerned with its overall well-being and progress, at any rate in so far as that well-being can be furthered by successful exploitation of the computer. To be associated with a botched scheme does not add to his reputation.

The datacrat's commitment to data-processing, and his preference for the company of fellow datacrats is, however, reinforced by something in the way of an occupational style, almost an occupational subculture, which hardly eases the tensions in his relationship with management which are for the most part created by his explicit function, his mobility, and his youth.

A number of features of his values, manner and appearance help to emphasize his separation from other members of the typical concern. Some of these characteristics, as described by managers, are reminiscent of the manager's stereotype of, in particular, the industrial scientist – 'cliquey', 'condescending', 'big-headed', 'scruffy', an 'impractical brain-box'. So is the common assertion that 'They think they're still at university, and haven't the faintest idea about standard commercial procedure' (i.e. the idiosyncratic variant of standard commercial procedure practised in the aggrieved party's own department).

The present writer would be the first to agree that datacrats often vary in their style from other managerial groups. But, the occasional bearded programmer apart, few he has encountered readily fit the colourful portraits of them which are sometimes painted by their managerial colleagues. Their taste in dress may deviate from the decent clerical-grey business suit, though usually in the direction of alpaca rather than corduroy. In their manner they tend to be less ceremonious than is thought proper in the more formal, traditionalist concern; and they seem more at home where sudden problems can be discussed with sufficiently high-ranking personnel without having to go through the 'proper channels'. Some certainly make a freer use of technical computing vocabulary than may be wise, though this may stem from sheer enthusiasm rather than any wish to parade their expertise and underline the listener's exclusion from it. Far from wishing to mystify their objectives and methods they are characteristically eager to communicate them.

Even minor differences in style between groups can be taken as signs of antipathy, and the fact that the datacrat's appearance and

behaviour vary from important norms of business life is sometimes read by managers as a sign of criticism of business or
hostility towards themselves. It is worth asking to what extent
such supposed antipathy in fact exists.

A number of datacrats seem to have felt at some stage the
ambivalence towards a business career which has been a feature
of the outlook of some graduate entrants to management since the
war, which consists on the one hand of the sentiments graphically
conveyed in the film *I'm All Right, Jack*, when undergraduate-
representative Ian Carmichael, on a tour of his prospective
employer's factory, vomited into an agitating-vat containing the
firm's cherished product (a synthetic confection); and, on the
other hand, hearty enthusiasm for the financial benefits of a
'sell-out', and the immodest conviction that if some things about
business – for example its human relations or efficiency – are not
as they should be then the entrant himself is the man to set them
to rights.

Nor is it difficult to find systems men ready to deliver set
tirades against what they see as managerial shortcomings. In the
words of an operations researcher:

'Look at us. This country's up the spout. Why? We just don't use
our brains. I went up to this factory in Lancashire somewhere and they
showed me their steam-engine with all its brasswork nicely polished
which they'd had since about 1850 or something. Still working, and
weren't they proud of it. That's so typical of all British industry.
They're not interested in new inventions or new techniques. So that's
why we're where we are now. It runs through the whole fabric. I don't
want to be bossed by Yanks, thank you. So someone's got to sort out
the mess they [British management] have made of industry by their
sheer backwardness and ignorance.'

For those who feel so bitter about our industrial failures and
recoil so completely from absorption in the main body of
management, yet seek its rewards, a career in data-processing
offers a unique compromise and opportunity. The individual can
be in business but not of it, operating directly to remove some of
its inadequacies. But it is clear that practical success in doing so
must depend on a more diplomatic approach than individuals
such as the above may be able or willing to make.

In fact the vast majority of datacrats show no such missionary zeal, nor the arrogance that goes with it. This does not mean that they are uncritical of management. But the criticism is selective, being directed mainly towards the more traditionalist managers who blankly deny the relevance of computing science to their day-to-day problems, without showing much inclination to give its methods a hearing. Systems designers and operations researchers understand only too well the delicacy of their position and the tendency of managerial personnel to regard them with suspicion. They must display considerable tact in their dealings with those personnel if their work is to be at all productive. For the most part they do their best to generate a satisfactory relationship, and develop great patience in explaining the objectives, and likely benefits to users, of their work. Some may not enjoy having to devote so large a part of their time to cultivating the arts of soft salesmanship, but they usually have little alternative: computerization by diktat is perhaps possible if senior management are sufficiently determined, but it is evidently less preferable than mutual co-operation.

The function of the datacrat and his occupational perspectives and style certainly combine to create an image of him in some managerial eyes which makes the manager's refusal to come quickly to terms understandable. Datacrats are imported to sharpen the concern's operating efficiency to the ultimate benefit of its members. But they are also imported to modify its organization by reorientating it towards what to many people remains a puzzling machine. For their age they are highly paid. The heavy demand for their skills, supported by numerous other factors, encourages their profitable movement between employers.

To perform their work they must be awarded a certain freedom from strict supervision, and this independence from control is buttressed by an independence of mind supported by their training and marketability. They possess occupational values which mark them off from other specialist groups and encourage a strong *esprit de corps*. They are in fact agents of continuous change and may sometimes see themselves in a more grandiose light. Because they can acquire intimacy with its overall affairs they can become eminent candidates for rapid promotion to key positions in operating management at an early age. They are influential, they are highly paid, and they are different. They are, in fact, practically everything that can easily lead to envy and resentment in less advantaged members of the concern.

CREATING WORKING RELATIONSHIPS

Given, however, that some friction between them and other managers – ranging from little more than a coolness in manner to deliberate withholding of information – is a largely inevitable consequence of their role and occupational style, what can be done to keep it to a minimum?

First, of course, there are those overrated but still useful stand-bys of the change-maker – communication and education. Senior management must be no less careful to explain its plans to middle and junior management and to provide computer appreciation courses for them than it should be with lesser grades of staff. Curiously, some have been surprised at the need for this action, it being assumed that managerial personnel will more readily perceive the advantages of computerization than others and less readily adopt obstructive postures. In fact, it is note-worthy that managers faced with far-reaching technological change not infrequently display the very 'short-sighted' or 'unintelligent' opposition which managers themselves more readily ascribe to manual workers when changes occur on the factory floor. Two West German writers cite the following, perhaps extreme, example:

The head of a rolling mill had been in the habit of deciding alone how many slabs were to be rolled each day. When automation was introduced, the number was pre-calculated. Enraged by this fact, the director in question threw all the punched cards in the fire.[3]

In so far as communication and education can modify resist-ance to change in any occupational group they will modify it amongst managers. But they will probably be more successful if they are supported by certain organizations provisions.

These provisions aim at a deliberate structuring of the formal relationships of datacrats and operating managers to minimize

3. Jaeggi, U., and Wiedermann, H., in Scott, W. H. (ed.), *Office Auto-mation: Administrative and Human Problems*, OECD, Paris, 1965, p. 76.

conflict. It has been suggested that, unlike such conventional staff specialists as development scientists, personnel officers or economists, systems staff cannot be segregated from other personnel and awarded purely advisory functions, being called upon as need occurs. Their responsibility, the furtherance of change, is a positive one, and it has to be assumed that they are best qualified to identify both where and how it should be introduced, without having to wait till others happen on a similar viewpoint.

But if they cannot be segregated neither can they be given direct executive authority over departments being changed. Not only would they be for the most part too young to be acceptable as superiors by the majority of operating managers, but their ability to stimulate change would be compromised by the weight of routine administration. Emerging orthodoxy suggests that the systems development branch of data-processing should be given a semi-independent position with power to initiate new projects in collaboration with operating managers. Acceptance of systems thinking would be promoted by the establishment of project teams jointly composed of systems and operating personnel, whose 'democratic' nature would reduce resistance to change. Such arrangements can certainly be productive, as, given certain conditions, participation in the planning of change can be where change affects non-managerial personnel. But they seem to have their greatest success where the composition and outlook of the managerial group are of a kind that would anyway be favourable to the acceptance of systems thinking. In other cases they can easily deteriorate into ineffectual debating groups.

Stresses in the datacrat–manager relationship are an inescapable feature of computerization, and there is good reason to believe that they have retarded the development and compromised the quality of a fair proportion of computer schemes in the United Kingdom. Computerization is becoming more ambitious as more concerns turn their eyes towards 'third-generation', on-line and in-real-time applications. At this level of use the potential impact of the machine upon organization – and hence upon departmental boundaries, career ladders, and operating methods – becomes all the more far-reaching.

These changes will affect management more than any other occupational group. Hence managers' attitudes towards them become increasingly important. It has been suggested that these attitudes, which are partially displayed in the relationship of managers and systems personnel, depend to some extent on the manager's background and personal characteristics. The next chapter will try to explore this relationship in more detail.

Further Reading

'A.D.P. as a New Form of Office Employment', in Ministry of Labour, *Computers in Offices* (Manpower Studies No. 4), HMSO, 1965.

Boguslaw, R., *The New Utopians: A Study of Systems Design and Social Change*, Prentice-Hall, New York, 1965.

Clark, W., 'The Computer Training Myth', in *The Times* Business News, 28 July 1968.

Department of Education and Science, *Computer Education*, HMSO, 1967.

Mumford, E., and Ward, T. B., 'Hard Facts about Software Merchants', *The Director*, June 1966.

CHAPTER 8

Management and the Computer

INTRODUCTION

SENIOR managers and administrators have to decide whether to introduce a computer. Ultimately it is their responsibility also to maintain proper control over the overall changeover process. They can appoint systems staff, authorize feasibility studies, order a machine, build a computer centre, organize publicity, undertake consultation, lay on training courses, and initiate numerous other relevant activities. But there is one thing they cannot ordain – a commitment on the part of their staff to the objectives of the changeover. The importance of such a commitment has already been stressed. Given the fullest commitment by all parties it is still hard to computerize effectively. If it is absent, trouble is likely. If the scheme engenders positive hostility, trouble is a certainty.

But the commitment of some categories of staff is more relevant to final success than that of others. There is one category in which it is vital – that is, management itself. Middle and junior managers and staff specialists are in a stronger position than any other group of staff to influence the design and operation of the new system. Increasing attention has, therefore, been paid to their reactions and behaviour when a changeover is set in motion.

Theoretically, of course, middle and junior managerial personnel are the natural allies of senior management in their plans. One tends to assume that they will adopt the same sort of perspectives about the desirability of change and techniques of change-making as their superiors, or at least go along with senior management decisions once they have been made. Such assumptions are as natural and automatic for many people as their usual corollary, namely that it is shop-floor workers, 'led astray' by 'obscurantist' trade-union officials perhaps, who are the natural opponents of technical and organizational change.

Such assumptions have always been superficial and inaccurate, and computerization is demonstrating just how widely theory and fact can diverge. Far from the majority of managers responding to computer plans with the predicted enthusiasm, their reactions to the change and their behaviour during it show considerable and important variations. It comes as something of a surprise, too, that the most commonly reported managerial responses are characterized by suspicion about the consequences and scepticism about the advantages of what is being put in hand. The fact that such reports often emanate from frustrated systems designers or programmers in no way invalidates them. In fact, these people are better placed than anyone else to observe managerial reactions at close hand.

When manual workers come out in opposition to a technical change the great explain-all is the trade unions. When managers, explicitly or tacitly, adopt similar postures a favourite recourse of the analyst is individual personality. A manager can only oppose change, it is suggested, if there is something unusual about his 'psychology'. Of course, 'psychology' is very much affected by age. With age, 'psychologies' become more conservative. Another contributing factor sometimes brought in for good measure is that trusty stand-by 'communications'. Management opposition to computerization is quite widespread, so if the foregoing is a valid approach one is forced to the conclusion that British middle and junior management is composed predominantly of ageing misfits who never get told anything.

Up-to-date evidence fails to bear this out, and we do not need it to decide that this kind of explanation in terms of individual waywardness or senile irrationality is of no value whatsoever. If managers shy away from computerization they do so for the same sort of reason that other kinds of staff do. That is, because they perceive it for very often what it partly is – a genuine threat, to the relevance of the skills the individual has to offer, to his status and seniority, and to his hopes of advancement.

An important technical change inevitably leads to a reshuffle of jobs and responsibilities, undermining some individual positions and prospects just as it advances others. If some managers resist computerization it is not merely because it temporarily upsets a comfortable routine nor because they are psychological oddities. Rather it is because it impinges on major personal interests and investments in a specific *status quo*.

It should be remembered that many people argue that perhaps the most striking consequences of the switch to computers will occur in the area of management organization; that it will radically alter what the average manager does and how he does it; that as applications become more ambitious and comprehensive it will redistribute positions in the hierarchy of management power and authority; that it will transform managerial career ladders both in the individual concern and in industry as a whole. That it will call for an entirely new type of manager – with different aptitudes, experience and qualifications.[1]

Some of these forecasts are a little sweeping and premature. So far they have only partially been borne out. But it must also be remembered that the full potential of the machine has still hardly been tapped and if the past is anything to go by we can expect future breakthroughs in utilization which will rapidly antiquate today's most ambitious applications.

TECHNOLOGY AND ORGANIZATION

Forecasting the computer's organizational implications is more than a matter of guesswork. Experience with other kinds of technological change does provide a useful basis for such an exploration. One starting-point is the known interdependence between a specific technological apparatus and its accompanying set of work tasks and authority, reward, and social structures. Associated with any technology there is usually a characteristic method of work organization comprised of a given number of more or less specialized jobs, each with its own set of duties and related to others in such a way as to achieve an efficient flow of work and a sensible co-ordination of activities. So if important changes occur in the technology they will be reflected in the organization of work and workers.[2]

1. This theme is especially strong in the forecasts of Stafford Beer, Herbert Simon, and T. L. Whisler.

2. See Emery, F. E., and Trist, E. L., 'Socio-Technical Systems', in *Management Sciences, Models and Techniques*, Vol. 2, Pergamon, 1960.

Most evidence supporting this view has in the past been drawn from experience with changing production technology on the shop floor. If we take the case of mining, before mechanical coal-cutters and the moving conveyor-belt were introduced, the miners, equipped with little more than pick and shovel, were typically organized in small, tight-knit work groups of 'craftsmen colliers'. Each individual possessed and exercised a full range of skills to cope with any of the numerous tasks or situations which could occur at the coal-face. With the mechanization of coal-cutting and the arrival of the conveyor-belt this form of organization was no longer appropriate. It was replaced by an organization characterized by large work groups and a complex division of labour with highly specialized work tasks, fine distinctions of status and reward, and a much tighter discipline over work methods and work times. These changes seemed a natural requirement if activities were to be efficient and properly co-ordinated, given the much larger-scale operations which mechanization permitted. As further mechanization occurs the organization of work and workers is again changing as machinery absorbs more tasks formerly performed manually and the full importance of maintenance work in the automated mine becomes apparent.[3]

Numerous other well documented technological changes in the field of manual work demonstrate the intimate relationship of technology and organization. An intimate relationship, however, is not the same thing as a deterministic relationship. One would be wrong to claim that a given technology 'demands' a *single* specific mode of work organization. In the case of coalmining, for example, it has been amply shown experimentally that the highly rigid division of labour usually enforced with the introduction of conveyor-belts is only one of a number of forms of organization which can accompany this type of technology without loss of productive efficiency. Within a certain range, variation in organization is feasible.[4] A technology does not dictate a unique form of organization, then, so much as set certain

3. See Trist, E. L., *et al.*, *Organisational Choice*, Tavistock Publications, 1963.

4. Trist, E. L., *et al.*, op. cit.

organizational parameters which can be relaxed only if other requirements, particularly least-cost production, can be abandoned. On the other hand, these associated organizational forms will generally possess certain strong family resemblances.

That the organization of administrative work is also related to the available technology is less easy to recognize. This is partly because administrative and managerial work is undermechanized. Management structures take on their characteristic forms because until the advent of the computer the machine technology available for assisting the administrator was of comparatively minor importance.

At the core of all administrative and managerial activity are two crucial functions – communication and control – which themselves depend on the capture, dissemination, interpretation and utilization of significant pieces of information. In many respects information can be thought of almost as a physical substance. In economic activities its transmission, collection and processing is hardly less important than the manufacture of goods by the movement, shaping and assembly of a collection of raw materials. But while the manipulation of materials has become progressively more sophisticated the manipulation of information has been tied to a technology in many ways no more advanced than that available to historical bureaucracies such as the medieval church.

Admittedly, breakthroughs such as the telegraph and telephone have added important new instruments to the tool-kit of administrative technology. Significantly, they often modified administrative organization in quite radical ways. At an international level, for example, the telegraph reduced the independence and discretionary power and the status of distant viceroys, ambassadors and service commanders. The telephone profoundly changed the pace and rhythm of all administrative work. But until recently there were no equivalents in information technology for the power tool, the automatic lathe or complex materials-handling equipment.

In fact the most important artifact in the information technology of administration has, almost paradoxically, remained the administrator or manager himself. It may seem curious that we should regard human beings as a technological phenomenon, yet we talk readily enough of the government, civil service or political party 'machines'. A universal complaint of the less powerful organization member is that he is 'just a cog in a big machine'. Similar imagery is applied to the administrative echelons of the large industrial or commercial concern. In a very real sense the image is valid. For the head of a large administrative structure, subordinates are in effect tools – information gathering and processing tools, passing up intelligence reports about events inside and outside the concern and interpreting the policies he lays down by drawing up detailed plans and issuing specific orders.

Administrative work revolves around information processing to produce control instructions, and a group of specialized subordinates expand the productivity of a common superior no less than a power saw expands that of a lumberjack, a tractor that of a farmer, or a crane that of a docker. The technology around which managers are organized is composed primarily of themselves.

MANAGEMENT ORGANIZATION AND CONTROL THEORY

The nature of the information technology traditionally available to designers of administrative control systems has tended to produce a characteristic pattern of management organization. This pattern of organization is usually an uneasy compromise between the need to relate the key components (individuals) of the control system one to another in the most technically advantageous form for information handling and the need to ensure that this arrangement does not in the long term result in distortions stemming from the pursuit of personal objectives by the 'components'. It is well known, for instance, that delegation, which involves the transfer of an increased number of minor decisions to subordinates, thereby reducing the amount of information senior personnel are required to handle and providing more time for major decision-making, also expands the scope of the subordinate's authority and provides him with opportunities to increase his personal power – a power which will often be used to further purely personal aims.

THE 'SYSTEMS' APPROACH

This kind of approach to organizational structure and functioning, which has become increasingly popular in recent years, thanks in some measure to the development of information technology itself, has been set out in a number of highly generalized forms. Most of these statements would fall in the field of what is generally understood by *general systems theory* (usually abbreviated to *systems theory*). As it applies to organizations the 'systems' approach is the subject of a certain amount of dispute. Some people find the claims of its more enthusiastic exponents, especially for its universality and objectivity, pretentious and unwarranted. Because of these disagreements it is almost impossible to give a brief account of the systems approach, and suggest how it may illuminate the question of how management organization may be affected by the computer, without appearing to take sides.[5]

In the systems theorist's eyes an organization like a business concern is viewed as a self-regulating entity, or system, and as such it shares broadly similar needs, problems, and functioning characteristics with self-regulating systems as a whole. 'System' may refer to engineering devices, animal organisms, social structures, biological or demographic processes – in fact, to practically any collection of significantly linked parts which communicate with each other in some way and together constitute a relatively coherent whole existing in and interacting with a containing environment.

To maintain its existence the system must be able to respond to changes both within itself and in the environment. Its success in doing so depends on the adequacy of its agencies of communication and control. Changes must be monitored, interpreted and evaluated, and adaptive responses effected. The greater their frequency or severity, and the more elaborate the structure of the system, the more refined must be its response mechanisms. Conversely, the more sensitive and elaborate the response

5. A discussion of varying 'systems' approaches to organizational behaviour can be found in Emery, F. E. (ed.), *Systems Thinking*, Penguin, 1969.

mechanisms it can develop the brighter its prospects of survival in a wide range of different situations and, where such an opportunity is open to it, the higher its chances of successful growth.

Response mechanisms are constituted from three main types of interlinked equipment or organ: *receptors*, *translators*, and *effectors*. Receptors scan or monitor the environment, transmitting messages about changes in it or reporting feed-back data on the progress of previous adaptive responses. In animals receptors are represented by the nerve endings of the five senses, and in mechanisms by, for example, instruments for measuring temperature, speeds of rotation or rates of flow.

Translators collate, interpret and reconcile incoming messages from receptors, consulting stored information about past events or desired conditions, and issue signals for adaptive actions. In animals these services are provided by the various centres of the brain. In simple mechanisms little interpretation is required and can be supplied by arranging components to capitalize on the operation of known physical laws, as, for example, in the successive expansions and contractions of a metal thermostat in line with 'messages' about the temperature of the oven. More complex mechanisms have, until the recent development of the analog computer, generally met their translation needs by 'borrowing' a specialized human operator.

Effector devices execute control signals, appearing in animals as the limbs of the body, and in mechanisms as valves, gears or switches.

For successful response to occur it is obvious that receptors, translators and effectors must be individually adequate to their assigned functions. When they are not disaster can ensue. Bikini Atoll was saturated with radioactivity after the nuclear tests but animals returning there had no means of monitoring this drastic transformation of their environment: some of the more horrific consequences of this exposure were portrayed, not without relish, in the film *Mondo Cane*. Even when receptors are adequate to monitor the incoming signals they may be pointing the wrong way when the critical message comes. Translator organs especially are liable to seize up through being overburdened with incoming information.

No less important than the individual adequacy of receptors, translators and effectors is that of the communication channels between them. These channels are represented by nerve tissues in animals and by electrical wiring, pipes for pressurized fluid, and so forth in mechanisms. The extensiveness and direction of these links obviously influence how signals are handled. So too does the capacity of each channel. Too few links and low channel capacity will starve the system of information. Too many may overload some centres at critical moments. The system becomes 'noisy', the profusion of signals rendering individual messages unintelligible. Some kind of compromise is necessary. In man-made systems this demands a careful specification of the volume and type of information each channel is to carry and of the number and direction of links.

But this is very much easier said than done, especially in the case of management systems. As we have seen, there is a crucial interdependence between the structural form of a self-regulating communication and control system and the nature of its environment. The one must fit the other. Animals possess a highly complex and highly centralized control system as a matter of fact. Receptor and effector organs, themselves fast-acting and highly versatile, are closely integrated with a single general-purpose translator organ, the brain. The system can respond and adapt to a vast range of heterogeneous and largely unpredictable events. The environment has to throw something very special at the system to get the better of its general-purpose capabilities.

But the engineer or administrative scientist has nothing comparable to the communication and control technology of nature. The effectiveness of the control systems they can devise is constrained firstly by the limitations of the technologies they possess, and secondly by their ability to predict the behaviour of the environment in which the systems they design will operate.

Generally the engineer will not attempt to design a self-regulating mechanical system unless he can predict the range and type of environmental changes it will experience. If his technology allows he can then structure it specifically to cater for them. Otherwise he may 'cheat' by providing the system with a human controller. In those cases where he can predict and his technology is adequate he can design mechanical systems of high effectiveness, with an elegance stemming from the perfect matching of internal construction to environmental character. Yet such systems are usually of narrow scope. The administrative designer, however, not only often cannot predict more than roughly the environmental events which will occur but obviously cannot restrict his terms of reference in this way.

These problems seriously compromise the design of effective management systems. There are, however, subsidiary problems to be faced. The system's receptor, translator and effector agencies are supplied in the form of individuals acting in specialized organizational roles between whom communication occurs by word of mouth and written reports and instructions. This is technically unfortunate in many respects since each component is himself a 'subsystem' with private needs and objectives.

Not only is he liable, from normal human error, to fail to identify and transmit relevant information or execute orders at critical moments, but he can choose to fail; and if his failure is detected he can come up with any number of plausible alibis or justifications for his omissions. Consequently, his own performance needs monitoring and supervision, and appropriate incentives must be offered for correct and efficient performance.

These requirements and constraints are generally thought to work in favour of a hierarchical structure of power, status, and money reward. We should note that this design philosophy, however, is reinforced to some extent by the cultural values most often held by the individuals themselves: for example, ideas about inherent differences of ability and the desirability of a career in which the individual can demonstrate his personal excellence by rising to increasingly powerful, lucrative and prestigious positions. Historical experience also works in favour of hierarchical organization of the system. As concerns have grown, often from one-man businesses, successive layers of administrative personnel have been added at the bottom, until a complex power pyramid emerges. Thus the erection of pyramidal control structures easily takes on the appearance of a 'natural response' – or rather, *the* 'natural response' – when growth and technical change dictate some elaboration of structure. History itself seems to justify the creation of a hierarchical bureaucracy. (Whether History will turn out to be on this side of the fence in the long run is another matter.)

It can be claimed that all these influences in favour of a hierarchical organization support what is needed technically from a purely systems point of view. A severe problem of management systems is the frequent absence of valuable information about the environment, for example the likely demand for a new product or the plans of competitors. But an even more persistent embarrassment is the abundance and complexity of the information that *is* available. Once this information is filtered of its irrelevancies it will indicate a mass of decisions varying in their scope and importance. No single individual is capable of taking them all and overseeing their execution. The answer is delegation, the rationalizing of monitoring, interpretative and executive functions in line with a vertical scale of authority and a horizontal division of responsibility.

This arrangement appears to take care of the problem of system design and personal needs at the same time, theoretically in a highly effective manner. Individuals low in the hierarchy are allocated the task of monitoring all information for a certain sector of the concern's environment, for example the sales of a given set of products. As information comes in they can take decisions of a limited scope to achieve adaptation. A group of such low-level managers then pass condensed reports to a common superior. After he has reconciled these streams of information, and taken any decisions of a scope matching his status, he in turn passes an even more refined and general report to a superior he shares with fellow middle managers.

A decision at any level leads to the issue of control instructions – an order to cut prices, to buy new equipment, to work overtime and so on. The geometry of the arrangement being what it is the higher the origin of the decision the further its ramifications. Also, the broader the terms in which it is expressed. At very high levels the decision takes on the nature of a policy statement which is passed to successively lower strata for amplification into detailed instructions. It is an arrangement which has every appearance of economizing on the more senior manager's time, and fully exploiting his wider knowledge and experience, at the same time as providing for many of the private needs and objectives of individuals.

So runs the theory, and probably the majority of management systems are designed in the light of it. It is arguable too that this kind of structure is well suited to operations in a stable environment. However, even from a technical systems point of view it has certain severe limitations – limitations which the new information technology of computing may do much to overcome.

To begin with, as information is filtered and transmitted upward the nature of the message reaching a decision-maker undergoes substantial modification. It provides an increasingly broader picture but one stripped of detail. Yet the absence of detail can on occasion adversely affect the decision which is produced. Again, while the scope and importance of the decision increases with its level so does the delay in making it. Sometimes it may come too late. These delays derive from the hold-up of information at lower levels for collation and screening and the successive pauses on the return journey for the amplification of a policy decision into specific orders.

Moreover, the system is primarily designed for the vertical rather than the horizontal transmission of information. A manager with information valuable to another of equal rank in another department of the concern may be officially required to communicate it through a common superior. In practice individuals forge horizontal and diagonal links to short-circuit these 'proper channels'. But such informal working arrangements may be frowned on and suppressed by a superior who is disturbed at the idea of things 'being done behind his back'. In other words the system encourages 'red tape' and the red-tape mentality.

Another obvious drawback is that because information channels, and lines of command, often pass through a number of intermediate filters or amplifiers the risk of loss, delay and distortion of messages is multiplied at each node. Not merely by accident either. Promotion in the hierarchy is based to greater or lesser extent on personal performance. Personal performance is usually measured largely in terms of the quality of an individual's decision-making success, which is itself dependent on the quality of information he receives. It is possible, and tempting, to scupper rivals, or even to dislodge a superior, by withholding or doctoring the information passing through one's hands.

DEPARTMENTALISM

One particularly strong tendency in the system as it usually operates is towards departmentalism. The system is structured largely on the principle of judicious delegation. By not trying to retain control of everything senior management maintains ultimate control of the things that matter and this permits the concern to grow to a much larger size than would otherwise be possible. But given some autonomy departmental heads may be tempted to take more. This may be achieved by gradually cutting down the information passed to higher levels and steadily arrogating more important decisions. It can even be justified as an attempt to assist higher management by 'taking the pressure off them'. Such empire building also takes place at the expense of other departments. One consequence is the amassing of departmental files which unnecessarily duplicate those of other departments or of a central office. The general result is an incipient process of fission which reduces the operating success of the concern as a whole.

The communication and control system, in other words, is paired with a dynamic social system in which struggles for power and status often intrude on harmonious technical functioning. These interpersonal processes not only interfere with the passage of information for decision-making: they also invite individuals deliberately to ignore it. Decisions, as we have seen, are stratified according to their scope. Higher-level decisions not only have a longer periodicity and depend on very general information. They tend also to be ill structured and non-programmed – that is to say, one-off and unique, necessarily dependent to some extent on qualities of intuition and judgement. Lower-level decisions tend to become highly programmed and well structured: similar choices have to be made again and again and it often becomes possible to lay down precise operating rules for choice between alternatives. Decision becomes a routine affair as soon as information is presented.

But because high status in the concern is associated with unstructured decision-making it is flattering to the lower-level decision-maker's ego to behave as if his own decisions were mainly of the ill structured type. Consequently he may attempt to ignore the policies and operating rules which are laid down for him by superiors and skip over the information he should use in his decisions.

It should be emphasized again at this point that the 'systems' conception of organizational functioning and dynamics is surrounded by a certain amount of controversy. One complaint is that it is too abstract – that the comparison of organizational control structures with animal organisms and engineering devices tends to lead to an equation with them, thus artificially stressing their similarities at the expense of ignoring far more important differences. This suggestion overlaps a second, and more serious, complaint: namely, that with regard to organizations (and other social structures) it stimulates a biased refusal to recognize the full importance in organizational functioning of factors of personal psychology and group interaction. In some formal statements of the systems approach, for example, there is a notable scantiness of discussion of the influence on organizational dynamics of interpersonal and intergroup conflict. In so far as conflict receives a treatment it is in disapproving tones, which contrast strangely with the claims to rigid, uncompromising objectivity which many systems theorists like to make.

In adopting any sort of 'systems' framework in the analysis of organizations there is always a danger of reifying the system, of unconsciously ascribing to it a completely autonomous existence. While such a lapse may be acceptable in the discussion of engineering mechanisms as systems, in organizational analysis it is fatal. Once such a step has been taken, and it often is, the next invariably follows. One can only express this as 'siding with the system', or taking its 'point of view'. There is an inherent logical absurdity here, of course, and the adverse analytical consequences of this error are severe. Organizational systems cannot have any 'point of view' which exists in total independence from the individuals manning the system. In practice the organization's 'point of view' is usually nothing more or less than the 'company line' as determined by its highest policy-making officers. Clearly, what they interpret as the best interests of the organization as a whole may not be those which all other groups or individuals in the organization would lay their finger on, and they may indeed vary in line with the fortunes of individuals and cliques in power struggles within the controlling elite itself. (Though there is no room to elaborate on the suggestion here it can be maintained that these differences of opinion and struggles for policy-making and policy-changing power, far from threatening the stable continuity of organizational existence which the systems theorist so often venerates, in fact can be the very dynamic forces which hold it together.)

Sensitized to the limitations and dangers of the systems approach, however, we may nonetheless make some use of it in an effort to predict the possible consequences for management organization of the introduction of high-level computerized operations.

INFORMATION TECHNOLOGY AND DECISION-MAKING

To glimpse how the new information technology may change the nature of managerial control activities we have only to recall the computer's ability to marshal and condense an enormous volume of information, much of it remotely captured in real time, to transmit it to users over data links, to store it in large random-access memory banks, and where operations research techniques have been applied, to use it directly to produce the analogue of a decision and generate detailed control signals.

The overall tendency of these capabilities, admittedly nowhere yet harnessed to their full, but underlying an increasing number of schemes under development, may be illustrated in more detail by the following remarks of Professor T. L. Whisler, of the Graduate School of Business, University of Chicago, a prominent commentator on the subject.

Let us start with a typical managerial job chosen because it lies somewhere in the middle management area, and because it has many counterparts throughout business and government. The job is that of the manager of a regional warehouse in a steel distributing firm. This manager is responsible for the decision as to how much and what kinds of finished steel forms to carry in his warehouse. Under him he has, of course, a number of clerks, warehouse workers, and supervisors. He has an important decision to make and remake, constantly. The rules provided for him are general and simple. One rule is not to disappoint the firm's customers by being unable to fill an order. (This rule could be modified to be not to disappoint *important* customers, or not to disappoint them *too often*.) The other rule is to minimize the company's investment in finished goods inventory. These very general rules obviously introduce conflict, creating the need for a manager who is willing to risk the ulcers attendant upon getting such a job done while tolerating the pressures and complaints from customers and upper level management.

This manager needs various kinds of information, and the kind that he uses is usually left to his discretion, although a number of staff departments are willing to provide data on economic conditions, sales patterns, current mill production schedules etc. This manager can be expected occasionally to exert intense pressure against production supervision. He will also probably try to provide himself with as good a defense as he can against the criticisms and evaluations of upper level staff and line people. The cost-cutting campaigns initiated by corporate management at occasional intervals will probably motivate him to reduce his inventory and, consequently, assure an angry complaint from the sales manager at a later time. He becomes, in other words, a typical improvising, harried manager.

Enter now some computer systems or operations research people. They carefully gather information on past demand patterns, on mill output capacities, on the cost of capital, and on a number of other items related to this manager's major decision problem. After some rather sophisticated manipulation of information, and the derivation of inventory models, these experts can go to top management and say, 'We have a choice for you to make.' The choice is based upon a quantified rate of exchange between service to customers and amount of capital tied up in inventory. After top management is persuaded that it can and must make a choice between the level of service and the volume of finished goods investment, and does make this choice, for the various warehouses involved, a warehouse supply plan can be devised, and from it mill production schedules set. Usually a series of computer programmes are then developed to ingest continuously new data of the kinds used originally to modify warehouse stock levels at regular intervals.

Subsequent developments will likely follow. It will be necessary to consider cost of transportation among warehouses versus transportation from mills. If the company has several mills it will involve comparison of transportation costs against fabrication costs. A greater variety of information is considered as time goes on, and the scope of the problem to be solved – that is, the decision to be made – keeps growing. What was once a more or less independent decision at one warehouse evolves towards a decision involving the total distribution and manufacturing system.

Let us look at what happened in this hypothetical example. Perhaps most basic was the change in the conception of the nature of the decision. It changed from an intuitive, improvising kind of decision, to a rational, objective, and, in some degree, mathematical decision. As this happened, the kinds of information and the volume of information needed rose sharply. The sources of information changed. Crucial data once originated at the point of distribution, with supplementary information coming from mills, and perhaps from other staff areas. All these sources are now involved but so are additional ones, including information from financial markets, from economic analysts, and from production cost centres. The decision level, in the narrow sense of choice among alternatives, has shifted upward – has become more centralized. The job of the warehouse manager has been radically altered, with his former range of choice over ordering and inventory being sharply restricted. It probably no longer requires the full time and talent of a warehouse manager to manage a warehouse – he can manage several. Or maybe no warehouse managers are needed now. Middle management ranks (in the old structure) may, at least temporarily, thin out. Involved in the decision process are new kinds of people – the systems people, the operations researchers, the computer people, the economists, etcetera. And, unless the steel company is an exception, it continues to move in the directions just described because it gets better decisions, makes more money.

Those doing research on the impact of this technology find these effects replicated again and again in all kinds of organizations, both private and public.[6]

6. Whisler, T. L., 'The Impact of Advanced Technology on Managerial Decision-Making', in Stieber, J. (ed.), *Employment Problems of Automation and Advanced Technology: An International Perspective*, publication of the International Institute for Labour Studies, Geneva (Macmillan, London, 1966), Chapter 16, pp. 306–8.

This example points to at least four interrelated effects of advanced information technology on decision-making activity, and some significant associated effects on management organization.

RATIONALIZATION

Information becomes more precise, i.e. more quantified, and criteria for choice between alternatives are more carefully specified. Responsibility for particular decisions is clarified, and the discretionary element in them curtailed. Moreover, their quality, and repercussions, become more accessible to the scrutiny of superiors. The manager's freedom of action is pared down and he needs to rely less on his intuition and judgement, and can shelter less easily behind such a reliance. At the same time he will need to use his human-relations skills more intensively to ensure the execution of a decision.

(An interesting, complementary possibility, with even wider potential implications in the long term for the nature of administrative control, yet one which is seldom given an airing, is that the scrutiny of the decisions of superiors by subordinates or outside interested parties (e.g. consumers' associations) could in theory also be facilitated.)

WIDER SCOPE

Because a greater volume of information can be captured and more rapidly transmitted any particular decision tends to have wider repercussions, cutting across departmental boundaries. Because the affected area grows, responsibility for taking a decision tends to be pushed up to a higher level of the management hierarchy.

ALTERED RHYTHM

Because the technology permits rapid and continuous data acquisition and processing, tactical decisions, such as the purchase of more raw materials or the revision of a production schedule, can occur more frequently. This calls for more adaptability on the part of managers who must execute the decisions. It also tends to increase the pressure of time in some parts of their work. At a higher level simulation of strategic planning decisions enables planning to be taken further into the future. More of the senior manager's time has to be devoted to this work.

MAN–MACHINE INTERACTION

The new system depends on successful man–machine interaction. Individuals who understand and accept the relationship, which calls for great personal discipline, will be more valuable to the concern than those who can not. Managers have to acquire the habit of accepting the machine's rulings and ensuring that they and their subordinates take pains to feed it with 'clean' information. At the same time they should devote attention to improving and developing the system.

The most important effect on organization of these changes seems likely to be the centralization of control in the concern. The degree of delegation which the growth in the scale of business operations and the limitations of a man-based information technology made imperative is no longer necessary. Delegation cannot be entirely done away with, of course, and it is rather an exaggeration to claim, as some almost do, that we are regressing in the direction of the one-man business. Things are a bit too complex for that, or anything close to it. Nonetheless, a significant measure of power can be returned to the top decision-makers.

And because decision-making can be concentrated at higher levels, or even disappear into the machine system itself, as Whisler suggests, fewer middle managers may be needed to operate a concern of given size. (In another study, Whisler reports a reduction of thirty-four per cent in the middle management jobs in a large factory following the introduction of an advanced integrated system.[7]) The number of tiers in the management hierarchy could also fall in some cases, making the gap between tiers too wide for some individuals to jump.

7. Whisler, T. L., in Myers, C. A. (ed.), *The Impact of Computers on Management*, MIT Press, Cambridge, Mass., 1967, p. 31.

Although these predictions cannot be more than partially confirmed by experience so far, and there are other people who argue for rather different organization effects (particularly *de*centralization: but the few cases where this has occurred seem the product of a deliberate policy rather than the apparent logic of the technology), it is noteworthy that they are frequently anticipated by managers themselves. To differentiate between managerial receptiveness to the machine is largely a question of asking which managers will have more or less to lose by the change, or feel they have.

The more resistant individual, generally speaking, will be one who most values his delegated decision-making power, could transfer less easily to another concern if his position and prospects became shaky, and has fewer of the aptitudes needed to put the new system in perspective and make a contribution to planning. Concerns whose management teams are mostly composed of such individuals will find computerization more difficult to achieve.

ORGANIZATION DURING COMPUTERIZATION

There is a reason why firms of this kind may find computerization difficult which goes beyond the qualms its managers may feel about the impact of the change on their position and prospects. Inevitably computerization brings a period of upset. The whole system of control is changing and normal procedures are constantly interrupted. A very fluid situation is brought about in the firm's internal affairs. Relations with its customers and suppliers too may be thrown out of gear. Its newly acquired systems and programming staff have to be absorbed and working arrangements with them thrashed out. Certain forms of organization can help to meet these problems. But the very individual who recoils from the consequences of computerization is also least likely to accept these intermediate organizational practices.

In the description of management as a communication and control system in previous sections, one kind of organization, characterized by strict hierarchy and pyramidal communication channels, was stressed. Actual management systems do of course vary a good deal in their extent of approximation to this model. Accidents of personality and history, the nature of the business or industry the concern is in, and numerous other factors exert their influence. Nonetheless, one can argue that there has been a general tendency for all concerns of a certain age or size to drift towards this form. Some social scientists have even pictured the process as the product of inevitable laws, and until recently many administrative theorists joined with them in stressing its supposed universal technical superiority.

TWO TYPES OF ORGANIZATION

But if this type of organization has technically superior features, it has been suggested by two writers of the early 1960s, they may only apply given certain environmental conditions, these being conditions of stability. These writers, Professor Tom Burns and G. M. Stalker, of the University of Edinburgh, draw a contrast between what they call 'mechanistic' and 'organismic' management control systems.[8]

Mechanistic organization approximates to what we have been calling 'hierarchical' and what is often described as 'bureaucratic' organization. It is characterized by a high degree of specialization, the separation – almost the abstraction – of one job from all others. Responsibility and authority for each position in a strict hierarchy are closely prescribed. Vertical rather than horizontal communication is stressed. Much emphasis is placed on individual loyalty to the concern and obedience to superiors. Its head is attributed with 'omniscience' about its affairs. And expertise gained by experience with the concern is more highly thought of than generally applicable professional knowledge.

So long as the informal and external environment remains stable this kind of system functions in a smooth and predictable manner. Everyone knows his job (and his place), how he should go about doing it, who gives what orders and who takes them. All likely events and how to tackle them are known from

8. Burns, T., and Stalker, G. M., *The Management of Innovation*, Tavistock Publications, 1961, especially pp. 119–22.

experience. The communication and control structure is tailored specifically for a known pattern of environmental occurrences. Positions resemble the specialized components of a machine, being coupled one to another by reporting and order-giving procedures in rigid mechanistic fashion.

This is all very well until the environment becomes volatile. Externally this could occur through sudden changes in the concern's markets, internally through the introduction of complex new products. The information and decisions demanded for adaptation will be without precedent. It will be 'nobody's job' to provide them. The constant redistribution of authority and reporting needed to tackle these eventualities will disturb the organization as a comfortable social system. Hardly surprising, then, that the larger mechanistic organization seeks to head off such upsets by 'rigging' the environment, for example by tying up customers and suppliers in long-term agreements, fixing prices with nominal competitors, and, where it has a monopolistic position, restricting its development of new products.

Organismically organized concerns are the polar opposite. Jobs are either totally undefined or constantly redefined: the individual is expected to use his good sense to see how and where his expertise can be used to most purpose. This expertise is more often of a general, abstract kind – that, for example, of the qualified technologist, statistician or economist. Communication takes on a multilateral, network pattern, and consists of advice and consultation rather than formal reports and orders. Decisions tend to be collaborative, whoever is best qualified to tackle the particular problem taking the lead. Loyalty to the concern is not continually preached at the member, it being assumed that the mere fact of his membership presupposes a commitment to further its objectives.

This looseness of organization gives the concern a suppleness and versatility essential to face a fast changing environment. Each individual takes on general-purpose information gathering and transmitting characteristics and the profusion of communication channels helps to transmit messages quickly to whoever is best qualified to take a particular decision.

But under stable conditions such arrangements would be

wasteful and unnecessary. In fact, neither system is inherently superior to the other. Each is fitted to a specific type of environment. It needs stressing, too, that as described here each is a model, an abstraction from reality. Any organization can contain departments tending towards either model at the same time, or change from one to another over time.

This change, however, does not occur spontaneously. It has to be engineered. Exactly how this can be done is not very clear, though obviously top management influence is important in this respect. It would seem to be particularly difficult to initiate organismic procedures. At the best of times life in an organismically organized concern is a strain on the individual, who needs to be constantly on the look-out for problems he cannot recognize till they appear. His personal status and authority shift disconcertingly from month to month, and the largely collaborative nature of his work masks the effect of his own contribution, sometimes depriving him of a sense of personal achievement. Some people take better than others to such uncertainties.

TYPES OF MANAGER

The process of computerization, ushering in a period of fluidity in the affairs of the concern, seems to call for organismic organization and procedures during the transition. If such arrangements exist beforehand, the concern has a flying start. If they do not, attempts to procure them will depend very much for their success on the nature of the managerial material at hand.

Organizations vary a good deal in the kinds of manager they attract from outside or promote from within. This differentiation is not a chance product. Clearly, the more mechanistic concern needs individuals who fit comfortably into its neat and codified hierarchy of positions, who possess a rich fund of experience in the concern's affairs, and who accept its stress on personal loyalty. Its staff tend to be home-bred, steeped in its traditions, and emotionally committed to it as a unique entity. Outside recruits have to accept this culture or move on. More organismically organized concerns need individuals with expertise of a more theoretical cast. Abstract skills of this kind are acquired either from experience in a number of previous appointments, from a high-level formal education or professional training, or, even better, the two combined.

LOCALS AND COSMOPOLITANS

Sociologists and administrative theorists have been much concerned in recent years with distinguishing between types of organization member along such lines. A commonly used contrast is between the 'local' and the 'cosmopolitan'. Whether he is a university teacher, a trade-union official or civil servant, a social worker or an industrial manager, the 'local' is the kind of administrator who is embedded in his employing organization. He tends to remain with it most or all of his working life. The fact of membership is imbued with personal existential significance. The organization becomes his life, central to his opinion of his own worth and where he fits in the world. In sociological terms his occupational reference group coincides with his membership group. Belonging to it is valued for its own sake, and personal achievement is synonymous with promotion in it. Loyalty to it is regarded as an over-riding obligation, both for himself and for others.[9]

The cosmopolitan, on the other hand, is an itinerant who regards his membership of a particular concern as a kind of secondment, a provisional arrangement forming a stage in a complex career process in which he 'spirals' upward to a final position of power and prestige by a series of partly strategic and partly opportunist switches of employer. Membership of any one concern is not valued for its own sake but as a springboard for higher things, an opportunity to expand experience and thus add to his stock of marketable skills, and to a lesser, though often important, extent because it may provide him with work of high intrinsic interest.

His commitment to the aims of his employing concern is not necessarily low, but it lasts only so long as membership serves his

9. Gouldner, A. W., 'Cosmopolitans and Locals: Towards an Analysis of Latent Social Roles', Parts I and II, *Administrative Science Quarterly*, 2, 1957–8.

long-range plans. He cannot share the local's emotional involvement in its private traditions, culture and prestige system, especially where these attributes lend the concern something of the atmosphere of a big patriarchal family. His reference group is much more likely to be the more diffuse body of individuals who share his own background, qualifications and values. It is in the eyes of these people that he wants to shine and succeed.[10]

Behind these variations between cosmopolitans and locals in their mobility and loyalty to the concern are significant differences in education and training. Individuals whose cosmopolitanism is most distinct usually possess specialist professional qualifications; as scientists, engineers, economists, statisticians, and so on. Possession of common qualifications is a special bond between members of the group. But all high-level education or training tends to stimulate specific values and attitudes. Those who share them come to identify strongly with each other. As industry recruits more professional specialists and university graduates the proportion of managers with cosmopolitan characteristics will grow. Management itself may even become more of a distinct profession with the spread of business education.

Possession of high formal qualifications creates feelings of fellowship which link individuals in separate concerns. Given the present emphasis on them it also stimulates individual mobility. The degree or diploma becomes something of a runabout ticket. The cosmopolitan not only wants to expand his experience but has more opportunity to do so. He does not need any particular employer for personal success.

Locals on the other hand are relatively poorly qualified for such movement. Their stock in trade is experience in one concern, perhaps in just one of its departments. Their expertise is specific to its methods and problems. In industry, the local *par excellence* is usually the ex-shop-floor or office worker who has risen to management through long service, being promoted precisely because he knows more about the workings of his department from direct experience than anyone else. Sometimes exceptional

10. See Watson, W., 'The Managerial Spiralist', *Twentieth Century Magazine*, May 1960.

personal qualities and long years at night school combine to give him a high value on the outside market. But for the majority a career means a career in the concern that produced them.

Loyalty to the concern is perhaps a necessity for the local, but it is strengthened by the sheer fact of long service. Absorption in the concern's life grows with the years. Relationships with other long-standing members, extended and elaborated in the life of the local community, and the crises, triumphs and heroes of the concern's history, become inextricably woven into the texture of the individual's existence. To leave the concern becomes a rejection of a large part of himself. To change it or to permit others to devalues an equally profound emotional investment.

There are also contrasts between the personal style and technique in carrying out their work of cosmopolitans and locals, which derive to a large extent from the varying origins of their occupational expertise. The local is an empiricist and improviser, with little time for what he sees as the purely textbook know-how of the specialist or expert. The cosmopolitan has more time for such skills, which are often the very ones he himself possesses. On the other hand, he tends to be suspicious of wholly intuitive judgements and industrial folk-wisdom. Locals tend to rely more on the exercise of personal authority to secure compliance with their decisions. Cosmopolitans lay more stress on obtaining compliance through explanation, consultation, and rational argument.

Obviously these distinctions are very broad. Gouldner goes on to make further divisions, suggesting for example that locals break down into such subtypes as 'the bureaucrats' (those who are addicted to following and elaborating the concern's procedural rules), the 'homeguard' (who see themselves as wardens of its subculture and traditions), and the 'elders' (individuals grown old in its service and living on past glories); and cosmopolitans into 'true professionals' (who stand off from any organizational involvements not strictly dictated by their job) and 'empire builders' (who set out to maximize their control over resources with an eye to using the prestige thus gained as an aid to later profitable transfers).[11]

11. These are the refinements put forward by Gouldner in the articles cited above.

Such refinements are unnecessary, however, to appreciate the implications of this contrast between managerial types for responses to computerization. Locals obviously tend to resist the change. For a start it threatens to transform the concern as they know and like it. The technical logic of the computer system may demand an information grid which trespasses over hallowed departmental boundaries and a rhythm and form of communication upsetting customary procedures. Yet it is largely because of his familiarity with these procedures that the local has value to the concern. Positions on which he has long set his sights may be removed or demand differently qualified occupants. Lines of control over subordinates may be altered too. Conceivably he might be transferred to another department or function where his experience is of little value. At the worst – a very unlikely possibility, but one often entertained precisely because it is so alarming – he might be thrown out altogether.

At the same time the local's unfamiliarity with and suspicion of theoretical notions leave him ill equipped to appreciate the rationale and benefits of computerization. It all sounds like dangerous far-fetched nonsense divorced from the working world as he understands it. He is hardly likely to hit it off with the computer experts who arrive to procure the organizational transformation. Genuine scepticism of the relevance of the machine, reinforced by emotional factors, will drive him towards non-co-operation. When the machine arrives he will take considerable self-righteous pleasure in any errors resulting from misprogramming or faulty input. In the words of one such individual: 'We said this [system] is hare-brained, it'll never work. And by God it didn't. But we told them.'

Staff of a well-known computer supplier, asked by the author to describe the more resistant managers, replied in terms which lend support to the foregoing. The following are typical replies.

'It's someone in middle management usually. The computer threatens his security and he doesn't relish the elimination of his "empire". He's generally qualified by experience with the company, with the faithful retainer attitude.'

'. . . The company man, who obtained his present position by long service, is mediocre in management, with a low efficiency [manual] system which he knows better than anyone else in the company.'

'He's been in the same company and the same job in it for years . . . either not qualified, or he qualified a long time ago.'

And if the fluid organization and informal procedures of organismic management systems are indeed appropriate to the uncertain situation during the planning and implementation of a computer scheme, clearly the local is not one who will readily adopt them. They contradict his expectation of precise functions and lines of authority. He likes to know his job, and for others to know it. The replacement of the 'proper channels' by the fuzzy responsibilities and shifting power centres of an organismic management system is objectionable to him, and the collaboration it demands may overtax his social skill.

It would be rash to assert that computerization is always positively welcomed by the more versatile, better qualified, more mobile cosmopolitan. Yet clearly his outlook and background operate to make him less antipathetic to the change. His greater familiarity with theoretical concepts and keener interest in managerial techniques help him to a sounder appreciation of what computerization seeks to achieve. Computer applications are an important addition to the manager's tool-kit, and experience with them adds a valuable item to his personal stock of skills. Because he finds it easier to put the machine in perspective his responses are less influenced by scarifying ideas about its effects on his security and job duties.

Anyway, given his higher marketability, actual displacement from the concern is not the chilling prospect it is for the local. He is habituated to movement and a premature move could involve no more than the revision of his private career plans. A move to another department of the firm might actually be welcomed. Ironically, however, computerization may actually increase his value to the organization, since in the long run it may add to the need for general planning ability. The cosmopolitan's wider experience and higher general qualifications make him more valuable for this kind of work than a veteran in a routine departmental job.

Computerization also tends to increase the value of personnel skills. The local is often firmly convinced of his 'ability to handle men'. But whether his talents in this direction are necessarily superior to the more up-to-date personnel skills upon which the cosmopolitan tends to rely may very well be doubted.

Rapport between the cosmopolitan manager and the datacrat is more likely to be satisfactory. The datacrat himself is, of course, something of a cosmopolitan with his considerable reliance on theoretical knowledge and cumulative acquisition of a varied experience by movement between firms and data-processing specialisms, such as programming and systems design. This is not to suggest friction will not occur. But when it does it is not likely to stem so much from misunderstanding and distrust of the datacrat's objectives, style, or manner, as it does with locals.

Cosmopolitans take more readily to organismic procedures since such systems have an inbuilt recognition of contributive expertise: those who have specialist knowledge are encouraged to display it. This opportunity provides satisfactions for the cosmopolitan that are absent in more mechanistic organizations, where personal prestige is a direct function of distance from the base of the organizational pyramid and not necessarily connected uniquely with excellence of performance. A loose, informal type of system suits the cosmopolitan's preferred style of operation. And it gives plenty of opportunity further to enhance his skills by picking other people's brains.

A pilot study of two firms introducing advanced computer systems by the author and colleagues at the University of Salford seems to support these conclusions. The firm which had made most rapid progress in computerization had a more organismic management system and was staffed by a predominantly cosmo-politan management. But in both cases, those managers who were objectively more cosmopolitan – better educated, better qualified, more mobile, less emotionally committed to the firm – were markedly more receptive to the idea of computerization, more enthusiastic about its advantages, and more realistic in their appraisal of what it could achieve.[12]

12. Hebden, J. E., and Rose, M. J., *Computers and Managers* (cyclostyle), Department of Sociology, Government and Administration, University of Salford, 1968.

It is perhaps worth saying something briefly at this point about age as a factor in managerial receptivity to the computer. This is often reckoned to be the most important influence of all. A popular approach is the crudely biological one that advancing years bring a natural resistance to any upset in routine. A more plausible claim is that more senior managers become tied to a firm by pension rights and very touchy about any change which might threaten their security. The results of the above survey lend very little weight to either type of explanation.

Older cosmopolitans were no less receptive to computerization than younger cosmopolitans. If it seems to be the older manager who resists the machine it is probably mainly because he is more likely to be a local, having entered industry before the present demand for formal qualifications made itself felt, when the atmosphere in many firms was distinctly more paternalistic than is nowadays acceptable, and 'loyalty' was more frequently confused with personal efficiency.

All this suggests that wider and more ambitious use of the computer and an easing of the problems of the changeover depend closely on the rate at which the present changes in the composition of British management proceed in the next ten or so years. The educational qualifications demanded of management recruits have been steadily rising over the last twenty years. There is a growing recognition, too, that merely to attract more graduates and qualified technologists is not enough, just as it is no longer possible to rely primarily on personal experience. What is needed is more people who have been trained in specifically managerial techniques.

A final point is worth bearing in mind. The computerization of business and administration is occurring at a time when, in certain western European countries at least, discussion is growing of the possibility of widening participation in the control of the enterprise. Some representation of those categories of employees who are normally excluded altogether from policy-making already exists or is coming into operation in Western Germany and France in certain industries. It is probable that demands for such participation will increase. These developments would perhaps have occurred independently, but whether or not that is so the whole question of participation in decision-making will be strongly stimulated by the growing penetration of the machine and the increasingly sophisticated systems which are being established.

Whether, how soon, and in what form such a participation should take place are not questions which can be dealt with here. One thing, however, is clear. It is not a development which most managers would be ready to welcome, for obvious reasons – reasons which would for the most part apply equally in our own and in other types of society. Yet if such developments are to be pushed forward it is equally clear that those managers who come closer to the cosmopolitan profile will be better equipped to understand why they are occurring and to adapt themselves to the new institutions and procedures which will arise.

Further Reading

Emery, F. E. (ed.), *Systems Thinking*, Penguin, 1969.

Greenburger, M. (ed.), *Management and the Computer of the Future*, MIT Press and John Wiley, New York, 1962.

Katz, D., and Kahn, R. L., *The Social Psychology of Organizations*, John Wiley, New York, 1966.

Marenco, Claudine, 'Automation administrative et direction des entreprises', *Coopération*, July–August, 1966.

Miller, E. J., and Armstrong, D., *The Influence of Advanced Technology on the Structure of Management Organisation*, International Institute for Labour Studies, Paris, 1964.

Myers, C. A., *The Impact of EDP on Management Organization and Managerial Work* (cyclostyle), Alfred P. Sloan School of Management, MIT, 1965; (ed.) *The Impact of Computers on Management*, MIT Press, Cambridge, Mass., 1967.

Schultz, G. P., and Whisler, T. L., *Management Organization and the Computer*, Free Press, Glencoe, Illinois, 1960.

Simon, H. A., *Administrative Behaviour* (2nd ed.), Collier-Macmillan, New York, 1966; *The New Science of Management Decision*, Harper & Row, New York, 1960; 'The Corporation: Will it be Managed by Machines?' in *Management and Corporations, 1985*, McGraw-Hill, New York, 1960.

Wiener, N., *Cybernetics* (2nd ed.), MIT Press and John Wiley, New York, 1961.

Woodward, J., *Management and Technology*, HMSO, 1958.

CHAPTER 9

Computers in Britain: Official Policy

FOR reasons to be reviewed shortly it is impossible to keep the computer outside politics, whether international or domestic. The present (1969) British government came to power with a mandate to stimulate economic and technological modernization by more direct intervention in industry. Since 1964 the rate of computerization in the UK has accelerated markedly and the British-owned computer-making industry has struggled off its death-bed and for the present shows every sign of rude and dynamic good health. To what extent the connexion between these events is causal or coincidental will be argued for some time to come. But whatever the relationship, official involvement in the computer-making and computer-applying industries has become an economic and political fact of considerable significance.

BRITISH COMPUTERS OR A COMPUTERIZED BRITAIN?

Given limited resources official policy has had to face a persistent dilemma. If there is to be intervention should funds, advice, and personnel be channelled into developing new applications, training computer staff, and subsidizing companies which install the machine? Or should they be used to stimulate British computer research and development? In other words, should policy be aimed at assisting those who use computers or those who make them? Concentration on the first might increase the efficiency and competitiveness of industry as a whole. But the price could be the disappearance of an independent British computer-manufacturing capacity.

In the event a decisive choice has never been made though it can be argued that in terms of cash the second option has tended to be more favoured in practice. And in the present writer's opinion there are a number of good reasons why this bias can be approved

– reasons which, needless to say, have very little to do with narrow economic nationalism, although the first and best reason is that if British computer makers went out of business American ones would replace them.

THE AMERICAN COMPUTER INDUSTRY

American computer-makers supply over ninety per cent of the world's machines and essentially they have gained this position because their products are technically advanced, efficiently produced, skilfully marketed, and of high overall quality. If we were talking about automatic washers or pin-ball machines it would be reasonable to suggest that any attempt to preserve an independent British industry would be superfluous and mistaken when we are otherwise so well served. But the computer is not that kind of product. The computer is a modern strategic industrial and military good, and depending on a foreign source of supply carries the same inherent risks as apply in other advanced technological fields – nuclear energy, aerospace, production automation or telecommunications. In fact the risks are higher since the computer is the common strand in advanced technology as a whole.

The economy of the future – not to mention national defence – will need computers as it now needs electricity or steel. Computer-importing countries will be uniquely dependent on their suppliers. For the foreseeable future the only alternative sources of supply to the USA for a computer-importing UK would be Russia or Japan. Effectively we would depend on the Americans, and such dependence might increase potential exposure to unwelcome pressures. The State Department for example has already blocked the sale of one large machine to the French, a salutary reminder that the computer cannot be divorced from long-term political considerations.

Dependence on the Americans would also carry the risk of eventually being dependent on one private company, International Business Machines. Much of what goes on in the computer world on both sides of the Atlantic cannot be understood without saying something further about IBM's key position in the $5,000 million a year American data-processing market. Like every other market outside the UK, Japan and Eastern Bloc countries it is decisively dominated by IBM, whose share of it is around seventy-five per cent by value. (The remaining twenty-five per cent is divided between seven competitors: the Univac Division of Sperry Rand; the Control Data Corporation; Honeywell; National Cash Register; Burroughs; Radio Corporation of America; and (American) General Electric.)

IBM came late to commercial computing, its senior management persisting with the belief that there was no future in it well into the 1950s. Competitors like Univac had an excellent start, yet between 1953 and 1960 they were completely overtaken. IBM's success was built on several exceptional advantages, not the least being its marketing expertise, but above all on its strength in the conventional punched-card equipment field (which IBM offered to customers on a leasing basis only). The transition to office computers was a logical one, and IBM had an enormous ready-made market.

While it was developing its computer interests its punched-card machinery rentals continued to provide it with a massive income, and until 1963 more than half its profits were still derived from this source. Consequently it always had sufficiently massive liquid assets to finance research and development without becoming side-tracked into the vicious circle most of its competitors were entering. This cycle, sometimes known facetiously as the 'law of exponentially unprofitable innovation', is a process to which European computer-makers have been even more damagingly subject. Essentially, what happens is that before the development costs of a new machine can be recouped it usually becomes necessary to pioneer an even more sophisticated model to fight off the new machines that competitors introduce in retaliation against the original 'winner'.

IBM's research programmes also benefited handsomely from federal defence procurements (see SAGE, page 219) and while other American companies struggled to keep their heads above water it went from strength to strength, tightening its grip not only by superior salesmanship but through its before-sales service and advanced educational efforts. By the early 1960s it had reached the paradoxical position of being too big and rich to afford to follow the price-cutting tactics of its rivals. To do so would have driven several of them out of business. Since such an event would bring it face-to-face with American anti-trust laws the company is in a sense obliged to continue making excessive profits.

IBM's domestic strength in the USA is reinforced by its worldwide computer interests. Hoping to achieve similar economies of scale, especially by selling the profit-making tail-ends of their production runs in the fast-growing European market, its competitors stepped up their own overseas activities in the late 1950s. Control Data and Univac chose direct selling; Radio Corporation of America and National Cash Register initially plumped for licensing agreements with European companies like International Computers and Tabulators and Siemens; Burroughs, Honeywell, and – disastrously – General Electric decided on local manufacture. Whatever the method the overall effect has amounted to the export to Europe of the domestic American battle.

The European computer user has gained substantially from this competition, at any rate in the short run, and there is no reason why he should not continue to do so as long as it lasts. But the question has to be asked: how long will it last? The withdrawal of some of the smaller American companies from the race, leaving the user with moribund equipment and software, is a real enough possibility. The risks of a worldwide IBM monopoly, or monopolistic market-sharing agreements between it and the survivors, though not immediate, cannot be excluded.

THE MACHINES BULL AFFAIRE

Total dependence on American imports is perhaps only marginally less desirable than a completely American-owned European computer industry. An illustration of the sort of thing that can happen when the smaller American companies export their battles with IBM on the American home market is the takeover of the French Compagnie des Machines Bull by the General Electric Company.

Machines Bull was founded in 1931 to exploit office machinery designed by a Norwegian, Frederick Bull. It remained a small but profitable concern until the 1950s, when following the development of a small computer, the Gamma 3, Bull began to grow at an annual rate of twenty-five per cent, thanks to the French economic 'miracle', until 1960. This sudden growth and Bull's success in out-selling IBM in France led directly to its later troubles and the feelings of national involvement which exacerbated its subsequent painful relationship with General Electric. It had outgrown its administrative structure, production methods were out of date, its labour force unnecessarily large, and the co-ordination of financial control and research and development scrappy. More and more capital became tied up in leased machines (upon which a computer company must wait four years for a financial return: if leasings continue to rise a company can be put in the paradoxical position of becoming bankrupt because it is booming). But this danger was in Bull's case fatally aggravated by the development of a giant machine, the Gamma 60, which arrived in 1960. To cover its development costs rentals had to be fixed high. Worse still the potential European market for machines of this size was then very limited. Only a dozen machines were disposed of.

To head off bankruptcy, Bull was forced to take out a licensing agreement with Radio Corporation of America, producing a French-built version of that company's 301 machine. Sales were good but Bull had to split the proceeds with RCA and gradually went further into the red.

General Electric first proposed buying an interest in Bull in 1963. This elicited a sharp 'non' from the Elysée, and President de Gaulle ordered an inspection of the company's affairs with a view to a solution française. An administrative and financial mess of considerable intricacy was revealed, and swallowing their pride the French government sanctioned the American takeover in the spring of 1964. The terms were complex, but in effect GE got full managerial control in return for safeguards for Bull's research effort and employee security. Later in the year GE also absorbed Olivetti's data-processing division in Italy.

In theory all this made good sense. GE would attack the world market manufacturing its large machines in the USA, its medium ones in France, and its small ones in Italy. All national partners would stand to gain from GE's paternal control, backed by a worldwide marketing organization and considerable financial resources. Unfortunately, the very reverse happened.

The products which GE inherited from Bull and Olivetti were both mutually incompatible and in some ranges directly competitive with its own. The main clash was between a new Bull computer, the Gamma 140, and GE's American-designed GE 400 (which was now being manufactured in Europe in Bull's factories). French salesmen actually persuaded customers contracted for the GE 400 to swop to the marginally cheaper – but much more patriotic – Gamma 140. Even so, by late 1966 only fifty 140s had been disposed of. A high-level decision was made to discontinue it. This brought howls of fury from the French press and worsened labour relations in the Bull factories, which were already acid following earlier attempts to reduce the (admittedly bloated) labour force.

It brought into question the whole future of GE's research and development effort in Bull. Indeed GE's worldwide future in the computer business now appeared at stake. Its large computer, the 600, hurried into production in America to capitalize on IBM's development troubles with its giant 360:90, proved thoroughly unreliable. Three of these machines were to have been sold to the nationalized French electricity utility but the sale had to be cancelled, all preparatory systems work being a complete write-off. Redundancies were occurring at GE's American plants too. What had looked like the rock-solid saviour of the French computer-making industry now appeared to be itself tottering on the brink of commercial disaster.

Undeniably GE took over in Bull an insecure and badly organized company. Its difficulties were increased by problems of culture and communication. (Hardly any of the newly arrived American managers spoke a word of French or seem to have shown any inclination to learn: these sentiments were returned by their French counterparts.) But few people would claim the episode lends much support to a *laissez-faire* approach to international investment. It underscores the problems of maintaining an independent research and development effort in an advanced technology field on a narrow economic base. But above all it illustrates the hazards of handing over an independent computer capacity to concerns whose essential interests lie in the rich American domestic market.

Not surprisingly the French government, through its 'Plan Calcul', is now desperately reviving the remnants of the French computer industry. The strong vein of chauvinism in this project does not alter the fact that it is inspired essentially by a well founded and legitimate concern.

In the British case there are strong arguments for supporting the local computer industry in addition to the wish to avoid dependence on imports and exposure to the cross-fire between American companies. Firstly, the sheer cost of a totally imported supply is worth considering. In 1967, deliveries of computers, peripherals and closely associated services to the UK market reached £100.5 million. In 1968, they are expected to rise by up to thirty per cent. In addition, exports of British-made equipment in 1967 reached £35.6 million. Within ten years home deliveries are expected to exceed £500 million and exports £200 million.

The exact balance of payments implications of the present pattern of trade are unclear because some overseas (i.e. American) companies manufacture locally and export a substantial slice of their British-made output. Again, British-owned companies import components and know-how, some of which are re-exported in assembled equipment. It is probable, however, that when profit remittances and licensing royalties are added to visible trade Britain already has a net import bill for computers of around £10 million. Given the expected rise in deliveries this bill will continue to grow unless British-owned suppliers increase their 55–60 per cent present share of the home market and their share of British-made exports as well as cutting their purchases of American know-how.

Absorption of the British-owned sector would not perhaps be calamitous in the short run. But the danger that the American companies which absorbed it would choose to supply its former export customers from their other plants is a pretty strong argument for its survival. But above all selling out computers would be selling out a key growth industry and abandoning a stake in developing the universal technology of the future. Britain just cannot afford to do things like that.

When the question is raised whether the government is justified in supporting the British-owned industry, American experience itself is relevant. In the 1950s, during which the early British lead in some key fields of computer technology (particularly 'memories') was overtaken, American research and development enjoyed the advantage of vast direct and indirect support from the federal government. The American services had of course subsidized important first-generation prototypes such as the ENIAC (1944), the EDVAC (1948) and the SEAC (1950). From the early 1950s government departments and armed services began procurements of machines for standard data-processing jobs. These purchases soon grew to gargantuan proportions, contracts for several hundred machines sometimes being placed at one time.

Perhaps the most significant set of procurements – significant for their timing as well as their value – were those associated with SAGE ('Semi-Automatic Ground Environment'). SAGE, created at the height of the Cold War, is a highly impressive, rather alarming, military integrated data-processing system which collates aerial intelligence on movements in the skies around the USA in real time, and helps specify and control defensive movements to any incoming attack. Its original version, installed by 1958, absorbed several thousand programming man-years alone. Altogether it cost something of the order of $1,600 million, a substantial portion of which found its way to IBM.

The cash was, however, less valuable to IBM than the experience it gained at this early stage in the design of integrated systems. The software expertise thus gained was put to good account in the first commercial on-line integrated systems, such as the American Airlines multi-million-dollar SABRE seat-reservation system, established in the early 1960s.

The effect, if not the intention, of defence and administrative procurements by the US government has amounted to a massive inbuilt subsidy to the American industry as a whole, the scale of which expands in line with the growth of American world military commitments and foreign aid, and – a massive bonus – the voracious appetite of NASA for the space programme. And these are of course largely markets from which foreign competition is excluded by the 'buy American' strategic goods policy (which demands, for example, a minimum fifty per cent underbid by a foreign contender of the lowest domestic quotation).

THE BRITISH COMPUTER INDUSTRY

The American experience suggests the advantage, especially for basic research and development, which large and sustained government support can bring. The British experience supports it, but from the opposite direction. Until recently it is a story of official indifference, an ill structured industry, and a gradually weakening technological competence.

Although the first computers (the ASCC and the ENIAC) of 1944–5 were developed in the USA they made wide use of theoretical ideas pioneered in Britain, especially those of the mathematician Turing. In the late 1940s British designs leap-frogged the American. As noted elsewhere British memory technology dominated first-generation machines and the first commercially oriented computer, LEO, was put to work by Lyons in London. Programming theory (at least in mathematical and scientific work) also drew ahead.

Yet these early breakthroughs were never fully exploited and followed through. 1955, which marks the arrival of magnetic-core memories, the basic patent of which is held by the American Professor Jay W. Forrester, can be seen as a watershed year. Since then the majority of major technical and applications break-throughs have originated in the USA. (It is hardly any comfort that British brain-drain expertise has gone into a number of them.) Increasingly, British manufacturers have had to rely on licensing agreements with American firms to produce machines embodying novel features some of which began as theoretical ideas in this country but were never exploited because either no one would listen or no one could pay. It is a familiar story.

These failures could unquestionably have been offset by more positive government interest during the critical second-generation period. Like their American counterparts the British armed services and Civil Service have made use of computerized data-processing from fairly early days. But their organization, the outlook of their senior staff, and the eagle eye of the Treasury hardly made for a generally enthusiastic approach. Ministers of the time seem to have been quite insensitive to the need for intervention or assistance to promote wider and more ambitious utilization of the machine by what are, after all, its own office staff. Nor was there the slightest thought given to an effective 'buy British' policy. (The contrast with nuclear policy is striking.)

There was no effort to procure a rationalization of the British computer industry with its host of mutually competitive companies, each trying to corner a large enough share of the market to support its private research and development programme. The benign operation of market forces was supposed to see to that.

In 1959, when market forces did begin to bite in earnest, there were still over a dozen British digital and process-control computer manufacturers all competing for a nibble of an annual market of less than a hundred machines and worth a mere £10 million, plus £2 million exports. Admittedly many of these suppliers were offshoots of otherwise large and profitable concerns. On the business computing side, for example, the (British) General Electric Company, Electrical and Musical Industries, Ferranti, English Electric, Leo Computers, and Marconi fell into this category. Only International Computers and Tabulators and Elliott-Automation were predominantly computer companies.

One consequence of this fragmentary structure and its inevitable repercussions on product quality, customer service and marketing, was the successful entry of foreign competitors suffering no such handicaps. IBM, whose share of the UK market stood at zero per cent in 1954, had captured a third of it by 1960. Another consequence was an artificial dampening of the potential market itself. It is still hard enough to choose a computer. At that time the bewildering array of incompatible machines each with its own profile of plus-points and drawbacks was completely stultifying. Rather than blunder some potential customers held off, or bought American.

The only official agency with any prospect of bringing order to this chaos, the National Research and Development Corporation, was neatly sewn up by its terms of reference into something close to impotence. The NRDC could merely respond to requests for development capital. It had no powers to intervene on its own initiative, nor – formally at least – to influence industrial structure through its choice of projects to support.

Since its establishment soon after the war it had done a certain amount in its discreet and financially modest way to put the computer industry on its feet. Its funds lay behind such notable technical successes as the Elliott 401, the Ferranti Pegasus, and the EMI 2400 computers. But there was a definite limit to what it could do at any one time. It has also been suggested that borrowers were reluctant to approach it for political reasons. Dr Andrew Booth, who as inventor of the magnetic-drum store has some inside experience, has claimed that being set up originally by the Attlee government the NRDC was regarded by industrialists as 'a socialist body' and deliberately cold-shouldered.

In view of its balkanized structure, government indifference (some would say 'superciliousness'), the NRDC's piggy-bank funds and ambiguous position, the arrival of foreign competition, and the caution of potential buyers, an independent British computer industry, like the French, German and Italian, should have been virtually snuffed out in the early 1960s. What seemed like the symbolic knock-out blow was administered in 1961 when the government of the time (whose 'Science Minister' was the colourful lawyer Quintin Hogg) decided not to allow London University to purchase the giant ATLAS machine, itself partially government-sponsored via the NRDC, insisting instead (under Treasury influence) on a marginally cheaper American-built machine.

The decision was later reversed. Somehow too the British industry survived, thanks immediately to importing American know-how, less directly to a spate of mergers finally culminating in early 1968 in the creation of a single British business computer company, International Computers.

INTERNATIONAL COMPUTERS LTD

The developments which led up to this belated consolidation are worth reviewing since they not only illustrate the precarious, see-saw nature of the computer-making business but throw light on the question of how important the change in official policy since 1964 has in fact been.

Of the two remaining British business computer companies, International Computers and Tabulators (ICT) and English Electric Computers, which merged to form International Computers in 1968, ICT had had the more volatile history. Curiously enough it owed its original existence very largely to its arch-enemy, IBM. As noted elsewhere, before IBM turned to computers it had been a maker of conventional office machinery since its foundation in the 1890s to exploit the inventions of Herman Hollerith. The franchise for Hollerith machines in the UK and commonwealth was held between 1905 and 1949 by the British Tabulating Machine Company (BTM). When BTM's agreement with IBM lapsed in 1949 it was able to retain its valuable world-wide list of customers.

This gave BTM the sort of built-in advantage which IBM was to exploit so successfully in the United States once it had decided to go over to computers. BTM itself was fairly quick to produce a computer. The HEC 1, incorporating the Booth magnetic-drum memory and developed in association with Birkbeck College, University of London, was unveiled in 1952. BTM's progress during the 1950s, however, for the reasons mentioned already was not impressive. By 1959, when it merged with another office-equipment manufacturer (Powers-Samas) to form ICT, American financial strength and technical superiority were already beginning to tell.

Its own products, such as the ICT 1300 – a physically gigantic programmer's nightmare – were uncompetitive, and in the early 1960s its only chance of survival lay through importing American know-how, the ICT 4100 coming from Univac and the ICT 1500 from Radio Corporation of America. These difficulties were aggravated by ICT's absorption of the business computing interests of three other British companies in close succession, those of the General Electric Company in 1961, EMI's in 1962, and Ferranti's in 1963. Each takeover temporarily extended ICT's range of incompatible, mutually competing products.

But the acquisition of wider research and development resources, ICT's willingness to buy in American know-how, and the technical fall-out from the ATLAS machine (acquired with the Ferranti link) were blending to create a more saleable commodity. The ICT 1900 series of fully modular, compatible machines was announced in September 1964. At first it encountered a good deal of criticism. Several months before, IBM had brought out the 360 Series, a replacement for its highly successful 1400 Series machines. The 360 utilized an advanced type of circuitry while the 1900 clung to transistors, and the technical gap between the two series seemed certain to operate in IBM's favour.

The development of the 1900 had strained ICT's resources to the limit. It was obliged virtually to withdraw from the European market where leasing rather than outright sale of machines is standard practice. The cash to finance this sort of business was just not there. Its recent mergers had left it with board-room problems and it seemed unable to thrash out a decisive top management structure. At this time it would probably have been glad to find a takeover client itself. The reluctance of anyone to step forward despite its slumped share prices (they lost two thirds of their market value between 1962 and 1966) was indicative of the general pessimism about the future of its new machine.

However, the decision to play safe with second-generation technology in the 1900 soon proved a considerable advantage. Like many computer-makers IBM found that mass-producing an advanced machine is more tricky than building a prototype. The 360's micro-circuits began to give trouble and deliveries fell further and further behind schedule. The 360 software also failed to meet initial expectations. Users found that it was not so easy as forecast to adapt their programs for previous IBM machines. The promised new programming language, PL-1, also proved problematic.

IBM's difficulties were exploited to the full. The 1900 machines were technically square. But from the start they were highly reliable. Starting from such an initially weak market position ICT had fewer delivery problems. The 1900 software, based largely on the ATLAS experience, was of a very workmanlike overall quality and some items outstanding. ICT had modernized its marketing methods too and drove home the advantages of the 1900 with an energy and deftness previously not conspicuous in its approach.

By mid 1967 orders for 1900s stood at over seven hundred and the thousandth was announced later in the year. With a value well over £100 million this began to represent the sort of volume of business which is essential if a computer-maker is to support an adequate research programme. In 1967 too ICT micro-miniaturized the 1900, removing any residual doubts about its technical sophistication. By the time of the creation of International Computers, what had been the sick man of the British computer industry was its most dazzling success story.

The fortunes of English Electric Computers, ICT's partner in International Computers, have fluctuated less wildly. It acquired its present character and range of products largely as a result of mergers parallel to those of ICT in the early 1960s – Leo Computers were absorbed in 1963 and Marconi Computers in 1964 – and the takeover of the much more important Elliott-Automation Company took place in 1967. It is worth remembering that as an offshoot of the large and strong English Electric Company it had enjoyed all along the advantage of access to substantial development capital.

The acquisition of Leo, whose machines carried a high reputation for their technical features, provided English Electric with valuable know-how, which was supplemented by extensive licensing agreements with the Radio Corporation of America to produce an extremely advanced range of machines in 1965. English Electric poured £12 million into the development of this System-4 series. Utilizing third-generation integrated circuits and program-compatible with the IBM 360 machines, the objective was to sweep the British market by leapfrogging IBM's technology and making it simple for ex-IBM customers to adapt their software. (This ploy, which reflects IBM's dominance of the computer market, was first adopted earlier in the 1960s by the American Honeywell Company, who advertised it as the 'Liberator Concept'.)

But because of their advanced design the System 4 machines were soon subject to production delays. Although superior in central processing speed the smallest model (the 4:10) proved uncompetitive with the ICT and IBM 'babies' and was cancelled. Once over their teething troubles, however, the larger models (the 4:70 and 4:75) became comparatively successful and had won orders of £20 million by early 1968. Their prestige was considerably enhanced by their selection as the backbone for the GPO Giro payments system and, following the Flowers Report on computers for scientific research, for the first multiple-access Regional Computing Centre (currently being established at Edinburgh University). They have also sold well in eastern Europe, where American efforts are inhibited by the US strategic arms embargo.

The takeover of Elliott-Automation in 1967 certainly made good industrial sense. Elliott's computer interests were small in the business computing field but it had a large share of the scientific-academic market. Both companies had for the most part complementary interests in process-control computers and electronic components. Like the previously absorbed Leo company Elliotts were well stocked with development expertise. Moreover, because it is likely that the present distinctions between business, scientific and process-control computers will break down in future, suppliers who can offer complete automation systems will be in the best market position.

The emergence of International Computers from these two streams of mergers gives the British industry a fighting chance of survival. The unification of research and development and marketing will make for important savings. In theory at least the new grouping is strong in machines at both the top and the bottom of the scale of computing power, and competition between English Electric and ICT medium-power machines will be removed.

Although the integration of all manufacturing will not be possible for some time, the production of peripheral equipment – which generally fits a variety of otherwise incompatible central

COMPUTERS IN BRITAIN: OFFICIAL POLICY

processors – can be rationalized. The new company is also to be linked with the Plessey Company, whose data-transmission equipment will add to the variety of systems it can offer, as well as ensuring harmonization between new communication equipment and new computers.

But the problems should not be underestimated. There are basic design differences between the two main series of machines the company will continue to produce (the English Electric System 4 and ICT 1900) which make them mutually incompatible. The position is still further complicated by the continuance of the small-to-medium size 4120 and 4130 machines of the former Elliott Company. Again, there is the dilemma of what design to adopt for a successor to all three series. Such a machine should be compatible with *both* these present ranges and with IBM's own *next* machine. The System 4 technology is more advanced, and it is compatible with present IBM hardware (and hence very likely with its next series). But ICT's 1900 has sold in bulk and these customers cannot be left high and dry.

Whatever approach is adopted, however, one question is settled by the merger: that is, who is going to produce the giant computer that the government is eager to see developed. At present the Americans unquestionably lead in this super-computer field, which will become increasingly important as on-line and in-real-time, multiprogrammed computing grows in popularity.

These giant systems will be the skivvies of the future economy, at the heart of total systems in the individual enterprise which will control the automated factory and form the basis of managerial activity, and the core of public 'information-bank' utilities. They will be of key importance to future defence systems. But more immediately they will be needed for bureau work for smaller commercial users and for scientific and technical research.

The latter need is the most pressing. In January 1966, a committee headed by Professor B. H. Flowers reported that computing provisions in universities and research institutions already fell far below requirements and was likely to become a progressively tighter research bottle-neck. According to the

Flowers Committee large American machines alone would be adequate to these growing needs and it recommended the government to hire them.

The government initially accepted the Committee's plan for a vastly increased expenditure (£30 million by 1971) and three Regional Computing Centres (at Edinburgh, London and Manchester), under the Computer Board at the Department of Education and Science. However, the American solution later gave way to a compromise, and the first centre, at Edinburgh, has been given an English Electric 4:75. In fact, since the Flowers Report development troubles have even struck the American giant machines, such as IBM 360/90. At the same time, multiple-access computing, which gets more out of a machine of a given capacity, has become more sophisticated, temporarily removing some of the pressure.

All the same, the underlying need remains. In 1967 plans were announced to make the Atlas Computing Laboratory, at Chilton, Berkshire, the centre for the biggest scientific computing jobs, and to equip it with the largest system in Europe by 1971.

To do so will require some pretty swift development work if a British machine is to be used. Prior to the formation of International Computers the computer companies were too small to produce such a machine by themselves, though each had pressed its suit, for the most part with schemes for running several of its larger machines in tandem to produce a giant. Even Elliotts presented plans for such a 'number-crunching' machine shortly before its acquisition by English Electric. ICT followed soon after with a proposal similar to an earlier suggestion for a large machine in the 1900 Series. This 'Project 51' machine would have a power ten times that of the ATLAS, there would be a market for at least fifty models in the UK and Europe, and it could be ready by 1970. But it would need at least £10 million for development.

Time is hardly on the side of the new company. But the very fact that there is a British-owned company left to make the attempt is perhaps something which only a few years ago would have seemed highly unlikely. The revival of the British industry covers the period since the present government came to power and it is worth asking to what extent any claim by it to have salvaged the industry is justified.

Perhaps the first point to make clear is that there has been no bailing-out operation on the scale familiar in other fields (e.g. aviation), although that is the impression sometimes given. Money, channelled through a variety of agencies, has changed hands on only three main occasions. In early 1965 ICT got £5 million through the NRDC to help develop the 1900 Series, improve its software, and get on with designing a successor for the 1970s. This was a loan not a grant, although it did not have to be repaid until between 1970 and 1975 in instalments scaled according to the company's profits. (The NRDC also lent Elliott-Automation £2.4 million at this time for process-automation development, and a further £1 million was distributed in 1966 for computerized machine-tools.)

Negotiations for this loan, incidentally, had commenced under the previous government, which makes precise allocation of credit difficult.

The second major injection of cash, this time routed through the then newly established Industrial Reorganization Corporation, occurred in June 1967, when £15 million was provided to facilitate the merger of English Electric and Elliott-Automation. This too was a loan, to be repaid plus interest at market rates after a two-year 'holiday' period. In effect it amounted very largely to a sweetener to persuade the two firms to merge by removing worries about their short-term financial position.

Finally, £13.5 million was granted to International Computers on its foundation in March 1968. On this occasion the money was a grant to assist the development of the new concern's next machine and will be phased in over a number of years. In return the government, through the Ministry of Technology, acquired a 10.5 per cent stake in the new company.

The policy has therefore been one which has tied judicious openings of the purse to structural concentration of the industry. What has emerged, on the business computing side at least, is a highly rationalized industry which can develop its future equipment on a sufficiently broad scale, and – the government's stake in the new enterprise surely implies this – be sure of a future market. (On the process-control, computerized machine-tool, and electronic components sides further rationalization is still necessary for real viability.)

It can be argued that the firms in question – Elliotts, English Electric Computers, and ICT – would have merged by now anyway without official intervention; or even that given a continuation of its recent success ICT would have finally emerged as the only British-owned computer firm, while English Electric would have cut its losses by pulling out of the business computer field. How much pressure was required to produce International Computers is presently unclear. Negotiations dragged on an unexpectedly long time and the delay most probably stemmed from ICT's resolve to gain recognition as the dominant partner, an objective it finally achieved.

If government money has gone to the computer firms on only a modest scale there has been even less evidence of a resolute 'buy British' policy for government departments, the nationalized industries, and scientific and academic bodies. As we have seen, the government initially accepted the 'buy American' recommendations of the Flowers Committee. The one major exception occurred in 1966 when the Ministry of Pensions was obliged to switch a £1 million order for a Univac machine to ICT. The NRDC and Ministry of Technology claim to work by encouragement and example only. More British machines are now certainly being purchased by official bodies. But whether this is a result of pressure or because they now compare so well with imported machines is difficult to judge.

Foreign firms certainly feel there is a growing discrimination against them. It is noteworthy how intensely their public relations advertising has come to stress their British connexions. Those, such as Honeywell, with large UK production facilities and a big contribution to exports, are probably in better odour than the direct importers such as IBM. (When IBM applied to build an extension to its UK Research and Development Laboratories in the Green Belt at Hursely Park in Hampshire in 1967, for instance, it was obliged to put them on a designated industrial site nearby instead. Some people in IBM are thought to have interpreted this as a narrowly hostile act of direct discrimination against the company, an interpretation extended to the 1967 sterling devaluation which forced up their UK selling prices by ten per cent.)

But probably the most influential aspect of government policy so far has been the simple fact of its existence. Because a computer user invests so heavily in software when he buys a machine he has to be assured of product continuity. If a supplier seems in danger of going out of business the user will look elsewhere. Simply by announcing that it would abandon its predecessor's passive role towards the industry the Wilson government encouraged a more confident assessment of the future of British suppliers. Many users who had been wavering between domestic and foreign machines came down decisively on the domestic side, with less fear of being left with obsolescent equipment and programs.

The main emphasis in policy has been on the producing side so far. But a domestic computer industry will be useless without a satisfactory home market. Thus a complementary strand in official policy, aimed at stimulating computer usage, has gained increasing importance. Here the government has chosen to operate mainly through the provision of better advisory and information services rather than by direct financial stimulation.

THE NATIONAL COMPUTING CENTRE

Necessarily the effects of this kind of approach are of a more long-term nature, and forecasting their impact presents considerable difficulties. The main agency through which the policy operates is the National Computing Centre (NCC) at Manchester. Plans for the NCC were announced in December 1965 and the building of the Manchester headquarters began promptly. Operations commenced immediately after the establishment of the Centre as a non-profitmaking limited company and the appointment of Professor Gordon Black as its director the following May. By the time of its official opening a year later (by a Prime Minister whose credentials as a technological visionary were still impeccable) it had already acquired over three hundred subscribing member-organizations and was expanding rapidly.

Although part of the NCC's role is similar to specialist computer consultancy and bureau work, its main functions are to act as a general adviser to its members (particularly smaller firms who are unable or reluctant to acquire assistance on the open market); to collect and disseminate information; and to encourage research into new applications and software. The final aim has always been to make the Centre self-supporting by providing these services at an economic price. But in fact capital costs and its rapid growth have resulted in only twenty per cent of its income deriving from members' subscriptions (these are scaled according to their size). The balance comes from the Ministry of Technology whose grant climbed from £290,000 in 1966 to £800,000 in 1967 alone.

The pattern of its activities is determined by the needs of its members. As these needs have emerged more clearly four main areas have become especially prominent.

Firstly, there has been an attempt, still continuing against the grain of manufacturers' policies and in the absence of a firmer official lead, to reduce the number of higher-level programming languages, and especially to cut down the 'dialects' – over a hundred in one case – of supposedly 'universal' higher-level programming languages like COBOL and FORTRAN. The persistance of low standardization in this field is a major problem, as noted in Chapter 3, which hampers the transfer of programs and programmers between users.

Associated with this effort is a second one: the compilation of a National Program Index of proved software covering the whole register of commercial, technical and scientific applications. The Index already contains over 5,000 items. The customer's requirements are coded up and the nearest-matching item identified automatically in the files of one of the Centre's own machines. The Centre provides the user with the name of the organization owning the program and he must make his own approach and terms. It does, however, give assistance with securing the exchange, and advice on any necessary tailoring of the program.

While this facility is of particular value to the small user uncertain where or how to get a program for a special job at a fair price, organizations of all sizes up to industrial giants like ICI can and do make use of it.

A third area is collaborative work with particular industries whose member-firms share common data-processing problems which have impeded their exploitation of the machine. Work on such 'industrial packages' is being done with the textile industry and the building and civil engineering industries, for example, full liaison and consultation being maintained with the appropriate Ministries and industrial associations to secure the widest participation of interested parties.

Finally, what may turn out to be the Centre's most significant contribution to wider and more skilful computer usage is its educational and training work. For example, it has been prompt in exposing the lack of adequate technical and professional standards amongst some computer personnel. Again it has already made a substantial contribution to increasing the supply of trained systems staff.

As stressed elsewhere the shortage of systems staff, already acute, could grow much worse over the next few years, seriously retarding the introduction of the machine and compromising the quality of the systems set up. If demand is to be met, methods of selecting and training systems personnel must be simplified. In 1966-7, in collaboration with the Department of Education and Science and ICT, the Centre devised a packaged six-week course in systems analysis. By the autumn of 1967 the course (each package, containing full teaching notes and visual aids, costs around £500 and has already found a number of export markets including the USA) was being offered by about twenty technical colleges.

The speed with which the basic course (which is being further developed to provide more advanced training) was prepared is perhaps illustrative of the NCC's approach, which is generally thought to be more professional than originally expected. The policy of recruiting its consultant staff primarily from the data-processing industry itself is obviously the right one. Indeed, in view of its promising start it seems highly desirable that the Centre's other branches (in London, Scotland, the North and the Midlands) should be opened or expanded as soon as possible.

From the foregoing it is clear that the government has become increasingly involved in the last four or five years in the computer-making and data-processing industries. It is also probable that this involvement will grow in the future. It is not only the current vogue for and growing acquiescence to central planning of the economy as a whole which makes this closer involvement probable. The unique importance of computers in advanced technology generally, their potential contribution to economic vitality, their military and political aspects. and the present structure of the international computer-making industry all work in favour of some form of central involvement.

The American computer-making firms dominate the world market decisively and will do for the foreseeable future. They have the advantages of a vast home market and massive federal procurements. The latter advantage will continue so long as the United States maintains a world military role on its present scale and its sophisticated aerial defence of the North American continent, as well as running an ambitious space programme. Since such commitments are unlikely to contract in the near or medium-term future the American industry has an inbuilt guarantee for its research and development efforts, and hence of course for the maintenance of the product quality which is the key to its success in the commercial market.

The abandonment of an independent British, and more recently an independent European, aircraft industry has been resisted at considerable expense because of its military, political and industrial implications. Yet the same arguments which apply in this field hold even more strongly for computers. As we have seen, in the case of Britain the straight economic arguments for a domestic computer industry are persuasive enough in themselves. Total dependence on imports would put a disastrous strain on the balance of payments, as well as sacrifice a promising growth industry and a stake in the universal technology of the future.

Government intervention in the computer industry might perhaps not have been necessary if British computer-makers had been quicker to merge, if users had adopted the machine more readily, and if the government itself had spent more freely on its products. But the opportunity to secure viability in this less formal way had passed by the late 1950s, thanks largely to an almost entirely vacuous official policy.

The more positive line taken since 1964 has unquestionably had an important effect, though estimating it precisely is tricky. With its new 1900 Series of late 1964 ICT would certainly have staged an independent – though perhaps only temporary – revival. The technical merits of the System-4 machines would anyway have brought English Electric a fair number of buyers. But neither series would have had its present level of success without the assurance of product continuity prospective buyers have read into the government's determination to maintain the industry. Again, ICT, English Electric and Elliotts might well have merged of their own accord to form a grouping like International Computers. But most probably any such consolidation would have been postponed much longer without official pressure. Again it is most unlikely that any agency with the scope and influence of the National Computing Centre would have appeared spontaneously.

Official action was necessary and justified and has had some impact. One is still left with the questions whether it has been sufficiently vigorous and appropriately balanced between the making and using sides, and what direction it should take in the future. International Computers has probably not emerged too late to produce a successor to the machines it has inherited in time to meet IBM's next series of machines. But it will need to put in a good deal of overtime on its development work to make sure. More financial concessions could perhaps have been made to promote investment in computers by users. But what is needed more than wider computer exploitation is successful computer exploitation. The latter depends closely upon improving computer education, software, and the quality of computer staff. But no policy can produce such improvements overnight.

Yet it is in this direction, with the future of the hardware industry relatively secure, that policy could and should now be pointed more decisively. The National Computer Centre is already making a useful contribution to wider and better use of the machine. Its services should certainly be expanded as rapidly as possible over the next few years.

Taking a rather longer view, there seems no good reason why the provision of general computer education should not be improved. The machine will not only be the common denominator of industry and business in the near future but will have an important bearing on social, leisure and political life. Yet few schools provide even the scantiest introduction to computer concepts and applications. Barely a handful operate their own machines. A more generous and thoughtful provision of facilities at this level would surely be worthwhile.

Further Reading

Developments in the domestic and international computer industry, and in its relationship with government, receive wide coverage both in the general 'quality' press and in the trade press of management and business and the data-processing industry: for example, the *Financial Times*, *Economist*, *Management Today*, *Fortune*, *Data Systems*, *Computer Weekly*, *Dataweek*, *Computer Survey*, *Datamation*. See also:

Burck, G., and the Editors of *Fortune*, *The Computer Age*, Harper & Row, New York, 1965.

'Controlling the Real-Time Revolution', *Management Today*, September 1966.

'Crisis in Giant Computers', *Management Today*, August 1967.

'Out of the Computer Maze', *Management Today*, July–August 1966.

Report of a Joint Working Group on Computers for Research (the 'Flowers Report'), Cmnd 2883, HMSO, 1966.

Servan-Schreiber, J.-J., *The American Challenge* (especially Chapter 14), Atheneum, New York, Hamish Hamilton, London, 1968, Penguin Books, 1969.

CHAPTER 10

Conclusions

SOME attempt can be made at this point to draw together the major points and contentions which have been made in the foregoing chapters and to relate them to the issues raised in Chapter 1.

It was suggested there that the theme 'computers, managers and society' has two main aspects, between which there is a certain tension: in some eyes, a contradiction. On the one hand we can trace an association between computerization, society's material well-being, and the prevailing standard of business and official administration. On the other hand, and in contrast, there is a connexion between the apparent logic and tendency of computing technology and its associated systems, the human condition in and the social structures of advanced industrial society, and the nature of the managerial role and managerial authority in society.

We can now reconsider these two interwoven sets of relationships and ask again whether their apparent tensions and inconsistencies can be reconciled. Whether, to put it somewhat crudely, a rise in personal living standards from computerization must be bought with a deterioration in personal living conditions; whether we are faced with a world where the individual, though increasingly affluent, will be over-organized and progressively excluded from the decision-making process which shapes his life as employee and citizen. Or whether we can indeed have our (much bigger) slice of cake and eat it too.

Before this apparent dilemma is re-examined, however, it is worth reminding ourselves that, although the computer can deliver the goods in a purely material sense, its economic contribution is still peripheral. The glowing forecasts of the machine's wealth-creating potentialities have been only sketchily realized. These disappointments stem partly from the failure to install the machine on a wide scale, especially in Britain, but even more from the recurrent failure to make individual schemes financially worthwhile.

The user's image of the machine's potentiality is often a rather instable compound of optimism and disillusion. In fact, in view of the strength of the latter element, and the ample empirical justification for it, it is in some ways remarkable how rapidly British management is now beginning to adopt the machine. But the failure to make computers pay can for the most part be put down to quite concrete and adjustable factors, such as poor understanding of the technology, scratch-pad planning and indecisive control.

The success of individual schemes endorses the more optimistic predictions of the machine's economic promise. To take one example, the annual savings from the Rolls Royce Aero Engines Division's installation are already over £2 million. This represents more than two per cent of the Division's turnover. In fact the Division looks for and gets a *direct* return of fifteen per cent on its capital investment in computers. Benefits from improvements to customer service and other 'invisibles', which as we have seen can often justify a scheme in themselves, are treated as wind-fall gains.[1]

This is an outstanding performance from what is in other respects an outstanding organization. Unquestionably it is not unrelated to Rolls Royce's excellence in other technical and operational fields. But there is nothing inherently mysterious about it. Nor is it, for example, a consequence of the company's size. Concerns which have paid as much attention to planning, control and education, whatever their size, have had an equally favourable experience. What it is unambiguously related to is the quality of management.

Some early forecasts of the machine's potential were rashly optimistic, as sometimes are those of people trying to sell it or persuade their organization to take the plunge. But the basic case for adopting it in business, industry, and administration is now well enough documented to be quite unanswerable. This does not of course imply that every business can yet make worthwhile use

1. As reported in 'The Hard Road to Real-Time', *Management Today*, September 1967.

of the machine. The presumption that a computer, any computer, automatically brings benefits is as pernicious as the flat denial of its utility. The decision to computerize must remain based strictly on careful assessment of the need, the cost, and the pay-off. But as a unit of computing power cheapens and (one hopes and expects) programming is demystified it will become a decision an increasing number of users can rationally make.

At this point it is worth remembering that some of the most impressive gains from computerization will be of an indirect kind, from its impact on the economic infrastructure – education, government, communications, transport, and research and development in particular.

One has in mind here the development of directly accessible technical and business information 'banks', and the more immediate prospect of a more certain, larger-volume tele-communications system. Both types of development will depend on the fullest use of computer hardware. So will a third and equally attractive piece of streamlining, the extension of direct credit exchange, which opens the eventual prospect of a 'cashless society' in which money in the cumbrous, easily lost or stolen form we presently know it could largely disappear.

The planning (through computer-aided simulation) and operation of an integrated national transport system is another major field with great promise. Even the shorter-term possibilities of computerized traffic control in congested urban areas, which are already being explored, offer a significant disguised reduction in a host of personal, social and industrial costs. It almost goes without saying that the future quality of scientific research and technical development will depend directly on the availability of computing power. The minimum needs here have already been recognized. But an economy like the British would benefit from scientific computing facilities similar in scale, flexibility and pervasiveness to the electricity grid, and would be as handi-capped without the one as without the other.

Computerization in the health and education services, although more controversial, could also undoubtedly contribute significantly and validly to more economical use of resources. Computer-aided diagnosis, already being piloted, could follow the extension of computerized medical record-keeping on a wide scale, though it will have to contend with the substantial doubts of the general practitioner and the general public alike. Similar scepticism will probably arise over widespread use of computerized teaching aids. But from the point of view of the teacher the decisive attraction could be the removal of the donkey-work of information cramming, which would be achieved at the student's own pace in dialogues with stored learning programs and direct-accessing of library information, enabling the teacher to assume a more creatively educational role.

Finally, there are the potentially enormous savings, not primarily of data-processing costs, but of the citizen's and businessman's time and patience, which could be tapped from the computerization (desirably linked to the thoroughgoing structural and procedural reform) of government, and especially local government. Landscaping these administrative morasses, building roads through them, and installing a proper system of street lighting are urgent priorities, whether from the point of view of technical efficiency or bread-and-butter democracy.

Many departments and local authorities already have quite a creditable record in computer usage. But the more advanced use of the machine is rare and there is a striking incompatibility between individual systems. A hopeful development is the steps the National Computing Centre is at present taking to promote collaborative use of computing power between the forty-one county-level authorities in the reorganized government system in Wales, and to thrash out a local government software package which could be adopted in the UK as a whole.[2]

Yet it is the thoroughgoing exploitation of the machine for commercial and industrial planning and control which should provide the more impressive returns over the next twelve years. But will such exploitation occur? The Computer Revolution is only just beginning in Britain while it is far advanced in the USA, and there has been a significantly wider adoption of the machine in nearly all other industrially advanced countries, whether we are talking about total computer stocks, ratios of computers to the employed population, or the scope of the

2. *Sunday Times* Business News, 28 April 1968.

average installation. British management, taken as a whole, has fought shy of the computer. Further exploitation on a worthwhile scale demands the abandonment of this timid approach.

No attempt has been made in this book to minimize or dismiss the very real difficulties and risks of computerizing the business firm or administrative unit. The prospective user is faced with an almost endless string of practical problems and dilemmas. Securing accurate, reliable, and, it must be said, trustworthy advice is often difficult and usually expensive. Ill-informed enthusiasm can play as much havoc with the objective appraisal of costs and benefits and the establishment of and adherence to a workable plan as the bland patter of the huckster or charlatan.

Choosing the mix of applications to aim at, the best configuration of equipment to operate them, and setting a realistic time schedule for phasing them in; recruiting, training and retaining personnel; maintaining control over the changeover: all present the most testing difficulties.

Planning and control are persistently complicated not only by the involvement of the change-makers themselves in the change, the pressure and uncertainty of a fluid situation, and the arrival of new personnel, but by sheer difficulties of communication. The busy manager or director has little time to verse himself in the mysteries of the bits and bytes; COBOL and ALGOL; tapes versus discs; peripheral simultaneity; and all the rest of the computer man's stock in trade. But without some familiarity with them he can be courting constant minor and sometimes major disaster.

Besides the general problems of communication, planning and control two specific problem areas are worth emphasizing once more.

Firstly there is the recurrent software problem. Without penetrating analysis and design carefully oriented to the overall objectives of all operating systems computerization soon turns into a ruinous farce. The same goes for the preparation of the individual and overall programs which activate the systems. High-calibre systems men are scarce, and despite important advances in programming languages programming remains a prolonged and intricate chore. Exchange of programs, though growing, is needlessly impeded by incompatibility between machines, poor communications, and inter-company rivalries and suspicions. Many software packages are virtually unusable by the majority of their intended clients, or can be adapted only at an expense almost matching that of starting from scratch.

Closely associated with the technical barriers to good systems design and programming is the almost calamitous shortage of skilled personnel. Of necessity recruitment and training are expensive and lengthy processes, though more so with systems men than programmers. Fitting the datacrats into the concern and apportioning assignments in the most economical way, while allowing for the personal values and career objectives of these new types of staff specialist, demand a measure of organizational and personnel skill which is itself rare enough.

The resentment of other staff towards the datacrat's rewards, operating style, values, and to the degree of self-supervision and technical leadership which he needs and demands to do his work effectively is perhaps inevitable and is liable to crystallize into sometimes overt obstruction. But the data-processing manager and his senior systems and programming assistants are of sufficiently critical importance to a scheme's success that it is well worth paying above the market rates for the right men. Nor is it possible to allocate them a 'safe', purely advisory role. Their unfamiliar approach and attitudes may be disturbing for many but for the most part they are indivisible from their technical objectives.

Mention of the strained relations between operating staff and datacrats brings us to the second major problem area: staff acceptance of the aims of computerization. Acceptance should mean something more than acquiescence. There is a very big difference between simply avoiding opposition and securing general approval for computer aims, or, even better, a widespread desire to participate in achieving them. Staff identification with the success of the scheme, especially that of operating management, is a gold-chip advantage.

Yet it is as rare as the truly successful installation. The great stumbling-block to such involvement is the uncertainty, real or perceived, the changeover brings to staff security and prospects.

So far the machine has seldom effected anything like such a transformation of the work tasks and staff structure of the average computerized office as is commonly supposed. Nor has there been any significant dislocation of the general clerical labour market. Indeed, demand for office workers in the UK continues to rise and in the medium term computers hold the promise of alleviating genuine and serious staff shortages. Where appropriate staff organizations or trade unions exist they naturally demand suitable guarantees of staff security, proper retraining and relocation procedures, and the protection of individual career opportunities. Partly because of the internal structure of most office staffs in which young, unmarried women predominate, and partly because of the length of most changeovers, management can usually provide such guarantees. But what makes it easiest of all to do so is the generally moderate effect on staff that computers have in fact had in most offices.

But if widespread office workers' opposition to computerization is not an immediate prospect, it is another matter to engage their enthusiasm. Some users may genuinely believe that their new system will add to the interest, variety and responsibility of the average clerk's job; and some systems can certainly have this effect. They can argue too that by increasing the firm's efficiency it adds to the ultimate security and prosperity of all staff. For these reasons they can claim that the office worker should co-operate to the full with the systems man and programmer. Unfortunately, however, the fact remains that basically the new systems will be oriented to needs identified jointly by management and computer staff. And it is very rare for office workers to be allowed to participate effectively in the design of a new system. As with technical change on the shop floor, management tends to expect workers automatically to adopt its own perspectives on innovation. At the same time the concrete participation and influence over events which may help to nourish such perspectives are withheld.

But it is not the possible opposition and probable apathy of clerical workers which are the main human obstacle to computerization as applications grow in scope and pervasiveness. Integrated computing and the drift towards the total system concept, with their implications for planning, communication and control – the core processes of managerial activity itself – and for the structures and prerogatives which accompany these processes in the classic models of business administration, precipitate a crisis of identity and values amongst managers themselves.

Doubts about the machine's consequences for personal security and prospects, expressed frequently in the guise of scepticism about its technical value or disapproval of the data-crat's methods and style, are often strongest in management itself, whether at board or departmental level, amongst functional and specialist personnel alike.

As with lesser grades of staff, explanation of aims, education in computing and systems concepts, and participation in system building may go some way to remove the less rationally grounded elements in this approach. But in some quarters the residue of suspicion – which is by no means totally unjustified – will remain a powerful force blocking the change.

The fact has to be faced that the computer is likely significantly to alter conventional methods of management and, on most of the evidence, to outmode present organizational patterns. Managers who cannot adapt to the new techniques, structures and relationships will find themselves playing second fiddle to those who can.

Managerial attitudes towards the computer vary with all the complexities of varying experience, training, function and back-ground among management itself. It unquestionably does injustice to this complexity to draw a rather arbitrary line between those who are broadly in favour of computerization and those who tend to view it with real suspicion. But if such a line is drawn we do find that the majority of people in each category can be broadly characterized in terms of a number of concrete and associated attributes.

Who is the anti-computer manager? Usually he will be one who has stayed with one company all his life and held only one major function in it. He probably won his way into management from the shop floor or office. His general education was not to an advanced level and if he possesses further qualifications they will be related directly to his function. He is insistent on loyalty to the company, whose fortunes he often sees as revolving round those of his own department, and suspicious of technical specialists or outside consultants. When he is a production man – and he very often is – he may regard the increasing emphasis on such functions as marketing as wrong-headed and gimcrack.

He has a great belief in leadership (charismatically conceived) and 'flair' as the source of operating success. It is almost axiomatic to him that anyone who becomes a manager does so because of superior inherent personal characteristics. Hence his higher estimation of the snap decision and improvisation versus planning, and his homespun and paternalistic approach to industrial relations. If promotion has passed him by he may tend to withdraw into a comfy bureaucratic cocoon – scrupulously observing, and demanding strict observance by others of, all the 'usual methods' and 'proper channels'.

His traditionalism, departmental outlook, suspicion of 'experts', preference of experience to theory, and improvising approach make him naturally hostile to computing and systems concepts and computer personnel. It all sounds like high-flown nonsense which will merely upset day-to-day routine. The idea that he should familiarize himself with the new techniques, or that someone in his job will in future depend on them, is an affront to his whole outlook and set of personal values.

The profile of the manager more enthusiastic in his approach to the machine is the reverse in practically every respect. He has usually stayed longer and done better at school, probably going on to university or taking specialist professional training. He enters management directly, possibly as a trainee or staff specialist. He is much more mobile between organizations, between departments in them, and individual functional roles. In this sense he is less 'loyal' to any one employer than his 'local-oriented' counterpart. But his lack of personalized loyalty does not necessarily inhibit his commitment to the ultimate aims of the organization. In fact his refusal to be absorbed into its social system can make these new goals easier to perceive and pursue rationally.

To say that he has a more 'scientific' approach to his work is probably an exaggeration, but he does give greater weight to rational planning and objective analysis of problems. He too may cling to the notion that managerial success requires some innate personal qualities, but these are the qualities of the consummate technician and skilful negotiator. He is rather more likely to believe that such faculties are either the product of a formal training or can only properly be developed by such a training.

In the sense that he lays more stress on techniques than on personal qualities or long-service experience he is a professional. In his view the manager can no longer drive by the seat of his pants. He should make the fullest use of the tools and techniques available to define, analyse and solve the problems before him. He sees his personal success as importantly determined by his ability to understand and exploit these aids and to keep abreast of new ones. Rather than retreat into a comfortable routine role his impulse is to criticize and innovate.

His greater familiarity with and trust in theoretical ideas accelerates his appreciation of computing concepts; and his ability to reach a better balance in his assessment of the concern's overall goals as against those of his own department helps him to grasp the importance of comprehensive, integrated computing systems.

Because his career and emotional investments in established methods and management structures are lower he is less disturbed by the prospect of their modification. Without claiming that he sees the datacrat as a kind of blood-brother it is probably fair to suggest that his own outlook, approach, style and values are similar in kind. Being more likely to recognize the probable future importance of computers in management he is often eager to pick the systems specialist's mind and to participate fully in the development of the scheme.

This wish for involvement, and the accompanying personal commitment to the success of the changeover, do not stem from any fuzzily conceived 'loyalty' to the firm. If it is any kind of loyalty at all it is essentially a loyalty to himself, from which the concern gains incidentally. The most trustworthy explanation is that by gaining experience of a changeover and learning how to exploit the machine he increases his own effectiveness and hence his value on the market.

The relative prevalence of these two basic types of manager – the loyal, departmentally minded, improvising local, and the mobile, techniques-minded, careerist cosmopolitan – in a computerizing organization will have important implications for the pace at which change can take place, for the quality of the systems which are designed, and for the use they are put to once established.

But it is not merely a question of the relative proportions of individuals falling in each category. Whether they hold the really influential posts in the concern is equally important. In a very large number of firms in this country it is almost certainly true to say that the majority of senior departmental positions are held by managers cast more or less in the local mould, because promotion to such posts is so often based on the criteria of local experience, loyalty and long service. The values associated with localism are in fact associated with still powerful, though weakening, traditions in British industry.

It is not the purpose of this book to trace the origins of these traditions and the ideology which has supported them. Clearly they owe a good deal to the social relations, institutions (particularly educational institutions), and social philosophy which accompanied Victorian and Edwardian imperial power, as well as to the economic privileges and protection which, culminating in the Imperial Preference system, masked their growing inappropriateness in an increasingly competitive world.

What is more relevant to present purposes is the nature of these ideas and their continuing force. For in so far as they continue to pervade the outlook of senior management and nourish the values of localism they obstruct the wider and more successful exploitation, not only of computers, but of many other tools and techniques which others with a better industrial record than our own have shown no comparable hesitation in adopting.

The nature of the outmoded ethos which continues to stultify the growth of a truly competitive spirit and the will to innovate in a large section of British industry can best be conveyed by a deliberate exaggeration. There is an enduring tendency to picture the enterprise as the warden of certain traditional technical standards and types of social relationship as much as a device for mixing men, materials and machinery in the most effective way to make money and grow. The self-image of the firm implicit in this approach sometimes comes close to that of the craftsmen gun-makers or the exclusive military tailor.

The product is conceived as inherently superior to others and for practical purposes incapable of refinement. Some customers may well be given the distinct impression that their orders are accepted as a condescending favour; and, once accepted, orders are discharged at a decent, gentlemanly pace, complaints at delay being viewed as an unmistakable sign of ill-breeding. Relations between proprietors and staff are intensely personal. Long service with the firm is conceived as a vital qualification not only for full competence in the technical mysteries of the craft but for the complementary prize of assimilation into its managerial elite.

This is undeniably an extreme characterization. But it is disturbing to what extent attitudes and practice in British management continue to be in one way or another inspired by such a complacent and somnolent traditionalism. It is equally certain that the docility and insular taste of consumers, the indifference of government, and the protectionist policies which helped to preserve it can no longer be taken for granted. As its insulation from competition – and competition for the traditionalist and local is a good thing only so long as it happens to someone else – is stripped away British industry faces a crisis which revolves predominantly around its managerial cadres.

The British experience with the computer to date is merely an index, though perhaps the most dramatic and unambiguous one (thanks to the machine's universal relevance to effective management), of the extent and nature of the upheaval.

There is of course no quick short-term way of meeting it. The market, the take-over wizards, and bodies such as the Ministry of Technology and the Industrial Reorganization Corporation will certainly make an impact in the medium term. But for the eventual solution, the removal of the traditionalist outlook and hence the people who hold it most strongly, and their replacement by more professionally minded individuals, we must rely mainly on biology on the one hand and educational changes on the other.

The cosmopolitan and local syndromes are the product of many influences, but perhaps the most important is formal education and training. Even amongst occupational groups like university teachers who are necessarily highly educated as a whole, cosmopolitan-type characteristics tend to be accentuated in individuals who have the most impressive attainments. At present the more cosmopolitan managers in British industry are mainly those who enter industry as one or another kind of staff specialist – engineers, chemists, economists, statisticians, accountants and so on. Owing to the until recently patchy and indifferent provision for management education *per se* their specifically managerial expertise has usually been accumulated in an opportunist way rather than in a period of formal training.

Thanks to the discipline of their specialist or academic training they are usually equipped with a set of methods which can be applied to self-education in distinct managerial skills. They are better able, as well as more inclined, to systematize the gleanings of their reading of management literature, discussions with colleagues, observation, and attendance at short courses and seminars (for which they show a distinctly higher enthusiasm than their local counterparts). In this way they synthesize their own management education. Even a small minority of outstanding individuals who in terms of their formal education and background one would expect to adopt a local orientation succeed in systematizing their managerial skills by a similar self-educative effort.

But it is now accepted that British management will never attain the degree of professionalism modern business demands, and which is exhibited so convincingly by the Americans, by relying on this kind of individual initiative. In the last five years management education has consequently become something of a growth industry.

This development should be welcomed. It is to be hoped too that the provision which eventually emerges will match the need. But such is by no means yet the case. Objectively, and by the general consent of those engaged in it, the structure of management education is chaotic, and the attitudes of those who are supposed to be promoting it are often ambiguous. Naturally one would expect some confusion until the demand for different types of course becomes clearer and course structures and teaching methods are adjusted to these requirements. But such questions as whether one should stress the social sciences or mathematical techniques, the business game or the case study, are not what is really at issue.

The basis of the present trouble is that too many institutions have jumped on the bandwagon with inadequate resources (especially in terms of staff), and no single body is charged with guiding rational growth. (One is thinking here of the public provision. The internal courses run by individual organizations or professional associations do add certain complications but can be left aside.) In the public system three main types of institution provide courses: the graduate Business Schools at London and Manchester, the universities, and the technical colleges. Of these it is the fifty-odd technical colleges whose standards and ability to attract suitable staff cause most concern, though similar worries arise over some of the smaller university departments.

Experience so far seems to have shown that the most urgent need arises at the early postgraduate level, for university students switching from other disciplines and for young 'post-experience' entrants from industry with professional qualifications of graduate equivalence. The London and Manchester schools can hardly be expected to cope with this demand, and are anyway supposed to devote a good deal of their attention to high-powered shorter courses for experienced senior personnel. It would therefore seem reasonable for any rationalization to stimulate the selective growth of the better university courses at present functioning.

But who might oversee this operation is unclear. At least six bodies – the Foundation for Management Education, the British Institute of Management, the Confederation of British Industry, the University Grants Committee, the Department of Education and Science, and the Department of Employment and Productivity – at present have some control over the shape and financing of management education. Admittedly the possibility of a new co-ordinating body is under study, but the wheels are grinding very slowly and there is no guarantee that whatever authority emerges will have the power to carry out the necessary restructuring and lay down the right long-term policies.

An associated reform should be in the financing of the management education effort. Shortage of funds at present affects both the quantity and the quality of what can be done. The same problem that crops up in the training of computer personnel recurs here in that the best qualified potential teachers can usually earn far more actually managing than teaching others to manage. One possible solution to this problem, to some extent already adopted, is to allow teachers plenty of spare time for private consultancy work. Another is to undertake such work for industry on a departmental basis. This practice is already followed in one or two institutions, notably by the University of Lancaster. But such involvements on a large scale might tend to conflict with normal university administrative practice.

A further problem at present is the financing of students. Some finance themselves, a rather larger number are supported by the companies who release them, and a few more get grants from bodies such as the Social Science Research Council. But the majority, about two thirds, have to rely on local education authorities, whose varying resources and sometimes puzzling means of selection add an unnecessary element of uncertainty and sometimes unfairness.

One possible solution to this problem (and perhaps the foregoing one too) would be to finance students from a central fund financed by a direct management education levy on industry comparable to the general redundancy and retraining levy. (A by-product of this solution would be the highly desirable one that firms reluctant to release staff for the longer residential courses would become more co-operative.) But again the conventional methods of university financial and administrative control would have to be relaxed.

An alternative solution would be some form of loan scheme. This too conflicts with the present methods and philosophy of student support. But in its favour are two special considerations: firstly that a fair number of management students, being older, have higher personal commitments (such as mortgages); secondly, that upon re-entry they are likely to obtain posts which guarantee their ability to repay. Perhaps the greatest virtue of this kind of arrangement, however, is that it would prevent the present absurdity whereby students considered amply qualified by an institution can be refused grants by their local education authority.

It can be argued that the modernization of British industry will depend on more than the spread of professional management through improved management education; or even, though less convincingly, that the spread of management education itself is merely one index of some spontaneous process of professionalization already occurring. In the case of computers it is sometimes claimed that more generous investment allowances, or positive financial incentives such as interest-free loans or subsidies, are what is really required. But such economism ignores the technical, managerial and human problems which must be overcome if computers are not only to be used more widely but used better. These are not the problems which the outlook and approach of the local and the traditionalist are well adapted to overcoming.

But there are reasons in addition to the need for greater operating effectiveness why the more professional – and imaginative – qualities which good management education can nourish should be welcomed as computerization proceeds. These relate to the second aspect of the theme of this book.

With cybernation – the computerization of decision and control and the automation of production – industrial society enters a new phase. For the pessimistic humanist romantic it promises the greatest erosion yet of human dignity and freedom, for which its material abundance is a poor compensation. The gloomy insistence that this erosion is irreversible is defeatist and mistaken. Yet it could occur if the majority of us are prepared to stand idly by.

We must surely begin to evolve novel industrial and political institutions, as well as developing some that have been with us for some time, if we are going to check, and eventually reverse, the many tendencies towards oversystematization and overconcentrated bureaucratic rule which are so apparent at present. No one would minimize the difficulty of doing so. The natural self-interest of those who run government and industry will incline them to warmly resist this 'interference'. They will argue that the sort of institutional changes likely to be put forward are unnecessary and – rather firmer ideological ground – that they stultify the pursuit of a technical rationality which serves the higher consensual goal of material prosperity. But the supposition on which such resistance is based – of the necessary conflict between initiative and participation on the one hand, and technical rationality on the other – although ideologically forceful is empirically extraordinarily shaky. Consequently, there is reason to hope that if our technocrats and administrators have undergone a period of training which has included some effort to sensitize them to this fact, and to the broader social and political implications of the systems they design and operate, some of the more blimpish forms of resistance may be headed off.

One is not suggesting – it would be rash – that of itself an advanced professional training will convince the administrator of the gathering concern about his power, and the appropriateness of the demands that it should be regulated and shared. Though his idealism and democratic spirit may be roused in the lecture room they may soon languish before the situational pressures of his work role and the exigencies of his personal career aims. Still, some appreciation of why these demands are being made, and being made more loudly, will remain. His realism may enable him to recognize them as practical constraints, however he comes to feel himself.

Previously the attack on technological values was largely concentrated on their manifestation in the mass-production factory. The scientifically managed assembly line, with its fractionalized, repetitive tasks, its dehumanizing monotony and its gruelling pace, and all its associated deprivations for the worker, was the prime target of criticisms. The demons of the piece were Frederick W. Taylor and Henry Ford. But production automation is outdating this kind of 'alienating' working environment. Concern and criticism have shifted already, and as the cybernation of industrial society proceeds they will focus increasingly on the problems of controlling the elitism and the exercise of power by the administrators and technocrats of government and industry.

In the case of industry especially they are also to some extent bound up with subsidiary doubts about the shape and nature of the working systems which may accompany advanced computerization. The computer, as used at present, unquestionably tends to enhance the centralized control of the enterprise. True enough, in very large organizations it may permit the apparently reverse process of devolution of control to individual divisions or 'profit-centres'. But what really occurs in such systems – as currently designed and operated – is that computerization permits a swifter assessment of divisional performance by the centre. Local management can be given greater autonomy in controlling day-to-day operations purely because any deviation from overall policy is much easier to spotlight. But essentially the tendency everywhere is to centralize information, thereby enhancing the ability to control of senior decision-makers.

At present this centralizing process has been relatively modest. Yet the future sophistication of hardware and software could multiply the number of decisions transferred upward – or, of course, absorbed into the machine system itself. The corollary could be the increasing routinization of the work of not only middle management but every grade of personnel downwards. Individuals might thus be relegated to roles well below their ability, with much diminished prospects of rising to a higher position, part of this career blockage resulting from the starvation, created by the system, of wider experience in other roles or duties.

Clearly such an outcome would make for a good deal of personal frustration. To counter it, the organization – or rather, its controlling elite – might resort to a number of adjustive mechanisms. As William Hyde Whyte Jr has argued in his book *The Organization Man*, many large organizations already employ an impressive set of applied socio-psychological techniques to cement the loyalty of their middle management members to the concern and reconcile them to its bureaucratic discipline and highly restricted functional roles. Such efforts could be intensified, perhaps, as Whyte argues, to the eventual detriment of the organization itself through their suffocating effects on individual explorativeness and initiative.[3]

3. Whyte, W. H., *The Organization Man*, Simon & Schuster, New York, 1956, Penguin, London, 1960. Surprisingly, Whyte says nothing specifically about the possible effects of computers on corporate ideology.

But must such a routinization of work occur for technically optimum operations? It is by no means proved that it needs to or will. Why should routine duties not be leavened by more creative work, in planning or research for example? Why should there not be suitable personnel training and development programmes to equip junior and middle ranks for higher responsibility? The structure of responsibilities and positions which could emerge, far from being rigid and narrow, would offer the individual much more variety, interest and scope for self-development than he has at present. Rather than conflicting with the notional technically 'one-best-way' of the computer system it might substantially improve on it.[4]

An alert and imaginative top management would perhaps realize the value of experimenting with such arrangements. In other cases the staff themselves are not entirely without means of influencing the top to move in such a direction.

But the main human risks of advanced computerization stem less from these possible internal effects on staff structure and work organization than from their more general implications for the location and nature of major decision-making. Put at its simplest, a centralized computer system necessarily enhances the power of the central controlling group since it creates a monopoly of comprehensive information about actualities. In private business this concentration of intelligence gives enough potential cause for concern. In government it is still more alarming.

4. In a study of a computerizing steel-mill, E. J. Miller and D. Armstrong reach precisely these conclusions. As they put it: 'The solution may well lie in devising dispensable forms of task organisation. These are sometimes found in research bodies and the construction industry. In such situations the individual is affiliated to the enterprise not so much through the task organisation itself, which is accepted as temporary, as through a more stable and enduring membership in, for example, a professional group. One counterpart of this in an industrial enterprise might be the provision of relatively stable part-time roles in a "development organisation", which would have the task of monitoring and implementing changes in the more ephemeral task organisations that are concerned with production etc. Affiliation to these would take second place. Other ways of achieving dispensable task organisations could doubtless be devised.' See Miller, E. J., and Armstrong, D., *The Influence of Advanced Technology on the Structure of Management Organisation*, International Institute for Labour Studies, Paris, 1964.

It is not simply the fact of exclusion from major decision- and policy-making in itself which is disturbing. Equally it is the possibilities which arise because the bases and processes of decision-making are allowed to become relatively immune from inspection.

This secrecy and the opportunities for abuse that accompany it are compounded by the genuine power of the machine as a decision-making aid. Properly used a computer is certainly an impressive tool. But some of us are perhaps a little too willing to be impressed. The fraudulent Fire, Auto and Marine Insurance Company, for example, made great play in its sales promotion of its supposedly sophisticated computer-based management. Any cynical controlling group could exploit public credulity equally systematically and probably with greater success, not merely to defraud the consumer, but to hoodwink and manipulate employees, shareholders, and, in the case of government departments, the mass of citizens.

A further consequence of centralized decision-making and our impressionable view of the computer could be the emergence of a potentially dangerous mystique of the higher administrative and business elite.

In our society most people are not unsympathetic to the idea that certain groups or individuals should receive exceptional rewards, in terms of money, status and power, if they either show themselves to be exceptionally clever or hard-working, or take on some exceptional responsibility. But we have to recognize that once people gain such privileges they tend to view them more as a natural right than a payment for services rendered. Power is enjoyable and the powerful like to have things their own way, becoming increasingly impatient of the 'interference' of lesser mortals.

Our willingness to exert control over their activities and influence is of course substantially lessened if we feel that on balance we gain from letting them have their heads. Today most people are concerned above all with their personal material welfare. Anyone whose expertise seems harnessed successfully to furthering this end can lay claim to a good measure of public approval. One would hardly expect it to be otherwise.

The quality of overall economic, and general business management in Britain is at present variable. But things – one certainly hopes so – will not stay as they are in these respects. Future economic and industrial success will derive in large measure from better government and industrial administration, which themselves will stem from the exploitation of tools like the computer.

Our administrative leaders, quite properly, will take a great deal of credit for any such improvement. But we shall have to ensure that our appreciation does not run away with us. For the development of any sort of cult of the managerial, administrative, and technological elite would be a first step towards the situation where the values and outlook of the mass of people would become favourable to a decisive move in the direction of total political centrism.

Some observers claim, as we have noted, that the drift towards political dictatorship, a benign and sophisticated one, but a dictatorship nonetheless, has already gone some way. These claims are perhaps exaggerated, but – the experience of the United Kingdom in economic management and planning in the last ten years is not irrelevant here – they are something more than whimsy.

It is worth remembering that such dangers certainly attend the spread of the computer (and all the other techniques and apparatus of modern economic rationality to some extent). But we are by no means trapped by our drive to exploit technology. We should recall the remarks of the sociologist Alvin Gouldner mentioned at the beginning of this book. As he argues, we are too ready to believe the worst. If we are talking about the industrial organization, or the State, we rush into assuming that there is a 'one best way' of structuring control and allocating responsibilities for effective operation. We morbidly project the bureaucratizing trends of the last two hundred years into an 'inevitable' future.[5]

5. See Gouldner, A. W., 'Metaphysical Pathos and the Theory of Bureaucracy', *American Political Science Review*, 49, 1955, pp. 496–507, of which a shortened version is reprinted in Etzioni, A. (ed.), *Complex Organizations*, Holt, Rinehart & Winston, New York, 1964; also Gouldner, A. W., *Patterns of Industrial Bureaucracy*, Free Press, Glencoe, Illinois, 1954, pp. 231–45.

In so doing we implicitly deny the value of a search for alternative, humanly superior, and equally or almost as technically advantageous methods of organization. We forget too that any form of organization must ultimately depend on the consent of the people being organized or being ruled.

The technical logic of computing appears to accentuate the 'inevitable' systematization of activities and centralization of control in organizations, from the State downwards, which Gouldner is talking about. But this 'logic' may be merely a relative one, whose validity depends intimately upon prevailing social values and institutions. What appears to be the 'best way' to use the machine may be no more than a 'best way' which only holds if certain assumptions can be made about the nature of society and what its members want and believe in. When these assumptions become inappropriate, when values change, so must the notional 'one best way'.

Yet how often, following the technocrats, we talk as though technology were developed and applied in some kind of social vacuum. People, with their shifting values and mutating behaviour, are every bit as much a determinant of the technically viable and the technically-optimum as physical and mechanical properties and laws. Somehow, though, we slide into that cardinal error, that technologist's fallacy, of merging social and physical phenomena, of talking about them as though they were the same order of things, of muddling economics with physics and ergonomics with culture. You simply cannot talk in the same breath about what holds and happens in the world of mechanics or physics and what holds and happens in the world of men, where events are so often the product not of deterministic necessities but of intention, volition – themselves variable with time and occasion – and contingency; where any attempt to mathematize observed regularities into probabilistic 'laws' comparable to those of natural science is stultified not only by the complexity of the phenomena themselves but – among much else – by the cumulative and dynamic mutations of human culture and history.

Even the purely mechanistic problems the technologist faces in deciding the 'one best way' to structure an artifact, mechanism or process are hedged around with social constraints and socially transferred assumptions. Almost invariably the pursuit of the 'one best way' must, for example, be related to cost. The 'one best way' of putting a man on the moon would change dramatically overnight if one of the contending nations doubled, or halved, the percentage of its gross national product it was prepared to earmark for the space race. There is in fact, even here, no 'one best way' but a host of alternative 'best ways' each tied to a given set of resources and cost relationships. And behind these given levels of resource availability and sets of cost relationships we can work our way back to shifting and dynamic social values and forces influencing them.

The whole idea that there is always a single, technically best way, whether of designing mechanisms, laying our production processes, or structuring formal organization, which exists in serene abstraction from mobile human and social values is a ludicrous but pernicious illusion. It is dangerous because the 'technically best way', which is put forward as some kind of universal necessity, is itself almost invariably contaminated with the technocrat's personal values and priorities, those borrowed from the social system he lives under, or those of an elite whose interests, wittingly or otherwise, he serves.

The fact that the technologist himself usually fails to recognize the influence of these values on his decisions is of crucial importance. Because he likes to picture himself, and may sincerely wish to be, the honest broker of progress, and because we increasingly accept this self-image, he is of all the more value to those who wish to preserve or promote those values embodied in his vision of rationality. The technologist is the twentieth century's most accomplished ideologue because he so readily gains our faith and because the last thing we or he are ready to believe is that his decisions are ideologically coloured. For the Russian traffic engineer the concentration on public transport is common sense rather than an expression of dogma; for his American counterpart the primacy of the private car is equally of the natural order of things. The choice of technical means, and notions of the technically optimum, are everywhere bound up, however, with assumptions, themselves ideologically influenced, about what people and society do want and should want.

These considerations, however, only attain their fullest significance when we remember the attempts that have been and are being made to develop a technology based on the discoveries of the social sciences. There is of course no question that some of these discoveries can be formalized and applied, while the questions of whether, or when, they should be applied, and by whom, are justly controversial. But we should never pretend that any such 'social engineering' is some benignly rational application of a neutral science. If the 'best ways' of mechanical engineering technology sometimes give off a faint ideological scent the 'best ways' of 'social engineering' positively reek of it.

The foregoing is not intended either as an attack on technologists or as a denigration of those social scientists who feel that their research discoveries have a practical value. It is merely intended to suggest the existence of certain relativities and the need to subject to the closest scrutiny certain claims which get made about universal technical exigencies. To return to a central issue: is it really some universal 'logic' which stems from the 'innate' properties of computing technology which 'demands' increasingly centralized and increasingly secret decision-making in the large organization? Or is it rather that we have come to accept the *presumption* that centralization is the 'best way', the optimum overall strategy, for structuring control? That because we have brainwashed ourselves into believing that it is 'necessarily' more 'efficient' our root concepts of systems design are subtly biased and our exploitation of computing equipment consequently selective? Centralization – and it is only one of a close family of structural tendencies – may indeed be leading not only to adverse human consequences: it may also be relatively inefficient in the long run in terms of purely materialistic input-output arithmetic. For a last word on this we may go to Professor Jay W. Forrester, who as the pioneer of Industrial Dynamics and the inventor of magnetic-core storage can hardly be classed as an anti-computer zealot:

. . . I see data-processing opening a fork in the road. Most organizations in the short run will choose the path of greater centralization, more recording and storage of information, but probably more restrictions on the accessibility of information. This road will make less effective use of people, will produce organizations with less flexibility, and will eventually lead to competitive failure.

The other road leads to new types of organizations, new concepts of corporate government, and to organizations that serve people rather than organizations that suppress people. These will be the organizations that build on the lessons learned from national political history. They will release the forces of initiative and innovation. I am confident that the latter road to organizational innovation is more rewarding. The choice is before us; the path is not predetermined by the nature of electronic computers.[6]

This act of choice, and the forging of the new types of organization and new concepts of corporate government, will be far from a simple process. We can expect any number of false starts, wrong turnings and blind alleys before the kind of institutions and structures we are fumbling for begin to emerge. Any suggestions which can now be made must be comparatively feeble and tentative, perhaps premature. But for a start it might be worth agitating for a parliamentary standing committee to police the uses to which government departments put their machines, with especial responsibility for preventing the collation, storage and tabulation of data in such a way as to endanger civil liberties. Comparable bodies of expert assessors with the right to inspect programs, files and mathematical models in confidence on behalf of consumers, shareholders and employees could follow in large public and private industrial organizations. Expert in information technology, and legally privileged, the 'information auditor' could become an important new professional. Monopoly of 'information banking' – whether public or private – should be forbidden by law. Wherever individual files are built up, individuals should be given the right to inspect their own files and contest entries. With certain types of file – one is thinking in particular of those which might be developed from some of the credit-record files which already exist – it might be necessary to insist on automatic recording of every inspection, its purpose, and the person making it.

6. Forrester, J. W., in Myers, C. A. (ed.), *The Impact of Computers on Management*, M I T Press, Cambridge, Mass., 1967, p. 281. (Copyright © Massachusetts Institute of Technology, 1967; reprinted by kind permission of The M I T Press, Cambridge, Massachusetts.)

But these kinds of safeguard would perhaps form only the emergency first steps in a wider strategy for instituting a more active participation by individuals in the control and operation of government and big business, the elementary justification for which, though not created by computerization, is very much strengthened by it. The possible forms of such participation and the structures enshrining it are even more difficult to specify. One imagines that they will emerge only after a good deal of sometimes bad-tempered trial and error. But discovering them is a problem shared by all industrialized societies to a large extent, whatever the socio-political nameplate on their national door. The process of experimentation could therefore be as universal as the penetration of the computer, and when it should begin is a question it is unnecessary to answer.

Index

MORE ABOUT PENGUINS
AND PELICANS

Penguinews, which appears every month, contains details of all the new books issued by Penguins as they are published. From time to time it is supplemented by *Penguins in Print* – a complete list of all the available titles. (There are well over three thousand of these.)

A specimen copy of *Penguinews* will be sent to you free on request, and you can become a subscriber for the price of the postage – 4s. for a year's issues (including the complete lists). Just write to Dept EP, Penguin Books Ltd, Harmondsworth, Middlesex, enclosing a cheque or postal order, and your name will be added to the mailing list.

Some other books published by Penguins are described on the following pages.

Note: *Penguinews* and *Penguins in Print* are not available in the U.S.A. or Canada.

ELECTRONIC COMPUTERS

S. H. Hollingdale and G. C. Tootill

Although little more than twenty years old, electronic computers are reshaping our technological society. This Pelican explains how computers work, how problems are presented to them, and what sort of jobs they can tackle. Analog and digital computers are compared and contrasted, and recent syntheses of the two techniques described.

To survey a difficult subject so thoroughly necessitated the collaboration of two authors, both of whom hold senior posts directly connected with computers. With the general reader in mind they have taken particular care with the specialist jargon of their subject, explaining each term as it occurs. At the same time the technique of programming is given in sufficient depth to prepare a novice to cope with a manufacturer's handbook, and the computer, in its varying embodiments, is described in enough detail to give him confidence in learning to use one.

In addition the authors have devoted two chapters to the history of computers and the fascinating story of such pioneers of calculating machines as Charles Babbage.

MATHEMATICS IN MANAGEMENT

Albert Battersby

Sophisticated methods of planning, control, and decision-making, together with the advent of the electronic computer, have already brought mathematics well to the fore in modern industry and commerce. At the present rate of advance, mathematics will soon be an indispensable tool of the intelligent manager.

Mathematics in Management has been specially written, for managers and others, to provide a sound basis of knowledge about the methods of operational research now being applied in public industries and services, to save resources and prune expenditure. Some such account is urgently needed, since general education has not kept pace with advances in this field, and mathematicians have difficulty in 'talking' to managers.

Among the particular topics covered by Albert Battersby in this new Pelican are network analysis, simple functions, linear programming, simulation, and electronic computers. The author employs a minimum of mathematical notation in his text and, wherever possible, makes his points with the help of drawings. He has also included a set of exercises with full solutions.